JOHN PAUL JONES:
Man of Action

BUST BY ANTOINE HOUDON
This is regarded as the best likeness of John Paul Jones

JOHN PAUL JONES:
Man of Action

BY

PHILLIPS RUSSELL

Drawings by

LEON UNDERWOOD

Publishers ~ New York
BRENTANO'S · MCMXXVII

Manufactured in the United States of America

Foreword

We shall better comprehend the man with whom we have here to deal if we understand that though he was first of all a man of action, he was also intuitively an artist. With ships and men, instead of paint, pen or chisel, he strove to make real his dreams of a glorious world.

The imagination of the creative artist obeys laws of its own. It is therefore rarely understood by those persons who do not create but merely exploit, according to the custom of the Phillistines.

The mind of the artist creates a world other than that in which this body lives. When this other-world is shortened by impact with what are called Cold Realities, its creator suffers. This is due to the very sensibility which enables him to perceive relations where other persons behold only objects. Hence the artist encounters many frustrations. He is never, however, entirely defeated. He attains moments when this world and that other-world coincide and are one. These moments are his supreme reward.

[v]

CONTENTS

CONTENTS

ILLUSTRATIONS

ILLUSTRATIONS

JOHN PAUL JONES:
Man of Action

CHAPTER I

*A Bold Captain Boards a Saucy Ship**

It is an Ancient Mariner,
And he stoppeth one of three.

. . . .

He holds him with his skinny hand;
" There was a ship," quoth he.

I

HERE he comes now, striding down the wharf towards
his ship with that firm, supple gait which has been
compared to a panther's. He carries himself erect,
with the air of a man who thinks well of himself and does not
care who knows it. He is returning after a ceremonious visit
ashore, dressed in the uniform of an American naval captain in
accordance with the regulations of the Marine Committee of
the Continental Congress dated September 5, 1776: three-
cornered hat, blue coat with red facings, slashed cuffs, high
stock collar from which flows a cascade of delicate white ruffles,
flat yellow buttons, scarlet waistcoat edged with lace, blue
breeches, white stockings, and low, soft-leather shoes. One of
the seamen swabbing the deck calls to his companions in a low
tone, and they pause to gaze over the rail with appreciation.
There can be no doubt about the picture the young captain presents, brightly outlined in his gay uniform against the dinginess
of the wharf. Everywhere he is famed for the neatness, almost
daintiness, of his dress. Even his buttonholes are embroidered
with gold thread. Foreign diplomats who have received him

* The quotations in verse at chapter headings are from *The Rime of the
Ancient Mariner*, by Samuel Taylor Coleridge.

[3]

in the expectation of beholding a coarse pirate with hair on chest, a burly fellow with anchors tattooed on his arms, have been disconcerted when confronted with a courtier of the waves, bearing himself with an irrefragable aplomb, and speaking in a resonant baritone a language reminding them faintly of something read in leather-bound classics. From his slender legs his body stems gracefully outward to a pair of powerful shoulders, roomy chest, and a swart and thickish neck. Moving with a pronounced dignity, he appears to be a formidable figure; and yet there is only five feet seven inches of him. His mouth is soft, though a little hard at the ends. His hands and feet are small like a girl's. As he approaches the ship, it is seen that his powdered hair, tied with a queue at the back, is really a dark brown, and that his straight-gazing, restless black eyes are really a dark grey, framed between jutting cheekbones.

Now his foot strikes the gangway. A bos'n's whistle pipes the side. "Boys," some in whiskers, spring forward and form a rigid lane. Lieutenants respectfully move to the other side of the deck. The marine sentry, dressed in British red instead of Continental green, stands at attention. All hands uncover their heads in silence as the captain steps on board. He salutes the quarterdeck, but according to an ancient tradition, ignores "the people." The men of the crew have no existence until they are dead; their names appear only on casualty lists. As he crosses the deck, the captain's glance cuts the air around him, but finds naught to criticize; his ship is, as usual, a "sweet" one. Once his cabin door is closed behind him, officers relax a little, but "the people" resume their duties with a double busyness, for John Paul Jones is once more on board his ship.

II

One who knows ships and seas says of the naval captain of the period: "He lived alone like a little God in heaven, shrouded from view by the cabin bulkheads, guarded by a red-coated sentry armed with a drawn sword. . . . No man on board dared to address him, save on some question relative to the duty of the day. No sailor could speak to him with his hat upon his head. One uncovered to one's captain as to one's God." [1]

Such was the aloofness deemed to be good form on the British ship of that day. It was the attitude cultivated by John Paul Jones himself, who had been reared on British traditions of the sea. Hear him:

" The commander should always impress his crew with the belief that whatever he does or may have to do, is right, and that like the Sovereign, he can do no wrong."

This attitude was a singularly unfortunate one for John Paul Jones to maintain. It was partly responsible for the subsequent descent upon him of an amount of trouble which not all his genius upon the sea and his great heart in action were able to avert. Nor were the British, for all their discipline, able to maintain it indefinitely with unaltered rigidity, for the eighteenth century closed with a mutiny among British seamen at Spithead and the Nore; and the year 1797 saw a " general assembly " of sailors run up the red flag and take charge of all warships in the English harbor of Portsmouth.

III

Of John Paul Jones's ship, can aught be said except that she was " sweet and clean " ? Aye, we may be sure she was also fast, for, he once wrote, " *I will not have anything to do with ships which do not sail fast, for I intend to go in harm's way.*" A " crank " ship with crotchety ways he could endure; but a slow one never. In appearance, this ship was doubtless something like that one of which John Masefield has lovingly written:

[1] John Masefield, *Sea Life in Nelson's Time.*

" A modern sailor, accustomed to the keen iron-ships of the present day, would have called such a ship a sea-wagon, qualified or otherwise, before spitting and passing by. But when the great sails were set, and the keel began to move through the sea, the cumbrous bulk took on attributes of beauty and nobility. There has been perhaps, no such beautiful thing on earth, the work of men's hands, as an old 74 under sail."

The best ships of that day were built slowly and affectionately by men who were good craftsmen and sometimes great artists. They loved their material and handled their tools fondly. When a vessel was completed, they liked to vent their fancy in rich carvings on the bow, the figure-head, and the blunt square-cut stern. And they painted her exterior sides yellow, which under the action of water and weather often became a rich, golden brown. Interior sides and surfaces were sometimes stained scarlet, so that the splashed blood of battle would not show. Stripes, gilt, and painted symbols on hull or sail sometimes added fantastic touches.

Leaders in the shipbuilding art were French. A French eighty-gun ship at the close of the eighteenth century, writes John Masefield, " was bigger, more roomy, faster, a finer ship in every way than our English ninety-eight-gun ship. Our own men of war were so badly designed and proportioned that they were said to have been built by the mile and cut off as required." [2]

Not far behind the French were the Spanish naval architects, led by a stern hidalgo named Paddy Mullins, from somewhere south of Dublin. Recognizing the superiority of the French builders, John Paul Jones eagerly examined their plans and technique at every opportunity, and being by nature a student of whatever pertained to his occupation, he became no mean ship designer himself, and rarely accepted a vessel without in some degree altering it to his taste, especially in the direction of

[2] *Sea Life in Nelson's Time.*

speed.   He meant to go in harm's way, but he also, when possible, meant to sail out of it.   He and Benjamin Franklin once collaborated on the design of a warship that was to outdo any other existing, but numerous distractions prevented its completion.

We can be sure, then, that, though he never commanded one so large as a 74, the ship which John Paul Jones has just boarded is as comely as any in her class, and that, in accordance with his habit of accepting the best that circumstances and politics will permit, he takes a pride in her and intends to force her to give her utmost.   The ship is the renowned *Ranger*, thus described: " In outward appearance she was a perfect beauty, her sheer being as delicate as the lines of a pretty woman's arm, and as she was rather low in the water for her length and her masts raked two or three degrees more than any other ship of the day, she was on the whole the sauciest craft afloat."

IV

While he is seated in his solitary cabin, those men of his crew who are not on duty exchange snatches of gossip about him; for a man so mysterious in his origin and movements as John Paul Jones is lawful food for tongues.   A whispered story that he was really christened John Paul is once more brought up; certain people say they know it to be a fact.   Why, then, did he add the name of Jones?   And when?   And where?   Follows comment, mixed with derisive laughter, about his recent order that the sun be saluted twice each day, morning and evening. He's a queer 'un.   Bit of a poet.   Mebbe so; but he can lick his weight in wild cats.   In the middle of a party at Norfolk, didn't he fair knock a drunken English lieutenant's head off for saying something low about American women?   Didn't he once, in a French café, walk up to a spy twice his size, slap his face, and challenge him to come out and fight?   Yes, chimes in a second

[7]

voice, and he's a seaman, too. Didn't he drive the *Ranger* across the Atlantic from Portsmouth to Nantes in thirty-two squally days, with the ship a-layin' on her beam-ends half the time? He did, agrees a third. And he treats his men fair, too. Didn't he throw the cat-o'-nine-tails overboard from the *Providence* and say he knew how to sail a ship without floggin' her crew to death?

People were always expressing opinions, usually very decided ones, about John Paul Jones. He was the sort of man who, wherever he appeared, caused talk. People seldom agreed about him. An Englishwoman, although he was at that moment at war with her countrymen, once pronounced him to be " the most agreeable seawolf one could hope to meet with." A French duchess, a true *grande dame*, called him " the untitled Knight of the Sea," " the wrathful Achilles of the Ocean," and " the Bayard afloat." Benjamin Franklin said he was not a man but a nor'wester. The French found him " un poète à ses heures." The English called him a pirate, renegade and blackguard.

Even the nib of Abigail Adams's pen, usually so mordant, altered a little when it touched upon the gifted captain. Writing from Paris, where her husband, John Adams of Massachusetts, was one of the American Commissioners, she outlined for Elizabeth Cranch this portrait in pastel:

" Chevalier Jones you have heard much of; he is a most uncommon character. I dare say you would be as much disappointed in him as I was. From the intrepid character he justly supported in the American Navy, I expected to have seen a rough, stout, warlike Roman, — instead of that I should sooner think of wrapping him up in cotton-wool, and putting him into my pocket, than sending him to contend with cannon balls. He is small of stature, well proportioned, soft in his speech, easy in his address, polite in his manners, vastly civil, understands all the etiquette of a lady's toilette as perfectly as he does the mast, sails and rigging of his ship. Under all this appearance of softness he is bold, enterprising, ambitious and active. He has been here often, and dined with us several times; he is said to be a man of gallantry and a favorite amongst the French ladies, whom he is frequently commending for the neatness of their persons, their easy manners, and their taste in dress. He knows how often the ladies use the baths, and what color best suits a lady's complexion, what cosmetics are most favorable to the skin. We do not often see the warrior and the *abigail* thus united."

As for her husband, John Adams, who succeeded George Washington as president of the United States, he found it difficult to make up his mind about John Paul Jones. Half the time he hated the bold captain; the other half he praised Jones with faint damns. In the first place, the captain was not a New Englander but " a foreigner of the South " — a grave and well-nigh insuperable defect. In the second place, Mr. Adams's chilly eye was affronted by the gallant seaman's colorful uniform. What with its golden buttonholes and epaulets, the thing was scandalous if not, in tendency, immoral. But let us hear Mr. Adams himself. The scene is a cosmopolitan restaurant, the *Epée Royale*, at the French port of Lorient, where Mr. Adams, as the guest of Captain Jones, has come down from Paris to inspect the *Ranger:*

" An elegant dinner we had, and all very agreeable. . . . Some hints about language and glances about women, produced this observation: — that there were two ways of learning French commonly recommended, — take a mistress and go to the comedy. Dr. Brooks [3] (in high good humor): 'Pray, sir, which in your opinion is best? ' Answer, in as good humor: ' Perhaps both would teach it soonest; to be sure, sooner than either.' ' But,' continued I, assuming my gravity, ' the language is no where better spoken than at the Comédie. The pulpit, the bar, the Academy of Science, and the Faculty of Medicine — none of them speak so accurately as the French Comédie.'

[3] Dr. Lawrence Brooke of Virginia, afterwards surgeon on the *Bon Homme Richard.*

[9]

" After dinner, walked out with Captains Jones and Landais to see Jones' marines, dressed in the English uniform, red and white; a number of very active and clever sergeants and corporals are employed to teach them the exercises and manoeuvres and marches, &c.; after which Jones came on board our ship. This is the most ambitious and intriguing officer in the American Navy. Jones has art and secrecy, and aspires very high. You see the character of the man in his uniform, and that of his officers and marines, variant from the uniforms established by Congress, — golden buttonholes for himself, two epaulettes — marines in red and white instead of green.[4] Eccentricities and irregularities are to be expected from him. They are in his character, they are visible in his eye. His voice is soft and still and small; his eye has keenness and wildness and softness in it." [5]

John Adams's own eye had jaundice in it; but it could sometimes see with considerable clarity. The keen, wild look characteristic of the colonial sea-rover was a heritage, perhaps, from his Highland mother, but the high cheekbone was a characteristic often seen on the men of the Scottish Lowlands, in which John Paul, afterwards called Jones, was born, as nearly as it can be fixed, on July 6, 1747. The place was the fishing village of Arbigland, Parish of Kirkbean, Stewartry of Kirkcudbright, on the north shore of Solway Firth, in the southwest country which produced William Wallace, Robert Bruce, John Knox, and Robert Burns. That dark hair perhaps was handed down from the Danes, " the black-haired strangers," who invaded Strath-

---

[4] Certain historians and historical paintings are responsible for the erroneous impression that the Continental soldiery was dressed in buff and blue. These colors were actually found only on staff officers. American privates of the Revolutionary period fought mostly in green or brown. Green was the color officially chosen for the Continental Marines, this choice possibly being influenced by the popular Culpeper Riflemen of Virginia, victors in an early battle with the British. Their captain was named Green, and out of compliment to him his men wore green shirts. Mr. Adams erred, however, in finding fault with John Paul Jones for dressing his marines in British colors. Jones did this on his cruises in British waters in order to deceive enemy captains.

[5] From the *Diary* in the *Works of John Adams.*

clyde in 857. There's no doubt that John Paul Jones had combative blood in him, whether inherited or acquired.

A year before the dark little John Paul was born, the English had crushed, on April 16, 1746, the last hopes for Scottish independence at the battle of Culloden; in consequence there settled down upon those who had dreamed of a Stuart prince again upon the Scottish throne, a brooding despair which caused Smollett to write " The Tears of Scotland." Scotsmen who had fought for Bonnie Prince Charlie fled or were deported by thousands to Ireland, Canada, and to America.[6]

His having been reared in this atmosphere of resentment and defeated hopes perhaps accounts for the bitterness [7] which John Paul Jones, the half Gael, frequently manifested against the English as a race, though he was ever ready to admire individuals as seamen and fighters. He once wrote from France to a friend:

" My relations with the people across the Channel are known to all. .Their enemies must be my friends everywhere; those whom they hate, I must love."

Here, then, we have our picture of John Paul Jones: he is young, being only a few years over thirty; he is gallant; he is a bit of a poet; he loves danger; he is bold and ambitious; and as a Highland woman's son, he hates the English. He is a man of " irregularities." From such a one anything may be expected.

[6] The Lowlanders came chiefly to New York and Pennsylvania. The Highlanders, curiously enough, preferred Virginia and the Carolinas, where, curiously again, some of them fought for the English king, George III, in the American War for Independence.

[7] In his *Journal* he refers to " the revolting spectacle of horrors which desolated Scotland in 1745," doubtless meaning the events which led up to Culloden.

CHAPTER II

A Canvas and a Figure

The Wedding Guest sat on a stone:
He cannot choose but hear;
And thus spake on that ancient man,
The bright-eyed Mariner.

BORN as the son of a gardener, John Paul appeared like an obscure speck in the middle of the broad canvas of the eighteenth century — a canvas streaked with blood, murder, rebellion, greed, and many winds of doctrine. It was a century of transition during which nations were racked by internal as well as external wars. It saw the birth-struggle, rise, and eventual domination of a human stratum new to history — known in English history as the great middle class and in French as the *bourgeoisie*. This class was composed of traders, living chiefly in the port towns.

It was the discovery of the New World with its unoccupied lands and resources, combined with the opening of an all-water route to India, which first awakened this class to the possibilities of great profits. Its opportunity came with the improvement in transportation, particularly by sea. Trading vessels, laden both ways, soon dotted with white the green waters to those fabulous lands — America and India. Urged by commercial foresight, the trading classes of each of the *soi-disant* Christian countries then assiduously set about getting astride the great ocean routes of the world. Becoming powerful as gains mounted, they put pressure on their respective governments, and England, France, Holland and Spain, the chief sea-trading nations, were soon tearing at each other's throats. They fought each other singly and by pairs, and no nation could say which ally of today would be its loathsome enemy tomorrow; for governments then as now, conducted themselves with an absence of principle which would bring a private individual to the gallows as a scoundrel or horse-thief. First in the arena were the Spanish, with their romantic belief in valleys full of gold and gems to be found in the Americas; but the wreck of the glittering Armada had discouraged them beyond full recovery. Their cannier and more matter-of-fact rivals, the English, who were the first to become " a nation of shop keepers," wasted no time in credulous searches for yellow gold. Just seventeen years after the birth of John Paul Jones, Hargreaves invented the spinning jenny, and the Industrial Revolution began. Men now rapidly learned to make goods by machinery instead of hand-power, and the strife for markets which would absorb exports was initiated on a grand scale. As the century developed the English sought " black-gold " in the form of African slaves, which they collected, shipped, and sold, in addition to other merchandise, to their successfully expanding colonies. France tried very hard, but, distracted by wars and internal problems, gained no permanent success in either founding colonies or controlling trade routes. Holland did better, but its inferior resources were unable long to cope with those of England, to which it was in the course of a hundred years now a fond auxiliary, now a dangerous adversary. The latter part of the century also saw the entry of Russia, with its capture of the Crimea, as a world-power competing for open routes and warm ports.

As the years waxed the rivalry on the sea became ever fiercer. Armies embarked, sailed, and disembarked in remote lands as admiralty officers bowed obsequiously to the demands of powerful merchant companies. Ships were widened, deepened, and sharpened, and designs were repeatedly altered to admit of ever more and more guns. Admirals and commodores became no more than errand-boys and strong-arm men for huge commercial interests. Press-gangs scoured ports and even inland towns for recruits, dragging whimpering men from their beds to the cold decks of ships or to dark holds where scurvy, decayed food, pestilence, cruelty, and perversion made a foul feast for the latent sadism of the more callous officers and masters to grin upon. The pressure of the English merchants for results became more and more insistent, culminating at the battle of Minorca in 1756, when Vice-Admiral, the Honorable George Byng, was ordered to hurl his fleet upon that of the French Admiral, Galissonière. Byng withdrew after an indecisive battle. The mercantile classes of England, already choleric over recent successes of France at sea, boiled over. The newspapers echoed their fury. Byng was called home, court-martialed, convicted, and shot to death by marines on the deck of the *Monarch*.

Byng was a harmless commander of the humdrum sort, and never popular, but the navies of the world were horrified at the verdict. Across the bay from the English town of White-haven, on the Scottish side of Solway Firth, the incident made a deep impression on the lad John Paul, as his correspondence shows; while in France Voltaire seized his saturnine pen and wrote:

" In that country they consider it a good thing to shoot an admiral now and then, to encourage the others."

The very opening of the century was christened with blood. In 1704 the English, aided by the Dutch, attacked and seized Gibraltar from the Spanish. On returning, the successful commander, Admiral Rooke, encountered a French fleet and fought with it an all-day battle. This fleet was commanded by the Count de Toulouse, son of Louis XIV by Madame de Montespan. When John Paul, then surnamed Jones, came upon an account of this battle, he studied it with eagerness, and when, haloed by fame, he afterwards met the grand-daughter of the

Count, his approving comments so charmed her that she became his friend on the spot. And she was a friend indeed, for she was a great lady and a potent one in the France of her day.

This, then, is the canvas against which the figure of the Scotch gardener's son, when he stepped out into the world to earn his living, was projected. These were the forces which he was compelled to mount and ride, or else be overwhelmed and destroyed by underlying currents which had dragged down men far mightier than he. He entered the welter alone, friendless, and without influence; but he had as allies youth, physical vigor, a perceptive mind, personal charm, and a steely determination to win distinction, applause, and power. If at times he was barely able to keep his nose above the waves, he was sustained by that steadying life-preserver, his vanity. It was a tremendous vanity, in both width and depth, yet it rested upon a foundation of undeniable ability; and hence was, by more than a degree, forgivable. And he could be forgiven the more, because his romantic emotional temperament, in the very attaining of his triumphs, caused him to suffer much.

CHAPTER III

A Little Bark Is Launched

O Wedding Guest! this soul hath been
Alone on a wide, wide sea:
So lonely 't was, that God himself
Scarcely seemed there to be.

I

IT is a noteworthy fact that nowhere in his numerous collected writings does John Paul Jones allude to his father. For his mother he had an often expressed attachment, but regarding John Paul, the father, he was silent. Whether there was an enmity between them, and whether this enmity was due to the father's failure to perceive that he had a genius for a son, it cannot now be said, but there is no evidence of sympathy between the two. The elder John Paul, of a Fifeshire family, came to the west coast of Scotland from Leith on the east coast, where his forefathers had lived for years. He was engaged by Robert Craik, a member of Parliament, as a landscape gardener on the estate of Arbigland, which had been purchased from the third Earl of Selkirk, who retained another estate to the north, the castle of which sat upon a promontory called Saint Mary's Isle, at the mouth of the river Dee. On this Isle, his brother, George Paul, was also a landscape gardener for the Selkirks, and it was on Saint Mary's Isle, under the care of his uncle, that the little John Paul played, waded, and sailed toy ships during his formative years. His mother was Jeannie Macduff, daughter of an Argyll Highlander and gunsmith named Ian Macduff, who had come down to Dumfries from Inverary, possibly with the intention of teaching the Lowlanders how to " lay on."

She added to the family income through her employment as helper and lady's maid to Mrs. Robert Craik. Since it is largely through mothers that family and racial traditions are handed down, the boy John Paul doubtless learned from his own that love of arms and battles in which he later showed himself to be well steeped.

John Paul, Jr., was the youngest of five surviving children. Of these three were girls. His only brother, William, came to Fredericksburg, Va., in the wave of the Scottish immigration which followed Culloden, and died there leaving a will in which there was no mention of his brother John Paul. It is an odd fact that the birth of neither of the two sons is recorded. There was something queer in the relations between the other members of the family and the little John. Was it because he believed his veins contained a different blood from theirs and a superior one? "In after times," says one of his biographers,[1] "when the name of Jones became the subject of romantic interest, an effort was made to assign to him what was thought a nobler origin, as the natural son of the Earl of Selkirk, or of Mr. Craik"; and Thomas Chase, of Martha's Vineyard, Mass., who sailed on one of Jones's ships, has left behind a memoir in which he mentions his captain's belief that he was the son of the Earl of Selkirk.

If this be true, it explains much regarding Jones's repeated use in his letters of the word "gentleman," his occasional haughty attitudes, and his subsequent relations with the Selkirk family. There is no proof, however, that John Paul's romantic heart was fed by aught but common blood, for during his boyhood the Earl of Selkirk was a very old man living chiefly at Edinburgh, and as for Robert Craik, he did have a natural son, but he afterwards came to Alexandria, Va., and became the friend and physician of George Washington.

[1] Alexander Slidell Mackenzie, U.S.N., *Life of Paul Jones.*

[17]

II

All that is known about the childhood of John Paul is that he played freely about the shores of Solway Firth, sometimes crossing in fishermen's boats to the English town of White-haven, and that he was in time sent to school by his Presbyterian parents. An old anecdote says that John Paul was once whipped by his school master for some shortcoming, whereupon he way-laid the master that night and beat him fiercely with a huge stick.

His behavior in his mature years indicated that he had been a lonely, introspective boy, growing strong and energetic in the salty air, but holding himself a little apart from his playmates, and much given to books, chiefly naval history and poetry. It would not be strange to learn that his companions and fellow townsmen considered him an odd little fish and one not des-tined to amount to much.

At the age of twelve or fourteen came his first thrilling ex-perience. " Since his earliest boyhood," he afterwards wrote, " America had been the country of his fond predilection." He now got a chance to visit his fairyland and to launch himself upon those fierce currents of which we have spoken. It was as an apprentice on the brig *Friendship* — a title which in itself must have appeared immensely winning to an impressionable lad who, in all his later life, responded eagerly to affection. The ship belonged to James Younger, a Whitehaven merchant and over-seas trader. It carried young John and his thirsty eyes to the famed shores of the Rappahannock in Virginia. At the head of navigation here stood the little town of Fredericksburg, in which the Rev. Patrick Henry, uncle of the orator, was a rector of the Church of England, and here, at the Rising Sun Tavern, the very young Colonel George Washington, whose family lived across the river, often came to take, between discussions of the detested Stamp Act, his customary beating at cards.

Here William Paul had already established himself as a tailor and bought a half acre of ground for which he paid £120. Fredericksburg was in Colonial days an important market town and cultural centre, having inhabitants of some wealth, taste and leisure. It had a few manufactures and throve upon a growing trade with England and with other American colonies. " Wagon trains, miles in length, loaded with grain were frequently seen approaching it from the mountains, merchant ships anchored at its wharf to purchase flour and other products, and sea captains and sailors moved constantly through its streets." [2] Nearby were the iron mines fostered by Governor Spottswood, and it was here that Col. Fielding Lewis, husband of George Washington's only sister, Betty, built a gunnery which supplied small arms to the Continental armies during the Revolutionary War. In Fredericksburg, too, could be seen the graceful women who, a few years later, were admired by the gallant Jones, though he never succeeded in marrying one of them. Had he done so, his subsequent career would undoubtedly have been far less spectacular than it actually was.

III

In the course of numerous voyages to America and the West Indies, John Paul gained the experience and sharpened the ability which caused his promotion to a mate's berth, though he was still in his teens. On Younger's retirement from the shipping trade, John Paul seems to have obtained an acting midshipman's warrant in the British navy, apparently through the influence of the Duke of Queensbury, who happened to notice the vigorous youth when visiting Lord Selkirk at Saint Mary's Isle. The only evidence regarding his movements at this time, however, is contained in two somewhat vague statements later

[2] Vivian Minor Fleming, *Historic Periods of Fredericksburg.*

made by John Paul himself in letters to Robert Morris, the Revolutionary financier, when he referred to his having " sailed before this revolution in armed ships and frigates " and mentioned his acquaintance with " many officers of note in the British Navy."

This latter reference is characteristic. John Paul Jones liked to associate with persons whom he regarded as having superiority and distinction.

Young Paul's stay in the Royal Navy was brief, but there exists no record to show how and why he left it. One described simply as " a fellow lodger " of Paul's at an unnamed place asserts that Paul was aggrieved because " his juniors were promoted while he remained unnoticed." This sounds plausible; John Paul was always resenting something. At any rate, he was soon back in the merchant service, and found himself third mate on a ship engaged in the slave trade.

IV

Every century is stained with some unforgivable crime. The eighteenth's woeful contribution to history was the African slave trade. It was begun by Sir John Hawkins, famous for one other historic introduction — that of the potato to Ireland — in the reign of Queen Elizabeth, who herself profited from the traffic. It is estimated that in a hundred years seven million slaves were imported from Africa to America, and out of every 100,000 shipped over twenty thousand died during the voyage.

" The Negroes were chained to each other hand and foot, and stowed so close that they were not allowed above a foot and a half for each. Thus crammed together like herrings in a barrel, they contracted putrid and fatal disorders; so that they who came to inspect them in the morning had occasion to pick dead slaves out of their rows, and to unchain their carcasses from the bodies of their wretched fellow sufferers to whom they had been fastened." [3]

Ships of all nationalities engaged in the trade — British, French, Spanish, Dutch and American, some owners and masters going at the business brutally, others with Bibles in their hands. It laid the bases of fortunes on both sides of the Atlantic, and made towns like Liverpool, England, and Newport, R. I., plethoric and powerful. The acquisition by England of the chief islands in the West Indies, with their great sugar plantations, gave the trade a vast impetus, for it supplied the shipping business with a solid, triangular foundation — slaves, rum and molasses. British ships brought slaves to the West Indies, whence American ships carried them and their product, molasses, to New England. From the molasses New England traders made rum, which was then shipped to Africa to be exchanged for more slaves, which were sold to the Southern states.

On April 2, 1775, the master of a ship wrote to his employers, the Champlin Brothers of Newport, the great American slave port, from Annamaboe, Africa: " I have on Board at this time 20 slaves . . . I sold 30 Hoghh of Rum . . . Sum days I git two or three Slaves and then For a weeake not see one. Gardnier is sold all his Rum at 200 and 210 . . . I had the misfortune to Git the Measels among my slaves, loss one Boy with it and Have another of my own that Is very Bad." And again:

" I give 160 gals for men and 140 for women, as I cood not git them for less. I have but 15 slaves on board yet . . . the 22th day of August I buried Mr. Whyatt he Died with the feaver so that I am but poorly mand at present. It has been very sickly heare."

Here and there protests were raised, chiefly by Quakers, against the trade in black flesh, but the New World's desire for

[3] Ingram's *History of Slavery.*

[21]

cheap and sun-proof labor overbore all scruples; so that in the end the trade was participated in by some of the most pious inhabitants of Colonial America. Thus did the slave trade pass through the usual stages by which the human mind reconciles itself to all occupations: that is, a thing is first expedient, then profitable, next moral, and finally divine.

"The merchants of Boston quoted negroes like any other merchandise demanded by their correspondents;"[4] and even Phyllis Wheatley, the first and for a long time the only Negro poetess in America, was bought in 1761 in the open market at The Hub by Mrs. John Wheatley, wife of a genteel Boston merchant, as if she were a turkey or wild rabbit.

v

It is an odd fact that a letter has been preserved indicating that John Paul Jones was sufficiently interested in Phyllis Wheatley to write to her. It was found by the writer in the J. P. Morgan Library in New York. No date or place where written is indicated except that it was aboard the *Ranger* on a Friday. It is addressed to Hector McNeill, John Paul's fellow Scot and naval captain at Boston:

"I am on the point of sailing — I have to write to you — pray be so good as put the Inclosed into the hands of the Celebrated Phyllis the African Favorite of the Muse and of Apollo — should she reply, I hope you will be the bearer. I am, yours always,
                                        "JNO. P. JONES"

It is a pity John Paul's enclosed letter has been lost. Why did he invite a correspondence with Phyllis? Did his letter relate to the African slave trade, of which they both knew so much, or to poetry, of which John Paul was so fond?

[4] Weeden, *Economic and Social History of New England.*

VI

John Paul received an interest in the slave ship, *King George*, which made two voyages between Jamaica and the Guinea coast. He then transferred himself to another slave ship, the *Two Friends*, as first mate, when he was about nineteen years old. He remained in the slave trade about two years, and then quit it abruptly. "It is stated by his relatives," writes James Hamilton, "the only source of information that is either accessible or to be relied on, that he quitted this abominable trade in disgust at its enormities."[5] This may be correct; for John Paul was easily affected by the sight of suffering or oppression. On the other hand, the slave trade was, in that day, entirely respectable, especially in New England, where it built many tidy homes, supported pulpits, and paid for decorous comforts unknown before. It was not until slavery was suspected of being unprofitable in comparison with "free labor" that it began to be preached against.[6] It is a peculiar fact, as proved by the Declaration of Independence, written by Thomas Jefferson, that one of the chief grievances of the American colonists against George III was his nullification of their efforts to abolish the slave trade; and years prior to the Civil War the Southern states, which saw themselves being drowned in a superfluity of slaves, began to nurse a resentment against Northern slave traders which was voiced by Congressman Smith of South Carolina in this speech:

"Pharaoh was, for his temerity, drowned in the Red Sea, in pursuing them (the Israelites) contrary to God's express will; but our Northern friends have not been afraid even of that, in

---

[5] *Life of Rear Admiral John Paul Jones*, 1845.

[6] "An opinion is entertained by increasing numbers, that slave labor is too expensive to be continued in a grain-growing state, if its place can be supplied by freemen. In other words, that the free labor would cost less and work harder than the slave." — *Historical Collections of Virginia*.

their zeal to furnish the Southern States with Africans. They are better seamen than Pharaoh, and calculate by that means to elude the Vengeance of Heaven; which they seem to disregard if they can but elude the violated laws of their country." [7]

What seems likely is that John Paul abandoned the slave trade because it was sapping his health. It was notorious that sailors in the slave trade died faster and had more diseases than others, due to the foul conditions aboard slave ships and the pestilences exhaled from their holds. In his letters home about this period young Paul mentions his " poor health " and " several very severe fevers lately."

VII

Meantime the wheel of war had undergone several more spins. In 1759 England had triumphed over the land forces of France at the battle of Quebec and dealt another blow to French sea-power through Admiral Hawke's victory at Quiberon Bay. She followed this up with victories in the Seven Years' War, and then soon after the accession of George III, by triumphs over Spain, took Martinique, Havana, and Manila. The peace settlement of 1763 gave England the West Indian islands of Tobago, St. Vincent, and Grenada, and strengthened her hold on the trade-routes through the Caribbean Sea.

Being without employment, John Paul then went on the stage, joining the company of John Moody, the Irish actor, playing the island of Jamaica. John Paul's rôle was that of young " Bevil " in *The Conscious Lovers*. He was just 21 years old. His training as an actor, though not extensive, no doubt proved valuable to him in later years. It strengthened his latent histrionic gifts, taught him the use of his body and

[7] *Annals of Congress*, 16th Congress, 1st session.

voice, enabled him to face crowds with equanimity, and gave him that for which he was afterwards to become remarked — "presence." In later years his acquaintances used to wonder where this gardener's son acquired his distinct speech and easy self-possession in courts and palaces. His Jamaican stage experience is probably the answer. All the rest of his life he was at moments somewhat histrionic.

VIII

Having earned enough as an actor to pay his passage back to Scotland, he boarded the Scottish-owned *John*, sailing for Kirkcudbright. On the voyage, both the captain and the first mate died of fever, and the youthful John Paul, being called to the command, took the vessel safely home. This pleased the owners, who promptly made him master of the *John*. His first voyage was successful, and the precocious young skipper now looked forward to a rising career as master and trader. He was not yet in funds, however, for in 1770 he wrote from Grenada to Robert Craik: "I must beg you to supply my mother should she want anything, as I well know your readiness."

On his next arriving at Kirkcudbright he sought and obtained admission to the Masonic lodge there. The early part of the eighteenth century saw a tremendous spurt in the growth of Freemasonry. The period being a transitional one, and hence troubled, men instinctively sought to band themselves together, swearing to respect and protect each other in a democratic brotherhood of man. The most conspicuous men on both sides of the Atlantic sought the shelter of Masonry. Among these was George Washington, who joined Fredericksburg, Va., Lodge No. 4, in 1752. His example was followed by a host of Colonial leaders who afterwards became the generals and statesmen of the Revolutionary War. To this day American Masonry is proud to call John Paul Jones a member, and the lodge at Alexandria, Va., long displayed a flag which was said to have been one of his when he drove the bow of the *Bon Homme Richard* over the cracking side of the *Serapis*.

CELEBRATED EVERYWHERE FOR THE NEATNESS AND
GALLANTRY OF HIS ATTIRE.

CHAPTER IV

A Whip and a Sword

Ah! well-a-day! what evil looks
Had I from old and young!
Instead of the cross, the Albatross
About my neck was hung.

I

IN the early summer of 1770 John Paul's ship was lying in Rockley Bay, at the West Indian island of Tobago, which is the southernmost of the Windward Isles. Full of the pride of life in his capacity as a twenty-three-year-old skipper, he looked from the deck now down upon his sweating crew, now upward to the island's high crest streaked with tropical greenness.

There was one man on the vessel who was not working according to John Paul's notion of fitness. He was the ship's carpenter, a mulatto named Mungo Maxwell. The young skipper strode forward and bawled at him sharply. Maxwell replied mumblingly, rolled his sultry eyes, and showed no disposition to look alive. On a ship such conduct toward a captain is outrage, it is treason, it is mutiny. John Paul acted hastily but according to law and tradition. He seized a whip and lashed it many times across the carpenter's shoulders, raising long bruised welts. Maxwell, not daring to retaliate, went to the judge of the island vice-admiralty court and lodged a charge. Captain Paul was summoned. His defence was that Maxwell had deserved the beating, at the same time, according to the judge's subsequent statement, " declaring his sorrow for having corrected the complainant." This was characteristic of John Paul: he was often given to rash action, which he afterwards repented in misery. The case was dismissed as frivolous. The beaten carpenter then left his job and shipped on another vessel trading between Tobago and Antigua. A few weeks later he died, according to the captain of the ship, of " a fever and lowness of spirits." But when John Paul returned to Scotland he learned that rumors had accused him of Maxwell's death. This is how the incident was afterwards related in the *London Evening Post:*

" As the carpenter was, in one of the hot days of summer, laying fast asleep upon the deck, Paul anointed his hair pretty plentifully with turpentine, after which he led a train of gunpowder at some distance, which setting fire to the carpenter, he instantly bounded up, and in the confusion . . . jumped overboard and was never more heard of."

John Paul's family was doubtful and worried, the neighbors whispered, and Robert Craik announced that he would have nothing more to do with the young brute. At the same time Paul learned that the owners of his ship were dissolving partnership. His discharge was honorable, but it left him once more jobless, depressed, and uncertain where to turn.

For a time he tried trading with the Isle of Man, his cargoes being composed chiefly of rum. But the image of the dead carpenter gave him, in turn, fever and lowness of spirits; and he at last went to Tobago again, where the judge in the case and the lieutenant-governor, after a six months' wait, gave him signed documents exculpating him of crime. On returning to the British Isles he went to London, where he wrote to his mother and sisters a letter heavy with depression. He mentioned his poor health, which had " added very much to the asperity of my misfortunes," referred to his consciousness of innocence " before heaven," and concluded with a bitter reference to Robert Craik: " His ungracious conduct to me before I

left Scotland I have not yet been able to get the better of. . . .
It is true I bore it with seeming unconcern, but heaven can
witness for me that I suffered the more on that very account."

From this time John Paul closed a certain compartment
within himself. He never wrote to Craik, never returned to
Arbigland, and never visited his mother again. His father was
then dead. His gravestone bears this inscription: " In memory
of John Paul, Senior, who died at Arbigland the 24th of October, 1767, Universally Esteemed. Erected by John Paul,
Junior."

II

In London, after a long delay, things took a sudden upward
turn. Young Paul obtained backers and enough money to buy
the *Betsey,* a trading ship. He sailed for Ireland, took on a
cargo at Cork, and in April, 1773, after fourteen months of
trading among the West Indies, was again at the fateful island
of Tobago. He knew he had evil-wishers there, but, conscious
of his innocence, he meant to show them that he was not afraid.
His self-confidence, always ready to gush upwards, had returned; he was captain of his own ship, he had as partner
Archibald Stuart, a Tobago planter; and was making valuable
friends. This at the age of twenty-six. While discharging
cargo at Tobago he added several new men to his crew. They
were a rough lot, nearly all them stained and calloused by the
rum and slave traffic, in which though detesting it in their
hearts, they remained because of its high pay.

Almost at once trouble began. The older members of the
crew were already surly because of unpaid wages. The new-
comers, to show their sympathy, broke into the captain's cabin
and stole his liquors, on which they all started a carouse together. A spokesman was appointed to face the upstart of a
stingy Scotch skipper in his cabin and demand that wages be
paid up to date. John Paul, hard-pressed for cash, had nothing

[29]

to offer except clothing from the ship's stores. A loud argument resulted. It ended in epithets. John Paul snatched his sword from a table. The sailor ran, with Paul in pursuit. The former swept up a club from the deck and turned. The sailor made too wide a lunge. He left his breast open, and John Paul's sword, directed by a trained wrist, flashed and ran him through.

The account which John Paul subsequently wrote of this fight leaves little doubt of the horror which at once gripped him. He was a tiger in combat, but the instant it was over he was again the dreamer and man of peace and poetry. He fully realized the danger of his position. He ordered his men below and returned to his cabin, leaving flattened upon the quarterdeck a tattered thing from which a stream of blood slowly wormed its way across the calked planking toward the scuppers.

His first action was to send for his chief mate. The demeanor of this man made it plain where his sympathy lay. John Paul at once left the ship. He went to the town, and offered to surrender himself to a justice of the peace. Friends were summoned. They persuaded him to delay his surrender to some future date. Meantime he must get out of the country. The appearance of things was blackly against him. It was the second time in three years that a man had died at Tobago after receiving blows from him. Who would now believe in his innocence, no matter how genuine? Besides, revenge was to be expected; the island was full of men with grievances against overbearing ship-captains. His friends insisted he leave his affairs in the hands of an agent. They concluded by ordering a horse for him. They put him on it, and said: " Ride! "

And John Paul rode.

III

From that instant John Paul rode into a silence. As John Paul he disappeared, not only from the sight of his West Indian friends, but from history. When the forlorn individual who once bore this name reappeared on the pages of verifiable records, it was in a different land among a different people, and he signed himself with a new and different name. Why?

The documents that might solve the mystery no longer exist, if indeed they ever did. From this time forward, for a period of nearly two years, we must let go the plain, if unsteady, hand of history, as related to the former John Paul, and venture into the untrustworthy wilderness of half-history, reminiscence, and legend. Out of this nebulous material, threaded with a few unassorted facts, we will try to reconstruct the movements of a man who, except for this single period, welcomed the limelight's play upon himself and all his deeds.

" It may be said," he once wrote in his eighteenth century style, " that I have been unfortunate — but it cannot be made to appear that I have ever, even in the weakest Moment of my Life, been capable of a Base or mean Action. Nature has given me a heart that is highly susceptible to the finer feelings."

CHAPTER V

Twenty Months of Darkness

An orphan's curse would drag to hell
A spirit from on high;
But oh! more horrible than that
Is a curse in a dead man's eye.

I

WHEN the solitary young horseman rode away from Rockley Bay, it was with his chin upon his breast. Tobago had again proved itself to be his isle of misfortune. It was natural for him to wish to be quit of it forever; and so it is surmised that he rode southward across the island, reached the water, and there hired a boat to ferry him over the fifteen miles of sea to Trinidad, the nearest land. Trinidad, being in Spanish hands, offered an obvious refuge from possible pursuers from British territory. But his successful escape probably gave him only momentary relief. There can be no question about the tortures which danced in his dark-tinged mind, his colorful imagination, after the killing of the sailor aboard the *Betsey*. He afterwards described it to friends as an accident, and always referred to it as " the misfortune of my life." For a sinewy man of the sea, accustomed to the hardships of the deck from boyhood, John Paul Jones remained throughout his life strangely sensitive and affectible. He exulted in battle, as became one of Highland corpuscles, but he had no genuine taste for bloodshed, and he sometimes went to curious lengths to avoid a personal combat. Your man of action is often like that; for every intense moment he pays in hours of reaction and revulsion. No man is continuously a hero; the strain of being heroic is too great.

In taking John Paul to Trinidad, however, we are only in-dulging in conjecture. There is no record as to his movements until September of this unfortunate year of 1773. Thomas Chase, 3rd, at first a Maine clergyman and later a lawyer, then takes up the thread with a narrative which he offers as having been taken down from the lips of his grandfather, Thomas Chase, a Massachusetts sailor who afterward sailed with John Paul Jones on an American man-o'-war.

The story may be thus summarized: Chase was a stripling, living on the island of Martha's Vineyard, Mass., when one day "a rakish, clipper built craft, painted entirely black" sailed into the harbor of Holme's Hole and put ashore the body of an officer for burial. Chase himself made the coffin. The leader of the burial squad remained on the island several days, during which the inhabitants had time to notice that he was "about five feet six inches high," "had a very broad chest and shoulders," and "a resonant and powerful voice." The crew, numbering about forty men, "mostly Spanish with a few Portuguese among them," seemed to regard this man as their captain. He finally told Chase that his name was Paul Jones, and "it was evident at this time that he really believed himself to be an illegitimate son of the Earl of Selkirk, whose mansion was near Whitehaven, on the west coast of Scotland, near the border of England. He said that his first recollections were of the servants' quarters in the Earl's establishment; that he was called John Paul, and told that his father's name was Paul. He also said that he was ignorant as to the exact date of his birth."

Two years later, it is related, Chase was aboard a Colonial privateer when he was captured by a British ship and carried to Plymouth jail. Subsequently he was exchanged and sent to Lorient, France, where he encountered Jones, was recognized

[33]

by him, and taken aboard the *Bon Homme Richard* just before the battle with the *Serapis*.

When Jones was later harassing the British coast, the English newspapers insisted on calling him a pirate; and this narrative by Chase, though not a part of accepted history, would seem to indicate that they were right, although Jones was no pirate when they called him such, but a regularly appointed captain in the Continental navy. It is possible, therefore, that after his escape to Trinidad, Jones, lacking money and friends, had to take what employment he could, and so shipped aboard one of the Spanish corsairs which made a business of running down the British merchantmen which plied between America, Africa, and the Spanish Main. But he could not have been in the humor to remain long in such a trade, and no doubt he left it as soon as he had replenished his purse. Where then did he go? And for what reason did he cease to be John Paul and sign himself, as in the previously quoted letter to Phyllis Wheatley, as " Jno. P. Jones " ?

II

Concerning these two points the opinions of biographers differ widely; and unfortunately for the integrity of history they offer as fact what is no more than theory, or else an incautious leaping at conclusions. Previous biographers of John Paul Jones may be divided into three schools. The first of these rapidly pass over this obscure period of Jones's life, but make a somewhat unconvincing effort to account for his addition of a new surname by asserting that it was the habit of Welsh Gaels to create a surname out of what was at first a single " given " name. Jones, for example, was originally " John's son," contracted to Johnson, and then again contracted. But there is no convincing evidence that such a practice was common among latter-day Scots. The second school is led by Col. Augustus C. Buell, whose book, *Paul Jones, Founder of the*

American Navy, declares that the young captain about this time went to Virginia to take over a substantial Virginia estate, worked by slaves, left by his brother, who renamed himself " William Paul Jones " after a wealthy benefactor named William Jones. But William Paul's gravestone at Fredericksburg, Va., bears the simple legend: " William Paul, 1774 "; his will contained no reference whatever to his brother John; and the value of his estate was trifling. The two executors he named declined to act, and one John Atkinson was finally appointed administrator. Consequently, there would seem to be no adequate reason here for John Paul's change of name.

The third school comprises the Rev. Cyrus Townsend Brady and Mrs. Reginald De Koven. These biographers depict Jones as wandering to Edenton, N. C., where he met and was befriended by two brothers celebrated in North Carolina history: Willie (pronounced Wylie) Jones, statesman and born leader, and Allen Jones, later a brigadier-general in the Revolutionary War. They describe the wandering young Scotsman as having been the house guest of these two men, and Willie Jones as his particular patron and supporter. They suppose also that it was in the leisured home of these two brothers, educated at Eton, England, that John Paul learned the manner which afterward sat upon him so well and read the books with which he showed himself to be so well acquainted. It was out of gratitude to the Jones family, this legend says, that John Paul affixed their name to his, declaring he would " make them proud of it."

But though the writings and correspondence of Willie and Allen Jones are found in fair volume in the State and Colonial Records of North Carolina at Raleigh, N. C., there is nowhere a reference among them to John Paul Jones; and though the ardent captain never forgot a favor and was always prolific in his expressions of gratitude to benefactors, there is in his numerous journals and letters not one addressed to either of these brothers, and not one reference to their home. There is, moreover, despite the kindly legends handed down in Eastern North Carolina, no verifiable evidence that John Paul Jones ever visited that state, or was intimate with any of its citizens, save one. This man, however, had more to do with John Paul's fantastic career than any other. History, rushing forward by fits and starts, has almost lost sight of him, but he will later occupy a large space in this chronicle.

III

To discover where John Paul Jones, after his flight from the Spanish Main, at last found a refuge, and why he suddenly chose to be called Mr. Jones instead of Mr. Paul, it seems safer, although he was not always a reliable autobiographer, to accept whatever clues may be found among his own collected papers. On March 6, 1779, he wrote concerning the Tobago homicide to Benjamin Franklin:

" It was the advice of my friend Gov. Young among many others, when that great misfortune of my Life happened, that I should retire *Incog.* to the continent of America, and remain there until an Admiralty Commission should arrive in the Island, and then return. . . . It was the advice of my friends that I should till that wished event might be brought about, remain *Incog.* — "

The repetition here of the word " *Incog.*," which we have italicized, is a clue sufficiently important and reasonable. It indicates that John Paul called himself Jones, not because of fancy or gallantry, but because the name Jones, due to the wandering foot of the Welsh, was sufficiently common on the American continent to enable him to avoid undesirable attention and escape possible identification in case he should encounter any of his West Indian enemies or their agents. In short, " Jones " was a disguise. What could be more instinctive, more natural?

And he came to America because it had been from the first the country of his " fond predilection "; because his countrymen were already there in great numbers; because it was large enough to lose himself in; and because it provided solid and attractive land at a low price. What seaman does not dream, among the creaking timbers of his ship, of a neat and permanently anchored little farm? This is the unhappy young sailor's own statement:

" It had been my intention from the time of my misfortune to quit the sea service altogether, and, after standing trial, as I had the means, to purchase some small tracts of Land on the Continent, which had been my favorite Country from the age of thirteen, when I first saw it. I had settled my future place of retirement in ' calm contemplation and poetic ease.' "

IV

This concluding quotation was a favorite passage of John Paul Jones in his favorite book of poems. It will appear again in his letter to the Countess of Selkirk, one of the strangest of the many strange ones that came from his excited and sometimes incoherent pen. It is a line from *The Seasons*, by James Thomson, who was of course a Scot; the Scotch-bred Jones had little liking for the Sassenach poets below the river Tweed except Pope. In *The Seasons* the line, " In calm contemplation and poetic ease," is preceded by these:

> Oh, knew he but his happiness, of men
> The happiest he! who far from public rage
> Deep in the vale, with a choice few retired,
> Drinks the pure pleasures of the rural life. . . .

And the two lines immediately following are:

> Let others brave the flood in quest of gain,
> And beat, for joyless months, the gloomy wave.

John Paul Jones not only carried his countryman's poems constantly with him, but often gave copies away. He once wrote this to the Countess de Tomatis de Valery at Warsaw:

"I have spoken to you several times of the beautiful poems called the Seasons, written by the delicate author whose works I have deposited with your sister for your acceptance. There is nothing in the English language that surpasses his thoughts, and his happy elegance of expression."

The Baron de Grimm, whose business it was to know everything and everybody, and write entertainingly of them from Paris to Catherine the Great of Russia, once described Jones to his mistress as "a man of the world, of great intelligence and sweetness. . . . It is a curious thing that he makes many verses, full of grace and tenderness, and the sort of poetry which seems to have most charm for his genius is elegy and eclogue."

And it was to the same empress that John Paul Jones himself, then famous as a conquering captain, but surrounded by intrigue and tortured by calumny, addressed this despairing cry:

"*So far from being harsh and cruel, nature has given me the mildest disposition. I was formed for love and friendship and not to be a seaman or a soldier, to which I have sacrificed my natural inclination.*"

How strange a confession to come from the pen of a man who has somehow been assigned a place in history as a reckless bucko, avid for combat and gore; and a bold rover of the deep, contemptuous of softness and comfort. But then the life stories of the race of men is full of dispersed dreams. The ploughboy would be an aviator; the general of armies yearns toward peaceful barnyards; the sedentary banker leans his head on his hands and sees himself as Napoleon pointing southward from the Alps; and the schoolma'am is unhappy because circumstance has deprived her of her natural position as a great *artiste* of the stage.

v

We now come to a further clue as to John Paul Jones's movements and his state of mind during this period when he was utterly alone and miserable. It appears in his letter to his friend Stuart Mawey at Tobago, dated May 4, 1777. He refers to the lack of expected remittances from the agent, named Ferguson, in whose hands he had placed his affairs before his flight, and remarks bitterly upon " the unfair advantage which, to all appearances he took of me, when he left me in exile, for twenty months, a prey to melancholy and want, and withheld my property, without writing a word of excuse for his conduct."

He informs Mawey that he wishes the sums due him from his trading ventures, after settling his debts, to be used for the support of his mother, who has " several orphan grandchildren to be provided for." Letters, he directs, should be sent to " John P. Jones," care of Robert Morris, Philadelphia. But the most telling part of this communication follows:

" After an unprofitable suspense of twenty months, (having subsisted on fifty pounds only during that time), when my hopes of relief were entirely cut off, and there remained no possibility of my receiving wherewithal to subsist upon from my efforts in your island, or in England, I at last had recourse to strangers for that aid and comfort which was denied me by those friends whom I had entrusted with my all. The good offices which are rendered to persons in their extreme need, ought to make a deep impression on grateful minds; in my case I feel the truth of that sentiment, and am bound by great gratitude as well as honored to follow the fortunes of my late benefactors."

[39]

Who were the strangers that became his benefactors, rescuing him not only from homelessness and starvation, but from the introspective brooding which was paralyzing every faculty; and where and how did he meet them? If we can solve this puzzle, pertaining to which there are so few authentic documents, we will in a measure illuminate not only the most obscure portion of the young Scotch trader's life, but explain why he suddenly emerged from this obscurity on the deck of an American ship, dressed in a Continental navy lieutenant's uniform, and bursting with energy, zeal, and gratitude.

VI

If it be true that he did serve for a time on a Spanish pirate ship, he probably left her to go back to the one part of America with which he was acquainted and where he might find friends. This was Virginia, on the banks of the Rappahannock. He perhaps made his way to Fredericksburg, where he found his none too friendly brother, William, dead. Tradition says he lived for a time over William's tailor shop, which is today marked with this inscription erected by the Betty Washington Lewis chapter of the Daughters of the Revolution:

" This tablet marks the only home in America of John Paul Jones. He was appointed a lieutenant in the Continental navy while still a resident of Virginia."

During this period he somehow made friends. " Among these," he remarks in his previously quoted letter to Franklin, " I can mention a person whom I very much esteem, and who has always expressed great obligation to you. I mean Dr. John K. Read of Goochland County, Virginia."

How did Jones meet Dr. Read? Jones, when named John Paul, had been, as noted, admitted to the Masonic lodge at Kirkcudbright, Scotland. Dr. Read was also a Mason and a power in those Masonic circles which were highly influential in the America of pre-Revolutionary days; so much so that Washington was once accused of choosing Freemasons as generals to the exclusion of all others. Dr. Read was later Grand Master of Virginia and the author of an *Ahiman Rezon,* or book of Masonic rules and constitutions, published in Richmond, Va., in 1791. He had another influential connection. He was the nephew by marriage of Benjamin Franklin, being the son of James Read, brother of Franklin's wife, Deborah Read. Dr. Read was probably also interested in politics, since he was later elected Mayor of Norfolk, Va.

Jones and Dr. Read met possibly by accident at Fredericksburg, not far from the latter's home at that time in Hanover County, Virginia. One or the other probably wore a Masonic emblem, or Jones may have visited the lodge. The grip was exchanged, and Jones, confessing his difficulties, instantly obtained that " aid and comfort " which he so urgently needed. Read, who was gregarious and warm-hearted, at once took the Scotch wanderer in charge. The homeless one obtained a home. The friendless one gained friends. From that moment fortune, for him, took an upward turn.

Dr. Read, who was about the same age as Jones, doubtless took the young Scot to Hanover County, where he had married his first wife. After her death, Dr. Read married Frances Payne, a widow, and went to live on her farm in the adjoining county of Goochland. It was probably Read who introduced Jones to the Virginia leaders with whom he seems to have been on friendly terms — Washington, Jefferson, the Lees, and the Dandridges, all of them Freemasons. A few of Read's affectionate letters which have been preserved among Jones's papers indicate that the Scotchman was at once admitted to a family intimacy. On October 13, 1775, Read wrote to Jones, who was then in Philadelphia:

" Two letters have passed from me to you, and no return. What can you say for such neglect? Shall I beg of you to wait on my father and tell him of the method I have fallen on for a more convenient correspondence? It is long, very long, since I have heard from you. What can you urge in extenuation? — I wrote you by Col. Jefferson requesting you to purchase me a Cullau au Chasse, provided you staid in Philadelphia till Christmas, as I am become a military man. Make my duty to my father and family. Tell mother her little namesake is the finest girl in this government. Had it been a boy, there would have been no bearing with me."

Another admiring letter from Read to Jones in February, 1778, says: "It was with inefable (*sic*) satisfaction I heard of your success. You once more (& I want words to congratulate you on the subject) taste the pleasure of affluence, and taste it with feelings that do not accompany the generality of mankind — a nice sentiment of honour & the slow, though sure reward of merit."

This letter mentions a mutual friend, a Col. Fleming, known as a fox-hunter, who had moved to Richmond; also "the partner of the fox-hunter" — doubtless Mrs. Fleming.

This reference indicates it was in the society of slave-owning, leisure-loving, fox-hunting Virginians, to which the festive Dr. Read had introduced him, that the adaptable John Paul Jones perfected those airs and graces which afterwards drew marked attention upon him when he made his first bow to the titled ladies of France.

VII

There is further evidence in the same letter of Read's attachment to Jones: "Shall I tell you I had my fears that my friend had forgot me? — but those fears were momentary and gave place to other feelings when I reflected on the many sentimental hours which (solitary enough) passed between us at the Grove."

It was this reference to "the Grove" which has tended to strengthen the legend that John Paul Jones was at one time the guest at Willie Jones's home of the same name in Halifax County, North Carolina. But Captain Samuel A. Ashe, the North Carolina historian, to whom we are indebted for many of the facts cited in this chapter, is authority for the statement that Willie Jones did not acquire the tract on which his own home, called "The Grove," was situated, until 1785 — ten years later than the period of John Paul Jones's life with which we are now concerned.

"The Grove," says Captain Ashe concerning this reference in Dr. Read's letter, "was probably Dr. Read's place in Hanover County, Va. . . . abandoned as his residence on his marriage to Mrs. Payne and removal to Goochland County." [1]

Furthermore, Dr. Read's reference to "the many sentimental hours which (solitary enough) passed between us" indicates that at least part of John Paul Jones's mysterious exile was spent at the Read home in the interior of Virginia, possibly after the death of Dr. Read's first wife. But when Jones was not acting as the physician's companion, how was he employed? In a letter to Dr. Read, written from Lorient, France, in 1780, Jones remarked that "for these five years past military affairs have engaged my whole attention. I am as much a stranger to trade as if I had never been concerned in it."

This remark would seem to indicate that five years previous to 1780, that is in 1775, Jones had been "concerned" in trade, possibly up and down the James and Rappahannock rivers and Chesapeake Bay, with which he was familiar. And it was thus, perhaps, that he earned the means to buy two Negro slave-boys, Cato and Scipio, whom later he took on war-cruises, and with which he presented the prosperous appearance necessary for his entry into the infant American navy as an officer.

[1] *South Atlantic Quarterly*, vol. xvii, 1917.

CHAPTER VI

Who Was the Sailor's Sweetheart?

The bride hath paced into the hall,
Red as a rose is she;
Nodding their heads before her goes
The merry minstrelsy.

IN one of Jones's own letters appears a reference to a yet more mysterious phase of this buried period of his life. In the midst of his sea-raids he wrote to the Countess of Selkirk:

" Before this War began I had at an early time of Life, withdrawn from the sea service, in favor of ' calm contemplation and poetic ease.' I have sacrificed not only my favorite scheme of Life, but the softer affections of the Heart, and my prospects of Domestic Happiness."

Other references of the same kind in Jones's letters and sayings make it evident that about this time he was wounded in a very tender place, and since he never married it may be assumed that the wound was serious. Some confirmation is lent by what is called the Edinburgh biography of 1830, which remarks that he " formed an attachment for an American lady. Their affection was mutual, but circumstances forbade their union, and from this time he formed the resolution of never marrying."

A few years later when the then Commodore was basking in the shining admiration bestowed on him in France, a Mademoiselle de Menon approached him and asked if he had ever been wounded.

"Never on the sea, mademoiselle," he said, "but on land I have been bled by arrows which were never launched by the English."

For this gallant and poetical reply we are told that the mademoiselle sympathetically pinned upon his coat a *cocarde* — a rosette.[1]

For years it was not known to what or whom these confessions referred, and then a passage in one of Dr. Read's letters, received by the Commodore when he was in foreign seas, came to light:

"You tell me you are under some expectation of purchasing a Virginia estate, but some more agreeable idea will I fear call you off and deprive us of you. Miss Dandridge is no more, that is, she a few months ago gave herself into the arms of Patrick Henry."

This letter was written in 1778. The records show that Dorothea Spottswood Dandridge was married to the Virginia orator, then Governor of the state, on October 9, 1777. She bore him nine children and survived both Patrick Henry and John Paul Jones by many years.

This, then, was the news that shattered John Paul Jones's dream of "calm contemplation and poetic ease," and at the same time dashed, as he informed the Countess of Selkirk in his letter written later in the year 1778, his "prospects of domestic happiness." This was the lady who to him represented "the softer affections of the heart."

What could have prevented the match, and why did he write of his giving up this dream as a "sacrifice"? Here again we are thrown back on conjecture, for there is no record of John Paul Jones ever having uttered or written her name.

In 1775, when Jones was a companion of Dr. Read in inland Virginia, Miss Dandridge was about 19 years old. She was the

---

[1] *Correspondance Littéraire Secrète*, 1780.

daughter of Nathaniel West Dandridge, formerly a captain in the British navy. She was a descendant of the famous Governor Spottswood of Virginia and a cousin of Martha Washington. Her home, near the estates of Dr. Read and of Patrick Henry, who was her father's lawyer, was in Hanover County.

It may be assumed that since her father was formerly a naval officer and was also a Freemason, that Dr. Read's introduction of the magnetic young stranger into the Dandridge home was favorably received. The romance doubtless developed quickly. But at some stage fell the bar upon the path.

Did the family, proud and propertied, frown upon the too-frequent calls of a young man who, however agreeable, was after all only an adventurer blown in from the Indies?

Was the lady over-dazzled by the attentions of Patrick Henry, the orator who had made a continent resound with the shout, " Give me liberty or give me death " ?

Or did she finally reject John Paul Jones because he could exhibit neither property nor a great name?

All these conjectures are within reason, and yet there is another which may more adequately explain Jones's reference to his " sacrifice " and his subsequent plunge into the navy.

Before he could definitely have obtained the hand of his adored, he would, of course, have been compelled to present a clean bill of health. He would have had to explain his origin, his birth, his entire history. He would have had to confess that his real name was not John P. Jones, but John Paul; and as such had been engaged in the slave trade — a thing abhorred in Virginia, which was one of the earliest states to denounce it, for reasons that have already been described. He would have had to go further and confess that at one time he served aboard a pirate ship. And finally he would have had to tell the woeful story of the thing he most wished to forget: the mutiny aboard the *Betsey* because of unpaid wages, his killing of the sailor, and his hasty flight from Tobago, to which he must one day return to face an admiralty court. He would have had to relate that this homicide occurred after he had been charged with the death of another seaman at the same spot, starting a scandal which had caused him virtually to break off relations with his people at home.

What a skein of evil appearance to unravel before a young and impressionable girl, belonging to a proud and careful family! And yet he must tell it all, omitting no whit and not sparing his own errors of impulse and temper; or else incur the risk, through her family connections or the low-lying winds of rumor, of her some day discovering the decaying pile of unfortunate and easily misunderstandable facts.

One other alternative perhaps presented itself: to maintain silence for the present concerning his real identity and history; to return, as soon as he found the means and the right time, to Tobago; clear himself; and then come back to America; somehow do great deeds; and diademed with distinction and applause, win the pardon and approval in which all would be forgiven.

But the opening of the war with England and the closing of the ports made any voyage to Tobago impossible. Simultaneously a glittering opportunity was presented — the founding of a new navy which was to dispute the seas with England. This opportunity he eagerly seized. It gave him exactly what he needed and craved. And then, just as he was achieving his most audacious feats, came the news that she who was to be the crowning prize, the light on his tower of dreams, had given herself to Patrick Henry, then a middle-aged widower, as his second wife.

CHAPTER VII

The Man Who Put Jones in the Navy

This Hermit good lives in that wood
Which slopes down to the sea.
How loudly his sweet voice he rears!
He loves to talk with marineres
That come from a far countree.

I

JUST how John Paul Jones, an unknown young Scotchman, made the leap from the pines of inland Virginia to the quarterdeck of one of the first American fighting ships has never been adequately explained. The written records of the period are hasty and incomplete; so we must surmise what cannot be at present proved.

The letters of Dr. Read show that at some time during the year 1775 Jones was in Philadelphia. He arrived there from his remote refuge in Virginia to find the grave little old town astir with armed men, politics, and buzzing tongues. Though the staider population was certain that good King George III would compel the die-hards in the British Parliament to abate their oppressive taxes and what was more detestable, their strangle-hold on colonial trade by sea, there were actually hotheads who were shouting for a lasting break with the mother country. War had already begun. In Massachusetts the battle of Lexington had been fought; in Virginia a meeting had been held at Fredericksburg where the participants pledged themselves, if necessary, " to reassemble, and, by force of arms, to defend the laws, the liberties, and the rights of this or any sister colony, from unjust and wicked invasion "; and in North

Carolina the inhabitants of Mecklenburg County had adopted an outright declaration of independence. The Continental Congress was holding its second session in Philadelphia, and among its delegates was the man whom John Paul Jones afterward called "the Angel of my happiness; since to your friendship I owe my present enjoyments, as well as my future prospects"; and to whom he once made this grateful statement: " You more than any other person have labored to place the instruments of success in my hands."

This was Joseph Hewes, who had come up from his home in the port town of Edenton, North Carolina, of which we have this description: " Within its vicinity there was in proportion to its population a greater number of men eminent for ability, virtue, and erudition than in any other part of America." [1]

It is strange that so little has been written concerning this important man, who was strong in colonial councils, was a signer of the Declaration of Independence, and whose vote determined its adoption, according to John Adams, who wrote:

" One day while a member was producing arguments to show that the general opinion of all the colonies was for independence, and among them North Carolina, Hewes, who had hitherto constantly voted against it, stood suddenly upright and lifting both hands to Heaven cried out, ' It is done and I will abide by it? ' "

Adams adds this further comment, showing how obstinate was the opposition to separation from England:

" I would give more for a perfect painting of the terror and horror upon the face of the old majority at that critical moment, than for the best piece of Raphael."

Adams has also left this remark upon the character of the conservative but sturdy delegate from North Carolina:

" Hewes has a sharp eye, a keen penetrating sense, but what

[1] Life and Correspondence of James Iredell.

is of much more importance, is a man of honor and integrity."
Further testimony is added by William Hooper, likewise a
signer from the Tar Heel State: " He was my intimate friend.
I knew and had probed the secret recesses of his soul, and found
it devoid of guile and replete with benignity."

Hewes was born of Quaker stock at Kingston, near Prince-
ton, New Jersey, in 1730. He was therefore sufficiently older
than John Paul Jones to be able to advise the impulsive young
sailor to take in an occasional reef. Hewes when a young man
went to Philadelphia as a trader, but about 1760 removed to
Edenton, probably to be nearer the West Indies, commerce with
which was highly important. Here, while retaining his interests in Philadelphia, he built up a prosperous shipping business in partnership with Robert Smith, an attorney. In Edenton today a tablet marks the site of their establishment.

Being a man of property, Hewes at first opposed any change
in relations with England which might damage his interests,
but local pressure became insistent. On October 25, 1774, what
has since become celebrated in North Carolina history as " the
Edenton Tea Party," attended by 51 women, engaged themselves " not to conform to that pernicious custom of Drinking
Tea, and that the aforesaid Ladys would not promote ye wear
of any manufacture from England until such time that all Acts
which tend to enslave this our native country shall be re-
pealed "; causing Arthur Iredell to write from London to his
brother, James:

" There are but few places in America which possess so much
female artillery as Edenton."

The colonial female of the species being more deadly than
the male, and Hewes being a bachelor, it is small wonder that
he gave ground, abandoned Quaker tenets, and threw his interests in with the colonial lot; and was thereafter active in all
Continental and provincial councils. He subsequently wrote
that in Congress and its committees he had " sat some days from

six in the morning till five or sometimes six in the afternoon without eating or drinking." His devout overwork probably induced the ill health which caused his death in 1779, in his fiftieth year, thus depriving John Paul Jones of an anchor which might have saved the sometimes rash young captain from much errant behavior.

II

The circumstances under which Jones met the man to whom he owed his gleaming career are not known. Perhaps they were introduced by James Read, who was then in Philadelphia signing the colonial paper money. Or perhaps Jones was recommended to Hewes by James Smith, the sea-captain brother of Robert Smith, Hewes's partner. The voucher for John Paul, when he joined the Masonic lodge at Kirkcudbright, was signed by one James Smith, who may have been the same man. In 1776, just after Jones had taken one of his first prizes, he wrote from the Nova Scotia coast to Robert Smith, announcing that he was dedicating a prize to Hewes: " I have seen and do esteem yourself, but I knew your brother James well when I was myself a son of fortune." Jones's candid remark that he had been at one time " a son of fortune " may have referred either to his service in piratical seas, or to his period as a free-lance trader in Virginia.

At any rate, it may be assumed that Hewes, as a shipper and judge of seamen, was impressed by the confident manner of John Paul Jones, perhaps engaged him for a few trial voyages along the coast in his own vessels, and then, satisfied as to his ability, backed him with his weighty support.

III

While the Continental Congress was in session in Philadelphia in 1775, it became evident that means must be found to waylay the ships bringing supplies to the British army, and General Washington, as commander-in-chief of all the Continental forces, ordered several small ships posted in Massachusetts waters. Among these was the *Lee*, Captain John Manly, who brought in four prizes. Thus did a new world-power make its presence first felt on the sea.

The entry of this unexpected competitor into the arena of international commerce was a portent not comprehended by any of those who were to be most affected by it. It was certainly not comprehended by the delegates to the Continental Congress. A strong faction was aghast at the notion of buying and outfitting warships at national expense; they wanted to borrow ships from the states, such as Massachusetts and South Carolina, which maintained small vessels chiefly to do guard duty. On October 5, 1775, a committee comprising Silas Deane of Connecticut, later the unfortunate commissioner to France; John Langdon of New Hampshire, and Christopher Gadsden of South Carolina, was appointed to consider the question. Their favorable report was brought before Congress. Instantly that body was rent by a furious discussion. One element declared the proposal threatened the very foundations of the nascent union, and would lead straight to bankruptcy, ruin and eventual anarchy; while the opposing faction was equally certain that in no other way could the said foundations be preserved for the enjoyment of future generations.

It used to be taught and firmly believed that the Founding Fathers of America were alabaster saints governed in all their duties by a rectitude which was Grecian in its beauty and Roman in its classic nobility. However, the notes and records of their proceedings reveal that they acted just as men do in all ages when they are arguing about any project, whether it be a town pump, a church organ, or the robbery of a house. They vociferated, pounded tables, suspected low designs, made charges, r'ared, plunged, snorted, and fought for vanity and individual interests in the manner which has sometimes caused democratic parliaments to be compared to obscene spectacles. Thus we find Stephen Hopkins of Rhode Island, who took part in the debate, afterwards recording his conclusions as follows:

" When we draw aside the veil of words and professions — when we attend to what is *done* and what is *said* — we shall find that Liberty is a cant term of faction and freedom of speaking and acting, used only to serve the private interests of a party. What else can be the cause of our unhappy disputes? What other reason for the continual struggle for superiority and office? What other motive for the flood of calumny and reproach cast upon each other? Behold the leading men meeting in cabals and from thence dispersing themselves to several quarters to delude the people . . ." And John Adams wrote of Congress in his diary: " Every man in it is a great man, an orator, a critic and a statesman and therefore every man upon every question must show his oratory, his criticism and his political abilities."

IV

The " big-navy " men won. On October 13, 1775, Congress voted for the purchase of two warships to intercept the British transports arriving at Boston. The *Lexington* and *Reprisal* were bought and equipped. The former was given to John Barry as commander, and some authorities maintain to this day that this Irishman from County Wexford was the real " father of the American navy," and not Manly, as others contend. John Adams has left his opinion, and incidentally revealed his spleen against John Paul Jones, in his letter written in 1809 to Dr. Benjamin Rush:

" Vanity is one of the diseases of the mind. You and all the world know to what a scandalous degree I have been afflicted with it all the days of my life. Jones and Barry were leprous with it when the first said, ' My hand first hoisted the American flag,' and the last was not less distempered with it when he said, ' The British Naval flag first struck to me.' Both were

[53]

true only in the mouth of John Manly, whose prizes were of more importance to this country than all that Jones and Barry both performed."

The original Marine Committee of three was then enlarged to include John Adams, Stephen Hopkins, Richard Henry Lee, and Joseph Hewes. Because of his experience with ships and seamen, Hewes became the work-horse of the committee. In December, 1775, Congress ordered the number of ships to be increased to thirteen, and again increased the Marine Committee so as to have a member for each of the thirteen colonies.

It was decided to choose a naval commander-in-chief, four captains, and a list of first, second and third lieutenants. The struggle over these appointments resolved itself into a battle between North and South — a struggle based on difference in interests, reflected in a difference in temperaments, which was to run like a waving thread through American history until the war between the States ended it almost a century later.

The New Englanders were astonished that anyone should want to officer a navy with aught but New Englanders. They had their lists already hand-picked, cut and dried. They felt hurt that anyone should question these sacred names. But it must be said that they had a partly justifiable argument. " Haven't you," they said, glaring at the Southerners, " filled the army with your precious Washingtons, Lees, and other Virginians? Keep your army spoils, but the navy is *our* meat." And then they brought out the steam-roller. Only two members refused to be flattened. Robert Morris of Philadelphia, who was certain that no navy ought to be born without a Philadelphian in it, brought forward the gallant Nicholas Biddle, of the historic family of that name. Joseph Hewes, spurred on by Morris, then planted his feet and announced that North Carolina must have an officer on that list. He named a man whom nobody had ever heard of — John P. Jones. And the New

Englanders, with low moans and muttered threats to get even, had to take him. They then took a glass of the Jamaica rum which Stephen Hopkins ordered to be served every evening at the tavern where the committee held its over-time meetings, called it a day, and went home. The naval slate was given out as follows:

> Ezek. Hopkins, commander-in-chief.
> Dudley Saltonstall, captain the *Alfred.*
> Abraham Whipple, captain the *Columbus.*
> Nicholas Biddle, captain the *Andrea Doria.*
> John B. Hopkins, captain the *Cabot.*

First Lieutenants: John Paul Jones, Rhodes Arnold, Eli Stansbury, Hoysted Hacker, Jonathan Pitcher.
Second Lieutenants: Benj. Seabury, Joseph Olney, Elisha Warner, Thos. Weaver, James McDougal.
Third Lieutenants: John Fanning, Ezekiel Burroughs, Daniel Vaughan.

An examination of this list disclosed some luminous facts. Most of the appointees were either relatives or friends of Stephen Hopkins and John Adams, the very men whose criticisms, quoted a few pages back, indicted their colleagues for narrowness and factionalism! The new commander-in-chief of the nearly all-New England navy was Stephen Hopkins's brother; the *Cabot's* captain was his nephew; the *Columbus's* skipper was his relative; while the captain of the *Alfred,* the flagship, was a relative of Adams.

It was a rare navy that was thus launched against the devouring foe, and Neptune and Mars doubtless fell on each other's neck when the Hopkins-Adams relatives first flocked forth in their new blue and red uniforms. Within a few months most of them had lost their ships, been cashiered, tried on charges, or told to find a port and rest. A few of them did almost everything except prick themselves with their own swords.   Only two men in this historic list of the first American naval officers came out of their first tests with laurels, and they were the last two chosen — Nicholas Biddle and John P. Jones.   Because he owed his appointment to Hewes, the latter was thenceforth known as " the North Carolina captain."

JOHN PAUL FINDS EMPLOYMENT AS MATE ON A SLAVE SHIP.

CHAPTER VIII

The First Cruise

The ship was cheered, the harbor cleared,
Merrily did we drop
Below the kirk, below the hill,
Below the light-house top.

I

JOHN PAUL, then 29 years old, was appointed a senior naval lieutenant under the name of John Paul Jones on December 22, 1775. He was at once given the task of arming and manning the flagship *Alfred* moored off the foot of Walnut Street, Philadelphia. We can imagine the exhilaration with which he went about his new duties. His twenty months of wandering and uncertainty were over. He had made his confession regarding the Tobago misfortune to Hewes. He had that powerful man's friendship and support. He had stepped from the deck of an ordinary trading ship to that of a war vessel about to enter the lists against the most formidable sea-power in the world. Here was his chance to retrieve past errors and to win renown. His letters to Hewes and Morris written during this period reveal his hope, zeal, pride and anxiety.

In January, 1776, Commodore Ezek. Hopkins arrived in Philadelphia, and escorted by an eager throng of citizens, went down to the Delaware where lay eight ships of the new fleet. On his boarding the *Alfred*, Captain Saltonstall gave the signal and Lieutenant Jones pulled up to the masthead the first American naval flag. This was not the banner with thirteen stripes, but a rectangle of yellow silk bearing a picture of a rattlesnake and the legend " Don't Tread on Me." This device had been previously used by the Culpeper Riflemen of Virginia, referred to in a preceding chapter.

John Paul Jones afterwards was fond of recalling the occasion, but John Adams would never grant that his was the hand that first hoisted the flag. On January 24, 1813, Adams wrote to John Langdon:

" My recollection has been excited by the information from Philadelphia that Paul Jones has written in his journal, ' My hand first hoisted the American flag,' and that Captain Barry used to say the ' first British flag struck to him.' Both these vain boasts I know to be false, and as you know them to be so, I wish to have your testimony to corroborate mine. It is not decent or just that those emigrants, foreigners of the South, should falsely arrogate to themselves merit that belongs to New England sailors, officers and men."

II

At that moment the colonies were in a fever of excitement about the burning of Norfolk, Virginia, by the British. On New Year's Day Lord Dunmore, after a bombardment by his vessels, had landed troops in the town, then numbering about 6,000 people, and set fire to a row of houses suspected of harboring rebels. History has exaggerated the so-called malignant deeds of Lord Dunmore on this occasion. He seems to have been a somewhat pompous but kindly disposed man of the type usually selected as colonial governors by a bull-headed government, but he had little heart for his task of fighting the Virginians, as proved by the celerity with which he quitted the situation. His troops actually burned about nineteen houses. The rest were destroyed by the colonial militia either because they feared that the British meant permanently to occupy the town, or because the looting and destroying instinct, always released by the drums of war, got the better of the soldiery, as it frequently did in General Washington's own commands.

III

Commodore Hopkins was directed to go down and attack Lord Dunmore's ships. But he was also told to use his best judgment about the direction of his cruises. The Commodore, whose experience on the sea had been gained as a commander of land militia and on the deck of a few trading vessels, could not get ready. It was February 17 before he could push through the ice in the Delaware. He then sailed, not to Norfolk, but to the Bahama Islands, with the intention of capturing British stores of powder which the colonists urgently needed. His fleet sailed directly up to the island of Abaco in daylight, thus giving the commanders of the forts due warning, and enabling them to hide or send away their powder. That the expedition did not fail entirely was due to Jones, if we may believe the *Journal* which he afterwards wrote for Louis XVI. Hopkins wanted to land his marines on the west side of the island and attack the town of New Providence from the land. But Jones, having become familiar with these islands during his West Indian voyages, proposed that the fleet be anchored at a key three leagues distant and that the attack then be made by the eastern, or shorter, road. Two captured pilots were available, but Hopkins was afraid to trust them, so Jones, taking a pilot with him to the masthead of the *Alfred,* took the ships into the key's harbor himself. The marines were then loaded on two schooners and landed four miles from Fort Montague. They easily captured New Providence (Nassau), and sailed away on March 17 with a hundred cannon and the British governor aboard. All hands congratulated each other on this first successful venture, and Jones wrote to Hewes that " the commander-in-chief is respected thro' the fleet."

[59]

And then, on their return, they encountered off Block Island the British man of war *Glasgow*. Both the *Cabot* and the *Alfred* attacked her, the lower deck guns of the latter being directed by Lieutenant Jones. The *Glasgow* tried to escape and victory looked certain, when Hopkins lost his nerve and ordered the chase to cease, for fear of running into the British fleet hovering off Rhode Island. At once the *Glasgow* rounded to, turned on her foes, and gave both American ships a severe pounding. Hopkins made sail to New London, Connecticut.

There a hurricane of criticism smote the new navy for its ineffective showing with the *Glasgow*. This increased when it was found the ship was full of diseased men. Captain Whipple was tried and acquitted. Captain Hazard was convicted of cowardice and " broke." Even Jones was included in the public uproar. He wrote to Hewes of his having been " hurt as an individual by the censures that have been indiscriminately thrown out — for altho' my station confined me to the *Alfred's* lower Gun Deck, where I commanded during the action, and tho' the Commodore's letter which hath been published says: ' All of the officers in the *Alfred* behaved well,' yet still the public blames me, among others, for not taking the enemy."

His inability to bear criticism, however slight and indirect, was one of John Paul Jones's conspicuous weaknesses. He nursed a grievance until it filled all space, and his brooding over it kept it alive and growing long after a short-memoried public had forgotten it completely.

IV

There is evidence in this same letter to Hewes that Jones received " rude ungentle treatment " from his fellow officers, some of whom confessed to him, he reported, that they had little taste for their task, because they feared hanging by the British.

" It is bad policy in superiors," Jones complained to Hewes, " to behave toward their inferiors indiscriminately, and tho' they were of a lower species, such a conduct will damp the spirits of any man — men of liberal minds who have been long accustomed to command can ill brook being thus set at naught by others who claim a monopoly of sense."

Jones seems to have been aiming at Captain Saltonstall, the appointee of John Adams, who, as has been previously re-marked, looked askance at this " immigrant " and " foreigner of the South " dug up from nowhere by Joseph Hewes. On the other hand, it is probable that Jones, after suspecting his own inferiority, rebounded to a superior plane from which he was inclined to look down on his associates. " When I applied for a Lieutenancy," he wrote, " I hoped in that work to gain much useful knowledge from men of more experience than my-self. I was, however, mistaken, for instead of gaining informa-tion I was obliged to inform others."

The sensitive lieutenant was soon mollified, for on Captain Hazard being removed from the *Providence,* Hopkins gave his command to Jones. From New York Jones wrote on May 19, 1776, to Hewes in Philadelphia, where the Declaration of Independence was being prepared: " I was ordered to take the command of this vessel the 10th currt. I arrived here yesterday afternoon in 36 hours from Rhode Island with a return of up-wards of 100 men besides officers, which Gen. Washington lent to the fleet at N. London."

Most of the experienced men of the sea had been dragged into the army; so General Washington had been compelled to make up the deficiency on the ships by sending them land soldiers. It was under such conditions that the American War for Independence was begun. But such a situation is not strange to history, which loves to repeat itself. It was an exactly parallel condition which prevailed among the Powers for months after the opening of the World War in 1914. Michael is always going forth to slay the dragons without remembering to gird on his sword, and Crusaders are ever starting for the Holy Land with a song, and not much else.

CHAPTER IX

The First Independent Command

He holds him with his glittering eye —
The Wedding-Guest stood still,
And listens like a three years' child;
The Mariner hath his will.

I

ON the *Providence* the newly appointed captain found,
ready for orders, the only unquestionably 100 per
cent American who ever, as far as is known, served in
the navy. He was Anthony Jeremiah, a full-blooded Narragansett Indian and whaleman from Martha's Vineyard, Mass.
Jones noticed him from the first, took infinite delight in him,
and kept him on his ships as long as possible. The Indian afterwards helped Jones fight two of his most famous battles. The
crew called him "Red Jerry," which they later altered, in
token of his color and cheerful disposition, to "Red Cherry."

"I have seldom seen a person in whom I take such keen interest as in this boy," wrote Jones to Hewes, after he had seen
the red man in action. "Though not more than twenty-one or
twenty-two years old, I haven't a better seaman. He is small
in stature, but active and strong. . . . He tells me that ' he
likes to see the big gun shoot,' (and) that ' he likes to hear the
big noise of much battle.' " Jones added that the Indian was
never either sick or homesick, wherein he differed from the
young Captain's two negro boys, Cato and Scipio, who, like their
chief, often yearned for " calm contemplation and poetic ease."

Other men were added to the crew who became Jones's devoted followers, and fought, bled or died by his side. Among

them were Nathaniel Fanning, Henry Lunt, Henry Gardner, Owen Starbuck, Samuel Stacy, Charles Hill, and William Hichborn, of Massachusetts; John C. Robinson and Richard Wallingford of Pennsylvania; Thos. Porter of Maryland, and Nathan Sargent of New Hampshire. These young salts made the *Providence* " a happy ship." Jones loved to praise them, and many times afterward mourned that he had not these merry seamen always at his back.

II

Jones was now ordered to do convoy duty for ships carrying supplies for the defence of New York. To do this, he had to pass through the widespread fleet of Lord Howe, which was blockading the Northern ports. He got himself chased several times, beat off the British frigate *Cerberus* which attacked him near Block Island, and saved the supply ship *Hispaniola* from threatened capture.

It was in being pursued that John Paul Jones most enjoyed himself. At such times he proved himself to be a thorough seaman. He liked to linger until almost overhauled, and then tack and be off before the wind before the enemy had waked up. Such performances at first gave his crew heart failure, but eventually anchored their confidence in him; and this was never shaken, for though during his madcap career John Paul Jones was many times chased, he was never overtaken and never boarded. For two reasons: he knew what to do, both by training and instinct; and he never took a ship which was not a fast sailer.

He returned to Philadelphia from his successful convoy voyage three weeks after the signing of the Declaration of Independence. Joseph Hewes was now satisfied that he had made no mistake in his man. He was also convinced that this fellow had a spot of genius in him, and that he had not the temperament to endure incompetent or lackadaisical superiors. He therefore set to work to obtain for Jones a command in which his initiative would have elbow-room. Meantime Jones went to John Hancock and obtained from him, as president of the Continental Congress, confirmation of the captain's commission given to him by Hopkins. It was dated August 8, 1776, the first awarded after the colonies had pronounced themselves to be a separate commonwealth.

III

About this time, says Jones in his *Journal*, he proposed to Hewes that he be sent to the west coast of Africa, to intercept and harass British trading ships. Very early he began to press for a naval war that should be not only defensive but offensive. The Marine Committee offered him, instead, the command of the brigantine *Hampden* in Connecticut waters. Jones declined; he wouldn't leave the fast *Providence* for an untried and slow ship. And then Hewes took a hand. He emerged from a committee meeting with an unlimited order to Jones for a free-lance cruise to last " six weeks or two or three months."

IV

It may be imagined with what eagerness Jones hastened down to the Delaware to break this news to his cheering crew. They loaded stores at once and on August 21, 1776, aboard the little *Providence*, carrying only twelve long-four guns and seventy men, sailed for the Bermudas on the first extensive open-sea cruise ever undertaken by a lone American warship. One of Jones's first acts was to fling overboard the whip. After Tobago, no more floggings for him.[1] He rapidly took three brigs

[1] " I never punished any man more than talking to him like a father, or, in extreme cases, stopping his grog for three days." — Letter to Robert Morris, Oct. 17, 1776.

which he manned and sent home, and then on September 1st he ran into serious danger. He encountered a ship convoying merchantmen, and Jones was almost upon her before he made her out to be the British frigate *Solebay*, with twenty guns. She promptly opened fire, and Jones ran for safety. The *Solebay* was very fast and after a four hour chase, got within musket shot of the *Providence*, which, however, her gunners were unable to hit. Seeing the danger, Jones escaped through one of his feats of seamanship. A squall coming up, he set his light sails and putting his helm sharply over, was off before the wind unharmed, leaving the enemy helplessly trying to box about. His description of his escape as " saucy " reveals his high satisfaction with the exploit.

The next saucy incident occurred off Sable Island, after the *Providence* had turned northward. The British frigate *Milford* surprised him while his crew was fishing. She was within cannon shot before Jones made sail. Finding the enemy slow, Jones shortened sail so as to entice him into a " wild goose chase." Keeping just out of range, Jones permitted the frigate to chase him for eight hours, the latter meantime wasting valuable shot and shell. As the enemy laboriously rounded to give him a final broadside, Jones, who occasionally indulged a mocking humor, replied with a single impudent musket shot and sailed off into the darkness.

No doubt this final touch to the picture was enjoyed by the *Providence's* gay crew, and doubtless they reported it on shore with appropriate embellishments, to the enhancement of the new captain's prestige. John Paul Jones knew that to lead a crew well is only part of a captain's job; he must also occasionally give the boys a good show. It was " night with her sable curtains," reported Jones afterward, in the florid strain which he sometimes liked to employ, (which) " put an end to this famous exploit of English knight-errantry."

The *Providence* was out six weeks and five days, having

taken during this time six brigantines, one ship, and one sloop and destroyed six schooners, one ship and one brigantine. Jones also demolished the fishing at the islands of Canso and Madame, not forgetting to leave the fishing population enough small vessels to take them home. " Had I gone further," he reported, " I should have stood chargeable with inhumanity."

He returned to Newport, Rhode Island, on October 7, laden with spoils and glory, but with his crew weak from exposure and lack of clothing. " Officers and men behaved incomparably well," said his triumphant report to the Marine Committee. And then petty politics rose up from its lair on land and enmeshed him.

CHAPTER X

Triumphs and Treacheries

And now there came both mist and snow,
And it grew wondrous cold:
And ice, mast-high, came floating by,
As green as emerald.

I

COMMODORE HOPKINS was meantime working desperately but confusedly to build at Providence, Rhode Island, two ships of the eight new ones ordered by Congress. So slow was his progress that on August 23d he was ordered to go to Philadelphia and face an inquiry. Dismissal seemed probable, but John Adams girded himself and got Hopkins off with a vote of censure which was kept secret, causing John Jay to write: " I cannot think of it with patience; nothing but more than ladylike delicacy could have prevailed on your august body to secret the sentence they passed upon that petty genius."

Hopkins was then ordered to go to Newfoundland and attack the fisheries there, but he could not get ready. He was next ordered to sail on a southern cruise with the *Alfred, Columbus, Cabot* and *Hampden,* but he could not get ready for this either, complaining, with cause, that privateers were enticing away all the best seamen and shipbuilders. Finally, with exasperated curses for Congress, he directed Jones to do what he could not do himself, while he remained behind to fight for legislative measures aimed at privateers. Jones's orders were to destroy the Newfoundland fisheries and to attempt the rescue of a hundred American prisoners working in the coal mines at the

Isle Royale. Jones, though delighted with the task given him, was able to man but two ships, the *Alfred* and the *Hampden*. The latter was in command of Hoysted Hacker, the political appointee. Hacker promptly ran his ship on a ledge of rock just outside the harbor, knocking off the keel, and Jones, murmuring maledictions, had to put back.

The young commander, thus balked, made one of those mistakes into which his intense nature sometimes led him. He wrote to his superior, Hopkins, virtually blaming him for the aborted expedition. The harassed Commodore replied temperately enough: " I received your disagreeable letter. . . . If I can, I will be in Newport tomorrow. I am your friend, Ezek Hopkins."

But he was not Jones's friend any more. From this time on, he was his ambitious subordinate's enemy, and soon found means to show it.

II

It is a sad thing, but one too often true, that men in a difficulty will often begin to accuse each other furiously, instead of finding the root of the difficulty and venting their energy in the removal of that. It was so with Hopkins and Jones. Hopkins was absurdly unfitted for his high post; from the moment he assumed command, the baby navy began to descend from a mere nettlerash into infantile paralysis; but stupid politics and sectional factionalism were to blame for that. The source of the tangle was the tumorous disease which assails all countries engaged in war — profiteering. But on the marine side of affairs it was known by its ancestral word — privateering.

This was a word which never failed to arouse Jones's rage; and he, romantic idealist that he was, had an equally furious contempt for its twin sister — self-interest.

" Our infant Navy," he wrote to Hewes, " is by no means well-established, nor under proper regulations, while self-interest prevails. I am informed, and have reason to believe it to be true, that even some of the Gentlemen appointed to fit out the new frigates, are concerned in privateers, and not only wink at, but encourage and employ deserters from the Navy. What punishment is equal to such baseness? And yet these men pretend to love their country! "

Jones was not the only patriot who found maggots, many of them fat and highly placed, working at the thin foundations of the new republic. General Washington was even more emphatic in his disgust.

" Such a dearth of public spirit," he wrote on November 28, 1775, " and such want of virtue, such stock-jobbing and futility in all the low arts to obtain advantages of one kind or another in this great change of military arrangement, I never saw before, and pray God's mercy that I may never be witness to again. . . . Such a mercenary spirit pervades the whole that I should not be at all surprised at any disaster that may happen."

" Thousands of schemes of privateering," wrote John Adams, " are afloat in American imaginations," and Robert Morris declared: " In the Eastern States they are so intent upon privateering that they mind little else."

Despite criticisms and curses, however, the fitting out of private warships for personal profit, under letters-of-marque granted by Congress, went on; and to a certain degree, aided the American cause through the damage it inflicted on British commerce. On February 8, 1778, Alderman Woodbridge of London told a committee from the House of Lords that the number of ships so far lost or destroyed through the operations of American privateers had been 733, representing a loss of £2,200,000. And because the business was adventurous and appealed to the young as well as the avaricious, it produced both oddity and comedy.

III

" Your true privateersman," wrote Herman Melville, " was a sort of half horse, half alligator, with a streak of lightning in his composition — something like a man-of-warsman, but much more like a pirate — with a superabundance of whisker, as if he held, with Samson, that his strength was in the quantity of his hair."

An old Nantucket yarn says that a certain American privateer crew, having been captured, was taken to a village in New-foundland, where the inhabitants surrounded them and pro-posed to hang them. A genteel old lady was fetched to read the strangers' papers. She donned her spectacles and on coming to the passage in their letter-of-marque-and-reprisal authoriz-ing them to " burn, sink and destroy," she gasped with horror and turning on them, lectured them severely. Then noticing their youth and half-starved appearance, she converted the pro-posed hanging into a feast by ordering the inhabitants to feed the guilty crew on corned codfish and salt pork, which they obediently did, and so forgot about the hanging.

An English captain who had taken another American pri-vateer ordered the crew to be sent to the notorious jail at Ports-mouth, England, but was disconcerted to find that one member of the crew was a woman.

A third comic incident was the capture by a Massachusetts privateer of a British brig laden with Bibles destined for Africa. The captors took the books home and sold them to the Massa-chusetts Bible Society for twenty cents on the pound sterling, which was deemed to be good business on both sides, both from a patriotic and moral standpoint.

But perhaps the oddest crew in privateering annals was that of the British *Terrible* which, after encountering the French ship *Vengeance*, had only 16 survivors out of 200 men on board.

She had lieutenants named Spirit and Ghost, a bo'sun named Butcher, and a quartermaster named Debble. She sailed from Execution Dock, London.

IV

When on November 2 Jones again sailed for Newfoundland in the *Alfred*, it was with the hardy crew transferred from the *Providence*. To his disgust, he found he had to give this treasured ship to Captain Hacker and take the latter along. The season was late and trouble at once appeared. Gales tore the ships' rigging, ice almost locked them in, and, worst of all, they were blanketed by repeated fogs. In one of these Captain Hacker chose to disappear. He dropped behind and, without a word to Jones, slipped back to Rhode Island just in time to be taken by the British.

Another piece of treachery occurred on the voyage. On November 18 Jones took the British brigantine *Active* off Cape Breton and in compliment to his beloved sponsor, Joseph Hewes, manned her under a bo'sun named Spooner and dispatched her to Robert Smith, Hewes's partner and prize agent at Edenton, North Carolina, with this note: " I am happy in the opportunity of acknowledging the great obligation I owe to Mr. Hewes, by addressing my prize, the brigantine *Active*, to you." The rest of this note has been quoted in a previous chapter: " I have seen and do esteem yourself; but I knew your brother James well, when I was myself a son of fortune."

The *Active*, however, never arrived at Edenton. Spooner took her instead to Dartmouth, where his brother was a prize agent.

V

Treachery and disobedience of orders occurred so often in Jones's career as to be astonishing, and might lead to the conclusion that he was either lacking in the personal force which commands respect, or he had defects which earned his associates' contempt and hatred. The testimony of some of his most prominent companions, however, leaves no doubt that although he was often curiously lenient with malefactors and at times almost Quixotic, he was a strict disciplinarian, and that his personal courage and gift of leadership were never questioned. Hence we must otherwise account for the astounding cases of rank disobedience which repeatedly well-nigh wrecked his plans and his cause.

First, we have the fact that John Adams, who reflected the New England viewpoint, regarded Jones as lacking in true merit because he had come from an alien clime. Second is the fact that the colonial privates took seriously the statements that the war against the despotic mother country was to be truly a democratic conflict, with all ranks sharing alike. " Can it be wondered at," wrote Joseph Reed, Washington's adjutant-general, " that a captain should be tried and broken for stealing his soldiers' blankets? or that another officer should be found shaving his men in the face of characters of distinction? " [1] Having such a belief, Jones's men no doubt sometimes took offense at his solitary habits and somewhat aloof attitude.

Third is the fact that for some time after the beginning of the war, the strongest suspicions of the foreign-born officers who received commissions in the Continental forces, were entertained by the native-born, extending even to such men as Lafayette, DeKalb, and Kosciusko. This suspicious attitude was well reflected by Abigail Adams when she wrote to John Adams on July 30, 1777:

" Will a foreigner, whose interest is not naturally connected with ours (any otherwise than as the cause of liberty is the cause of all mankind), will he act with the same zeal, or expose

[1] *Life and Correspondence of Joseph Reed.*

[73]

himself to equal dangers with the same resolution for a republic of which he is not a member, as he would have done for his own native country? "

Even their French allies landed at Newport by Count Rochambeau were regarded by the Founding Fathers and Mothers as not quite human and scarcely worthy to associate with the native stock. "It is difficult to imagine," wrote the Abbé Robin, "the idea Americans entertained about the French before the war. They considered them . . . as a kind of light, brittle, queer-shapen mechanisms, only busy frizzling their hair and painting their faces, without faith or morals."

That Jones himself was not exempt from these suspicions is shown by this passage from a letter by him to Commodore Hopkins:

"I asked Captain Saltonstall how he could in the beginning suspect me as you have told me, of being unfriendly to America. He seemed astonished at the question and told me it was yourself who promoted it."

VI

Sailing up to Isle Royale, Jones found that his plan to free the imprisoned Americans had been balked by the winter ice. It was frozen solid, and the heavy cakes off shore made the navigation of his little ship difficult, but he carried out a successful raid on the Acadian coast, burned some fish warehouses, and took four transports. And then came three great pieces of luck.

He fell in with a sixteen-gun privateer from Liverpool and captured her. He next ran down a large armed transport, the *Mellish*, carrying a company of soldiers and a thousand uniforms, with blankets and stores for General Burgoyne's army in Canada, then preparing for its historic descent below the line. And then finally, off Boston, he met his old friend, the British frigate *Milford*. He was fully aware of his dangerous situation: he was convoying prizes; he was short-handed, and water and provisions were low; he was laden with prisoners, and more than ever he cursed Captain Hacker for his desertion; but he resolved to fight it out by strategy. The frigate came up about nightfall. Jones placed the *Alfred* between her and his prizes, ordering them to crowd sail. He then hoisted a top-light, and after he had thus lured the *Milford* to the chase, he tacked. The enemy followed his light, thus permitting his prizes to escape. The next morning he had to decide whether to fight the *Milford*. He accordingly signalled Lieutenant Saunders, in charge of the captured Liverpool ship, to drop back until he could discover the enemy's force. Saunders obeyed, but stupidly dropped so far back that the frigate overtook and captured him. Jones, after exchanging a few shots with the *Milford*, made sail for Boston, where he arrived with only two days' water and provisions left. He hastened to send the news of his valuable captures to General Washington, then planning to lead his frozen army against the Hessians at Trenton. Meantime Jones was compelled to pay off the crews of the *Alfred* and *Providence* from his own pocket, getting no refund until after the end of the war.

And then came a double-headed blow of the kind which Jones was least able to bear. The owners of a Rhode Island privateer from which, at Hopkins's order, he had taken four skulking seamen, served him in a suit for damages; and almost simultaneously he learned that he had been superseded in the command of the *Alfred* by a man who had been his junior officer by eight numbers.

CHAPTER XI

Chills and Fever

Day after day, day after day,
We stuck, nor breath nor motion;
As idle as a painted ship
Upon a painted ocean.

I

A MAN of action feels that his existence is justified
only when he is acting. Enforced idleness, while
about him there is hum and stir, is to him supremest
cruelty. His days are spent in a fevered hoping; his nights are
tortured with electric visions of what he might be doing if only
a fire could be built under those sedentary ones, the men who sit
in offices and council chambers. He whimpers like a chained
hound. When he sees or thinks of those who might so easily
slip his leash, he breaks out into despairing ululations. He is
like a spring in tension, which if not soon released, loses its
power, its *élan*, and suffers deterioration. All history is a record
of struggles between the dynamic and the static — between
those who want to do, and those who want to delay.

It was the fate of John Paul Jones to be repeatedly the victim
of men who love status quos. He passed through multiple
dangers without a serious wound, but these all but slew him. It
was so after his victorious return from Northern seas. It was
almost five months before he was again given an errand to do —
and this at a time when every foot-pound of his energy should
have been fiercely used. No one was to blame. No *one* ever
is. Situations may have more heads than any hydra. Congress
was absorbed with a thousand difficulties If it could pass over,

as it did, the claims of so brilliant a commander as Benedict Arnold to promotion, what chance had an insignificant sea captain?

II

While Jones was outfitting his ships at Rhode Island, he found himself sickeningly short of men, due to the higher attractions held out by privateers. He had Commodore Hopkins's order to search for and take deserters wherever found. He therefore raided a privateer schooner, the *Eagle*, and took from her four men hiding behind a bulkhead. In consequence, he found a suit lodged against him for £10,000, whereupon Hopkins disavowed Jones's action, because the order had not been " given in writing." Jones wrote a stinging letter to Hopkins for thus leaving him " in the lurch," and added: " I glory in having been the first who hath broke thro' the shameful abuses which have been too long practiced upon the Navy by Mercenaries whose governing principle hath been that of self interest." On January 12, 1777, he wrote to Hewes condemning Hopkins as " unfit " and stating his astonishment "that such despicable characters should have obtained commissions as commodores in a navy." Two days later Hopkins ordered Jones to give up the *Alfred* and go back to the smaller ship *Providence*. Jones at once complained to the Marine Committee in an open letter which contained a statement to which the Annapolis authorities still direct the attention of midshipmen:

" None other than a gentleman, as well as a seaman both in Theory and Practice, is qualified to support the character of a commissioned officer in the Navy, nor is any man fit to command a ship of war, who is not also capable of communicating his ideas on paper in Language that becomes his rank."

He added this bold request: " Could I, which I never can, bear to be superseded I should indeed deserve your contempt and total neglect. I am therefore to entreat you to employ me in the most enterprising and active service, accountable to your honorable Board only for my conduct, and connected as much as possible with Gentlemen and Men of sense."

Bold words, indeed, for a young blade of a captain who had scarcely been in the navy a year, and who a year before had been Mr. Nobody of Nowhere. But the Committee, instead of boiling him in oil and decapitating him for his effrontery, actually did as he asked. But not before there fell upon John Paul Jones another blow. This, one of the severest of all to one of his temperament, darkened his disposition for the rest of his life.

III

In April, 1777, Jones, perishing from inaction, left Boston for Philadelphia to lay his grievances before Congress in person. There he was pierced to the heart to find that in a new list of commanders drawn up by Congress in October, 1776, while he was at sea, he had been placed as low as the eighteenth, having been superseded by thirteen men who had joined the navy later than he. The head of the list was James Nicholson of Maryland, an unknown. The second was John Manly. Third was Hector McNeill, Jones's friend. Fourth was Dudley Saltonstall. Even the incompetent Hacker preceded him by two numbers. By every sort of count, Jones considered himself entitled to fifth place. His rank, that soul of a naval officer, had been ignored, and superior places given to men " with whom," he said, " as a private gentleman I would disdain to associate."

He hurried around to the door of Congress and hurled himself upon John Hancock, seriously upsetting that placid and ease-loving gentleman. Jones tremblingly thrust into Hancock's hand a document and ordered him to read it. It was Jones's commission, signed by Hancock himself, dated August 8, 1776. Jones pointed out that this must take rank of all subsequent commissions. Hancock was stumped. He played for time, pleading pressure of business. He asked that Jones leave the document with him a day or two, until he could look into the matter. When Jones returned, Hancock handed him a commission dated not August 8, 1776, but October 10, 1776, and numbered 18 on the margin. Jones announced this was not good enough and demanded his old commission back. Hancock hemmed and fumbled. Finally he " turned over various papers on the table," Jones wrote Morris, " and at last told me he was sorry to have lost or mislaid it." Hancock, too, had left him in the lurch.

IV

While this was going on, Hewes was absent, having lost his seat in Congress through a political overturn at home. The Marine Committee was afraid of Jones. They felt guilty about him, and as far back as February they had prepared a cruise for him, to extend by way of the West Indies to Pensacola, Florida, where there was an opportunity to capture a park of British artillery. They now gave him permission to go to the coast of Africa, if he preferred. The order was signed by Robert Morris, later the fertile and ingenious financier of the Revolution, who made much money in the course of it but died ruined. But Hopkins managed to avoid letting Jones have his ships for the cruise. He contrived delay after delay from February 1 until April, when Jones went to Philadelphia to beg relief. Hopkins, himself a victim of politics, now tried to play it, but got his hair singed, and eventually lost his head entirely. He began to call Congress names, and that body, recovering its nerve after its panic flight to Baltimore, broke him and dismissed him.

[79]

V

Hopkins and Jones were not the only victims of intrigue and maladministration during this period. Washington's head was sought by the Mifflin-Conway cabal. The embittered Benedict Arnold and Charles Lee thought, like Washington at one time, that the game was up, and went over to the enemy. The population seemed to care nothing for liberty, independence, or anything else that could not be cooked and eaten. In the cities " speculation ran riot. Every form of wastefulness and extravagance prevailed in town and country, nowhere more than Philadelphia, under the very eyes of Congress." [1]

But John Paul Jones, the romantic, held true, and resolved to wait a little longer, though it killed him. " When I entered into the Service," he wrote, " I was not actuated by motives of Self Interest. I stept forth as a free citizen of the world in defence of the Violated Rights of Mankind."

And he did not forget his loyal sailors, still unpaid. " It makes my heart bleed," he wrote, " to see them half naked at this Severe Season."

[1] Greene, *Historical View of the American Revolution.*

CHAPTER XII

Overseas in the Ranger

The fair breeze blew, the white foam flew,
The furrow followed free;
We were the first that ever burst
Into that silent sea.

I

EARLY in May, 1777, the Marine Committee thought of a new way to use the harassing Captain Jones. They sent him to New Hampshire to take command of the French ship *Amphitrite*, which had arrived there with a cargo from Beaumarchais, who when not making watches and writing operas, was sending supplies to America under the guise of Roderigo Hortalez & Co., for which he was seldom paid. Jones was to sail direct to France and report to Commissioners Silas Deane, Benjamin Franklin, and Arthur Lee, who would purchase a fine frigate for him and give him orders. This frigate was then being built in Holland. Her name was the *Indien*, later the *South Carolina*, aboard which a rare comedy was to be later played.

This was very fine — " generous indeed," as the happy Jones wrote to Hewes. But the Marine Committee neglected one small but important ceremony: they failed to notify the French commander of the *Amphitrite* that he was expected to step down and make room for John Paul Jones. Consequently they inflicted upon the latter the humiliation of being informed by the surprised and indignant French captain that he was willing to take him as a passenger but not as the commander. Jones saw the justice of that, and had no choice but to return to Boston to await a new suggestion as to what he should do.

[81]

On June 14, 1777, Congress voted these two resolutions, which in the record happened to be juxtaposed: " that the flag of the thirteen United States be thirteen alternate red and white stripes, with thirteen white stars on a blue field " ; and " that Captain Paul Jones be appointed to command the ship *Ranger*."

It is to be noted that from this time forward his official name was " Paul Jones." The " John " was dropped, or rather reduced to a " J," which in his signature was so involved in the whirling loop of the following letter " P " as to be almost invisible.

II

The *Ranger* had been newly built by Colonel John Langdon at Portsmouth, New Hampshire. She was " crank," causing Jones to cut down her guns from twenty-four to eighteen, and to shorten her masts, but she was very fast. Captain Roach had first been appointed to command her, but had been suspended under charges. Jones wrote him a sympathetic letter, saying he had no choice but to supersede him, though he had no cause of complaint against him. Weeks were spent in outfitting the *Ranger* and in enlisting seamen, to whom Jones had to guarantee their wages before they would sign for one year. Two friends, both fellow Scots, helped him while away the tedious hours of waiting: Captain Hector McNeill, of North Carolina, commanding the *Boston*, and Major John Gizzard Frazer, of Virginia, who volunteered to go with Jones as a marine officer for " amusement." At last on October 30, 1777, the *Ranger's* captain was ready to sail, being appointed messenger, to his great pride, to carry the news of Burgoyne's surrender to Deane, Franklin, and Lee in Paris. Among his officers were Thomas Simpson, First Lieutenant; Elijah Hall, Second Lieutenant; Samuel Wallingford, Third Lieutenant; all of Portsmouth, and Nathaniel Fanning of Salem, midshipman. John Calvin Robinson, of Philadelphia, was the bo'sun. The crew included men from Portsmouth, Nantucket, New Bedford, Boston, and Philadelphia. And conspicuous among those present were Anthony Jeremiah, the Indian, and Cato and Scipio, negro cabin boys set free by Jones in 1776 and now proudly surnamed Jones, after their young master. Jones made his will and wrote farewell letters to Hewes and Morris. That to Hewes contained two particularly interesting passages. One said: " I most ardently wish for the Command of some Spirited private Enterprize whereby I may be enabled to prove that I have not merited the disgrace of being superseded." And the other: " Major Frazer . . . hath given a description so truly Elysian to a small Estate on the Mattapony, Virgina, that I wish to become the purchaser . . . I wish you could satisfy yourself respecting the situation and properties of the Lands before the purchase."

And thus dreaming of " calm contemplation and poetic ease," he pushed the *Ranger's* nose out into the Atlantic, free at last of politics, free of intrigue, free of self-torture, and with exhilarating prospects before him. Such an occasion called for a song, and it was not long in coming from the throats of a cheerful crew, as written by the youngest midshipman, Charley Hill, of Barnstable:

SONG OF THE RANGER

So now we had him hard and fast,
Burgoyne laid down his arms at last,
And that is why we brave the blast,
    To carry the news to London!

Heigh-ho! Carry the news!
    Go! Carry the news to London.
    Tell old King George he's undone!
Heigh-ho! Car-r-r-y-y the news!

III

Brimming over with energy, Jones could scarcely be induced to sleep. He spent only three or four hours out of the twenty-four in his bed. He chose the northerly and more stormy passage and drove the ship dead into the wind. He crowded on the canvas till the *Ranger's* raking masts bent backward and her straining hull lay almost flat on her beam ends. The men were eight hours on duty and four hours off, but since their captain worked even longer, no one complained. When they grew chilled from exposure, Jones hurried about the deck, serving them grog with his own hands. Once when a squall struck the ship, he saved her from capsizing only by cutting her fly-sheets with a hatchet. But despite the strain and the cold, no one fell sick, and only Solomon Hutchings, a seaman, was hurt when a boarding sea bowled him over. And throughout the voyage no one was punished, no one was even reprimanded.

They saw no ships till they entered the Bay of Biscay. There they spoke a Dutch one. " I informed the Dutch captain of the surrender of Burgoyne," reported Jones, " and requested him to repeat the intelligence, with my compliments, to any British captain that he might fall in with." On the last day he paused to take two prizes, sent one to Brest, and convoyed the other. He cast anchor in the Loire, below Nantes, on December 2d, 1777, and hurried by coach to Paris with his dispatches. He placed them, with a bow, in Benjamin Franklin's hands on the 5th, only to find that Jonathan Loring Austin, the Boston messenger who had come on a fast French ship, had beaten him to Paris by twelve hours.

MORTAL COMBAT BETWEEN JOHN PAUL AND SAILOR AT THE ISLAND OF TOBAGO.

CHAPTER XIII

In France

The Sun now rose upon the right:
Out of the sea came he,
Still hid in mist, and on the left
Went down into the sea.

I

BENJAMIN FRANKLIN, who was a canny judge of men, must have looked curiously at this self-assured young sea-rover who had come to him with no introduction save that of a letter from the Marine Committee describing him as " an active and brave commander of our navy," but he was apparently impressed with him, for he introduced John Paul Jones to his good friend, the Countess d'Houdetot, with a letter which said: " When face to face with him, neither man, nor, so far as I can learn, woman, can resist the strange magnetism of his presence, the indescribable charm of his manner."

As for Jones, he regarded Franklin from the first with veneration. In letter after letter he addressed the sage in terms of filial piety, signing himself " with grateful and real affection and respect," and finally as " your most devoted and obedient foster son." It was to Franklin that Jones wrote the first full account of his killing of the sailor at Tobago, for which the sage excused him on the ground of self-defence; and it was to Franklin that he resorted for occasional counsel and for balm to his frequently wounded pride. Jones had an openly expressed scorn for certain men in high places, but a word from Franklin could bring him humbly to heel.

[85]

II

After settling down at Nantes to await the orders of the American commissioners, Jones wrote to his friend, Mr. Wendell, at Portsmouth, New Hampshire, a mock-poetic letter which revealed his exuberance:

" The *Ranger* was wafted by the pinions of the quietest and most friendly Gales along the surface of the Blue profound of Neptune, and not the swelling bosom of a Friend's or even an Enemy's sail appeared within our placid horizon until after we had passed the Everlasting mountains of the Sea (called Azores) whose tops are in the clouds, and whose foundations are in the center. When lo! this halcyon season was interrupted! The gathering fleets o'erspread the sea and war alarms began, nor ceased day or night until aided by the mighty Boreas, we cast Anchor in this asylum the 2nd current, but since I am not certain that my poetry will be understood, it may not be amiss to add, by way of marginal note, that after leaving Portsmouth nothing remarkable happened until I got to the eastward of the Westward Islands. . . . My heart glows with the most fervent gratitude for every unsolicited and unexpected instance of the favor and approbation of Congress, and if a Life of Services devoted to the interests of America can be made instrumental in Securing its Independence, I shall be the happiest of men. . . . I must rely on you to make my best compliments to the fair Miss Wendell, and to the other agreeable ladies of my acquaintance in Portsmouth."

Another letter was to the American commissioners at Paris. It summarized certain proposals which Jones had previously submitted to the Marine Committee at Philadelphia, and revealed that even at the age of thirty, Jones had a studious and fertile mind, with a grasp of the broad principles of strategy as well as the narrower ones of tactics.

" I have always, since we had ships of war, been persuaded," he wrote, " that small squadrons could be employed to far better advantage on private expeditions, and would distress the enemy infinitely more than the same force could do by cruising either jointly or separately. . . . We cannot yet fight their Navy, as their numbers and force are so far superior to ours, therefore it seems to be our natural province to surprise their defenceless places and thereby divide their attention and draw it off from our coasts."

On the same day, December 11, 1777, Jones wrote to Robert Morris giving some news of his friend, Major John Gizzard Frazer, who had come as a volunteer marine officer to France for "amusement." Jones was no longer so smitten with the gallant major, who, knowing everybody and everything, had selected for him a neat little estate in Virginia which could be had at a wonderful bargain. The major, Jones lamented, was "subject to drink." Later the major confessed to Jones he was short of funds and negotiated a small loan, upon which he took himself to Bordeaux where the inhabitants lived, he wrote, "in more fashion." He left his servant in Jones's care and thanked him in advance for settling a few small debts which would be brought to his attention.

War always stirs up dregs and France was soon full of American adventurers and cadgers of a similar stripe. They hung around the cafés in port towns, conversed affably with ladies of leisure, and graciously allowed fresh arrivals from the States to buy them meals and drinks. When pickings at the ports dropped low, they moved on to Paris and tried to borrow from Benjamin Franklin. If that failed, they earned a desperate livelihood by amateur spying. In return for these cargoes, France sent over in Lafayette's train a number of seedy but pretentious gentlemen of the same kidney, and one of them for a time became the chief bane of John Paul Jones's life.

III

While Jones was thus trying patiently to await develop-
ments, he was cheered by being told that he was to receive command of a splendid new frigate being built at Amsterdam for
the Continental government. This was the *Indien*, the story of
which, hitherto incorrectly told, forms one of the most curious
chapters in American naval history. She was almost ready for
launching when the British government discovered her real
ownership and at once threatened to seize her. To prevent this
the government of the Netherlands hastily transferred her to
France, and on January 16, 1778, Franklin and Deane, two of
the three American commissioners in Paris, were compelled to
write Jones that " it is not in our power to procure you such a
ship as you expected." This must have been a sharp disappointment to John Paul, who was so easily elated by promises,
but he accepted it philosophically, remarking that " my un-
feigned thanks are equally due for the intention as for the
act."

The *Indien* was subsequently " lent " by the King of France
to the Chevalier Ann Paul Emanuel Sigismont de Montmorency Luxembourg for three years. This was a subterfuge
adopted because France was not yet ready to break with Britain
by coming out openly for America. About this time there arrived in Holland Alexander Gillon, of South Carolina, the only
American state possessing a commodore exclusively its own.
Gillon, who was a Hollander by birth, had been authorized by
his state to borrow $500,000 independently from France, and to
buy ships for an independent South Carolina navy, greatly to
the annoyance of Benjamin Franklin, who was himself trying
to borrow all the money that France would part with. Gillon
complained that Franklin refused to reply to his letters, adding,
" This is doing as he has done on every matter I applied to him

on." [1] However, Gillon obtained the *Indien* from the Chevalier Luxembourg on a lease contract, with the privilege of subsequent purchase. After enormous efforts, fantastic financing, and many delays, Commodore Gillon, who had been a merchant and estate owner at Charleston, South Carolina, sailed the ship out of the Texel, the Amsterdam roadstead. He had renamed her the *South Carolina* and carried several passengers, including Capt. William Jackson, a South Carolina officer who had been sent over to " accelerate " Gillon's oft-delayed departure. The *South Carolina* cruised north, captured a privateer, and then turned southward to put in at Corunna, Spain. Here Jackson and most of the other passengers, quarreling fiercely with Gillon, left her. Gillon continued his voyage to Havana, taking five ships on the way. He then proceeded to Philadelphia where he was forced to quit his ship due to a suit lodged against him by the Chevalier Luxembourg for non-fulfilment of contract. The *South Carolina* then sailed again and was ingloriously captured by the British off the Delaware Capes.

Thus, due to confusion and factionalism, was a ship, much the finest of her class, lost to John Paul Jones. He had to go back to the little *Ranger,* which needed much repairing before she was again fit for service.

IV

Meantime Franklin and Deane had been listening to Jones's proposals for harassing Britain, and they now dispatched a letter to him giving him virtually a free hand.

" We advise you," they wrote on January 16, 1778, "after equipping the *Ranger* in the best manner for the cruise you propose, that you proceed with her in the manner you shall judge best for distressing the enemies of the United States, by sea or otherwise, consistent with the laws of war, and the terms

[1] Quoted by D. E. Huger Smith in *S. C. Historical and Genealogical Magazine,* vol. 9.

of your commissions. . . . We rely on your ability, as well as your zeal, to serve the United States, and therefore do not give you particular instructions as to your operations."

This was an order exactly to Jones's liking, and in his joy he scarcely noticed it was not signed by the third Commissioner, the sulky Arthur Lee. Lee's excuse was that he had no confidence in Gourlade, one of the prize agents named by Franklin and Deane; but the real reason was his incessant feud with Franklin and Deane, due to his own megalomaniac vanity and to the scant respect showed him during the negotiations with the French court. In addition was his peculiar hatred of Jones as a Scotchman. " Beware," Lee, who had been educated in Edinburgh, repeatedly counselled his friends, " of the Scotch."

v

While Jones was hastening the repairs on the *Ranger* at Nantes he received the invaluable help of the zealous young prize agent there, Jonathan Williams, with whom he formed a friendship in which he was the David to the other's Jonathan. Williams was a son of Benjamin Franklin's niece in Boston. He was able, alert, and businesslike. There exists a record of the sale of the *Ranger's* prizes by Williams, on which Jones noted that it was the only one ever received from any of the numerous prize agents acting for the American colonies. And then when John Adams arrived in France to take the place of the deposed Silas Deane — the victim of Arthur Lee's suspicions — Adams, who was only too ready to listen to the half-crazy Virginian, ordered Williams to be discharged! His successor was a German named Schweighauser, afterward known to John Paul as " that pig of a Schweighauser." Williams returned to the United States, where he organized and became the first superintendent of the Military Academy at West Point.

Anyone examining the historical records of that period is compelled to pause and wonder, in such a stew-pot of incompetency, confusion, intrigue, and self-seeking, that the feeble little American colonies ever survived the war at all. Their salvation was due to the fact that, in addition to the possession by the colonists of a few hardy and resolute souls, the British were equally incompetent, if not more so. Few of their army commanders, dispatched by a corrupt and lumbering government, had any adequate notion of what constituted effective fighting in the American wilderness; and their navy was often sent out wretchedly manned and badly equipped owing to the robbery and jobbing of supplies by officials in the home government, notoriously fostered by the Earl of Sandwich, first Lord of the Admiralty, and the " Jemmy Twitcher " of ribald and cynical songs.

However, revolutions, even at best, are exacting enterprises. There probably never was a revolution, or any grandiose human rising, which was not conceived in dirt and carried out in mingled foolishness and anguish. The fact that from such swamps a lily ever rises, is one of the wonders of history. And yet the lilies do rise, and have their blooming.

CHAPTER XIV

Plans for the Grand Cruise

The skiff-boat neared: I heard them talk,
" Why, this is strange, I trow!
Where are those lights so many and fair,
That signal made but now?"

I

ON February 6, 1778, France made public her Treaty of Alliance with the American colonies and Jones at once saw an opportunity to shorten the war. On February 10 he wrote to the commissioners at Paris advising a plan of attack on the English which " would prove their Ruin and insure our Success." He proposed that ten or twelve French ships of the line, accompanied by frigates, should secretly sail, attack, and overwhelm Lord Howe's blockading fleet off the American coast. " Small squadrons might then be formed, to secure the coast and cut off the Enemie's supplies while our army settled the Account current." This plan Captain Alfred Mahan, author of *The Influence of Sea Power*, accepts as a token " of the great general officer that might have been." It was finally laid before the French court, and Jones afterward, without adequate grounds, accused Silas Deane of presenting it as his own. Count d'Orvilliers, admiral of the Brest fleet, approved, but de Sartine, minister of the French marine, was a hopeless dilatory, and it was midsummer before the French fleet, under Count d'Estaing, reached the Delaware, just too late to catch the British squadron which had helped General Howe evacuate Philadelphia. It was the assistance of another French fleet under Count de Grasse, who drove the British Admiral Graves away from the Chesapeake, which later cut off General Cornwallis's supplies and made possible the victory at Yorktown.

II

On February 12th Jones sailed for Quiberon Bay, taking with him Jonathan Williams as a witness to a certain diplomatic victory he meant to win. There he demanded a salute from the French commander, the famous La Motte Picquet, " gun for gun." The latter answered that he would reply with the salute customarily given to any republic. Accordingly Jones sailed the *Ranger* into the harbor and at sunset proudly fired thirteen guns. There was a moment's tense pause, while Jones and Williams waited side by side on the *Ranger's* quarterdeck; and then came the leisurely first gun from the French admiral's flagship — " Boom! " There was another pause, and again " Boom! " Eagerly Jones and Williams counted until the last gun had echoed over the harbor. Nine! Four less than John Paul had wanted, but not so bad for a beginning. Jubilantly he ran back to his cabin and dashed this off to the Marine Committee:

" I am happy in having it in my power to congratulate you on my having seen the American Flag for the first time recognized in the fullest and amplest manner by the Flag of France."

To make matters certain, however, Jones the next morning sailed a brig through the French fleet and again saluted the admiral, who " was exceedingly pleased and returned the compliment with 9 guns." John Paul then received the visits of the French officers with high satisfaction, writing home:

" This squadron is officered by a very well-bred set of men. They have all visited the *Ranger* and expressed great satisfaction, calling her a ' parfait bijou ' " (perfect jewel).

And now he girded himself for his first great enterprise in

[93]

foreign seas. " It is true," he wrote, " I must run great risk, but no gallant action was ever accomplished without danger; therefore, although I cannot ensure success, I will endeavor to deserve it."

On April 10 he drew out of Brest and headed north into the Irish channel through the teeth of a gale. He carried with him as company, two " gentlemen volunteers " — Jean Meyer, a Swedish army officer, and C. F. Morris, an American. The watch was doubled and changed often, for the word of his coming was out, and Jones had been warned that if captured he would be hanged to a yard-arm as a renegade and pirate. He was no sooner out of sight of land than he discovered eight of his crew had deserted him and that his first lieutenant, Simpson, was sulky and had little stomach for the enterprise.

CHAPTER XV

Raids by Sea and Land

Almost upon the western wave
Rested the broad bright Sun;
When that strange shape drove suddenly
Betwixt us and the Sun.

I

IT is an odd fact, but one not in itself strange, that John Paul should have chosen Whitehaven as his first landing place in his first descent upon the English coast. From the hill the hunter always returns home; the child yearns to go back to the matrix; and the wisdom of the East declares that life traces itself in circles or spirals; the end, at least in thought, being not far from the beginning.

Whitehaven, opposite the top rim of Ireland, was Jones's home port, the spot where he began his career. It was also just across the bay from the place of his birth. It was the neighborhood in which he had been reared, and where, as a rather queer child, he had been lightly regarded. The fact that the bay was full of enemy shipping, and but scantily fortified, was incidental. In the past " they " had scorned him. He was coming back to damage English shipping and to raid an enemy stronghold, yes; but he was also going to " show them."

The wind was unfavorable, but in the dark hours of April 22 his raiding expedition dropped off the *Ranger* in two boats and rowed for the sleeping town. He took with him Lieutenant Wallingford, Midshipmen Arthur Green and Charles Hill, and twenty-nine men. It was dawn before he swept down upon the fortification. He surprised the two forts and waked up three snoring sentinels to inform them they were prisoners. He spiked all the guns and turned to await the blaze upon the shipping which Wallingford was to start. But that officer's light had gone out, and Jones had to set the nearest ship afire with his own hands. The townspeople now came running up, but fled when they saw the gleam of arms. Daylight having come, he ordered his people to return to their boats. He himself remained behind, pistol in hand, alone, standing silhouetted upon the ramparts, enjoying the gaze from " the eminences around the town " which were " covered with the amazed inhabitants." He loved it all. It was one of his glorious moments.

When he finally took to his boat, he was fired upon, but the shots fell short. " The shot," he wrote, " instead of doing us any damage, afforded some diversion, which my people could not help showing by discharging their pistols, etc., in return of the salute." He counted noses and found only one man missing. " I was pleased," he wrote, " that in this business we neither killed nor wounded any person."

The alarm caused by this raid was absurdly out of proportion to its actual accomplishments; but beneath the hysteria was a very real fear born of the realization that England's long untouched shores had been violated by a daring enemy who might soon strike again, and that retaliation might be expected for the burning by the British of Fairfield, Conn., Charlestown, Mass., and Falmouth (Portland), Maine. Whig newspapers attacked the government for having brought this upon the people, demanded that Lord North make peace, and excoriated the population for its panic. The raid had another serious effect. It enormously increased the insurance rates on British shipping, thereby adding another burden to the growing expense of the war.

II

From Whitehaven the *Ranger* stood up Kirkcudbright Bay, passing through waters of which Jones remembered the formation of almost every wave. He landed a boat at Saint Mary's Isle and walking up the familiar paths where as a child he had played under his uncle's eye, he stopped and sent a squad up to the home of the Earl of Selkirk. This had no sound military purpose, though Jones afterward explained that he meant to seize the Earl as a hostage to be exchanged for American prisoners who were being treated as pirates in English jails; and this visit would be almost inexplicable did we not know that at one time Jones believed he was the Earl's natural, and neglected, son.

The Earl was not at home, but the Countess, who was about to become a mother, answered the doorbell. Two officers, one dressed in green and the other in blue, demanded all the plate in the house, though, said the Countess afterward, " I must say they behaved civilly." They put everything in sacks, and then, " Where is the teapot and the coffee pot? " The Countess replied there was no more plate, whereupon Lieutenant Wallingford walked through the house, and then ordered his men away.

" It was immediately known," wrote Lady Selkirk, " that this Paul Jones is one John Paul, born at Arbigland, who once commanded a Kirkcudbright vessel belonging to Mr. Muir and others, a great villain as ever was born, guilty of many crimes and several murders by ill usage, was tried and condemned for one, escaped, and followed a piratical life till he engaged with the Americans. He seems to delight in that still, as robbing a house was below the dignity of the States of America. The sailors at the door told, their captain was born at Berrick, knew my Lord (whose name and the name of the place those in the house

[97]

pretended ignorance of) had a great opinion of him, and for that reason had given orders that no harm should be done."

It is entirely probable that this letter accurately reflected the notions concerning Jones that still prevailed in his home territory. Lady Selkirk's opinion of him after he had bought the plate back from his men at a cost of £140 and returned it to her from Brest — "to gratify," as Jones wrote, "my own feelings" — is not recorded. The returned teapot, with its tea leaves still intact, was long visible at Castle Douglas on Saint Mary's Isle.

III

The next day Jones crossed the Channel and came abreast of the Irish port of Carrickfergus. There some fishermen, whom he took on board, told him that the British war sloop, the *Drake*, which had been at anchor in the roadstead as a guardship, was coming out to look for him. This was welcome news to Jones. He had been itching for a fight with the English in their own waters, and here was an opportunity laid in his hand.

"To save trouble," he writes, "I ran down again, hove to off the mouth of Belfast Lough, and waited for the *Drake* to come out, which saved me the pains of going in after her."

Though already informed of the Whitehaven raid, the *Drake's* captain had no suspicion of Jones's presence, but on sighting the *Ranger*, he sent out a boat to reconnoitre. The midshipman in charge could not make her out because Jones kept his ship's stern toward the boat, and he finally boarded her. He was astounded when informed he was the prisoner of the dreadful John Paul Jones. The *Drake* moved out slowly, attended by several small vessels full of sight-seers who scented spectacular trouble. But on alarm-smokes suddenly rising from both sides of the channel, these hastily put back to shore. The *Drake* came up astern, hoisted her colors, and hailed: "What ship is that?"

"The American Continental ship *Ranger*," bawled Nathan Sargent, the New Hampshire master, as the American banner went up. "Come on; we're waiting for you."

The ships gradually wore close together, and then there burst from each a broadside, Jones's being a trifle the first. The action at once became furious and the English officers began to fall, among them being the captain and the first lieutenant. "I have never before seen men," wrote Jones of his gunners, "handle guns as they handled the *Ranger's* nine-pounders."

Holes began to gape in the *Drake's* hull, and Jones ran up to ask Owen Starbuck of Nantucket what he was trying to do. That gunner and his companion, Anthony Jeremiah, the Narragansett Indian, gaped at the question.

"To sink the ——s, sir," they replied.

An idea was running through Jones's imaginative brain, What, instead of sinking the English ship, if he could take her and carry her into a French port? What a sensation that would be! Instantly he ordered his gunners to cease firing at the enemy's hull and to aim instead at her sails and rigging. This was a favorite French tactic of the period, of which John Paul had doubtless been advised by the French officers back at Brest. The gunners took the hint and as their muzzles rose at the swell of the sea, they brought down the *Drake's* fore and main topsail yards in a heap and the rigging soon came tumbling after. In a moment the ship was as helpless as a log. Jones then ran back to the wheel of the *Ranger* to order a luff. But Nathan Sargent had already put the helm down and as the *Ranger* responded, her gunners raked the enemy's decks fore and aft. The *Drake* could endure no more. Her only remaining officer, a second lieutenant, struck her colors, and Jones boarded the enemy after a fight lasting an hour and four minutes. She had lost forty-two men out of 160. Her captain, Burden, was conscious but died in a few minutes. Her first lieutenant died later. "They were buried," wrote the punctilious Jones, "with the

honors due to their rank and the respect due their memory."
He also wrote to the young lieutenant's family.

Jones lost only two killed and seven wounded. Among the
dead was Lieutenant Wallingford who had taken part in the
raids on Whitehaven and Saint Mary's Isle. Among the English dead lay an army officer in full uniform who had come
aboard the *Drake* to see the sport. Nearby lay the remains of
a barrel of rum, burst by a cannon shot. In the *Drake's* hull
were found 107 shot-holes, some of them piercing the ship
through and through. Her upper works and rigging were a
wreck, and most of her guns dismounted. But William Hichborn of Salem, Mass., the *Ranger's* carpenter, soon had the
captured ship seaworthy again and she followed in the wake of
the *Ranger* in command of Lieutenant Simpson.

IV

The battle with the *Drake* ended just at sunset, and Jones
then turned north around the end of Ireland. One of his first
acts was to release the Irish fishermen whom he had taken on
board and who had been compelled to stay with him through the
fight. He gave them a boat to replace the one they had lost,
added money for new outfits, and sent with them two sick men,
with their fares paid to Dublin. " The grateful Irishmen were
enraptured," wrote Jones, " and expressed their joy in three
huzzas as they passed the *Ranger's* quarter." Jones then came
down the west coast of Ireland, taking a prize on the way, and
when in sight of France, turned to pursue a strange sail. On
returning, he found the *Drake*, with Simpson in charge, dis-
appearing over the horizon. It soon became evident that
Simpson, who ignored all signals, meant to desert him. All that
night Jones pursued the fleeing ship, being thus compelled to
pass by several valuable prizes. The next day he overtook her,
and on Simpson's failure to explain his conduct, Jones suspended

him and put Elijah Hall in command. That night his Swedish *compagnon de voyage*, Lieutenant Meyer, told Jones of something he had learned from a Swedish sailor. It is thus given in a memoir left by Meyer:

" The crew supported by the majority of their officers had decided to seize the person of their captain, whom they disliked because he was a Scotchman, with the intention of throwing him overboard, or at least to put him in irons. They intended afterward to choose Lieutenant Simpson for their captain, to take them back to America, where all ardently desired to return."

Jones's leniency with Simpson on this occasion would seem to be astonishing, did not his subsequent actions indicate that he suspected Simpson of having been incited by men in high place. Jones was convinced that treachery was being carried on somewhere in an American office in Paris. He knew that the English had been informed of his coming, and had even learned in advance of his departure from Quiberon. He had complained to the American commissioners about the flow of secret information to London. " Strange " he wrote, " that nothing can remain secret! " But no action had resulted. He meant to deal with the situation himself at the proper time. Meantime he regarded Simpson, who had fought well in the *Drake* battle, with half-amused contempt. " The trouble with you, Mr. Simpson," he wrote, " is that you have the heart of a lion and the head of a sheep."

v

Jones sailed into the harbor of Brest at sundown on May 8 with the *Drake's* colors inverted under his own flag. He had been out of port twenty-eight days, during which he had achieved feats of the kind in which he most delighted. As the *Ranger* glided up the roadstead in the darkness, she was challenged by a French guard-frigate. Jones replied with a pri-

[101]

vate signal. He was ordered to stand by until the frigate had summoned another ship. The two ships then bore down on him suspiciously. " Who are you, and what is your prize? " came the hail in French.

Jones's sonorous voice replied proudly:

" The American Continental ship *Ranger* of eighteen guns, Captain Paul Jones. The prize is His Britannic Majesty's late ship, the *Drake* of twenty guns! "

But the proud captain was seldom able to enjoy his triumphs long. On going ashore he received the news that Miss Dorothea Dandridge, of Virginia, had become the second wife of Patrick Henry, and that the American commissioners had dishonored the draft with which he meant to feed and clothe his victorious crew.

JOHN PAUL SEEKS REFUGE ON BOARD A PIRATE SHIP.

CHAPTER XVI

Spies and Counter Spies

And now the storm-blast came, and he
Was tyrannous and strong:
He struck with his o'ertaking wings,
And chased us south along.

I

ONE morning after his return to Brest, Jones suddenly entered the courtyard of a post-inn where a man in American dress was about to step into a diligence bound for Paris. This man was of large dimensions, about six feet high and weighing perhaps 200 pounds. Without warning Jones sprang at him. We have the word of Nathaniel Fanning, who was an officer under Jones and at one time his secretary, that the little captain " was quicker than chain lightning — when roused he could strike more blows and do more damage in a second than any other man I ever saw could do in a minute." It was so now. Jones's fist caught the fat man on the jaw and knocked him flat. Jones then seized the whip of the amazed driver of the diligence and began to lash the prostrate man furiously about the body, at the same time kicking him with unmistakable signs of rage and contempt. Passersby and servants ran up and caught Jones's hands as he reached for one of the three pistols in his belt. The fat man meantime covered his face with his hands and bawled like a calf. When pulled to his feet, he made no attempt to fight back but hastily hid himself in the diligence. Jones would make no explanation, and the surrounding Frenchmen gave up the matter as evidently being a private one among those Americans, who beyond a doubt were given to dementia.

[103]

We learn the name of the fat man from Jones himself.   In
his *Journal* he afterwards wrote that " to this day I cannot understand, even if I excuse myself for it, why I spared the reptile
life of Hezekiah Ford in the courtyard of the post-inn at Brest,
when he was at my mercy and I had every justification for
it."

Hezekiah Ford was one of the numerous secretaries surrounding Arthur Lee, of the American Commission in Paris.
He usually wore an expression which was half cleric and half
crocodile.   He came from Virginia where he " passed for " a
minister of the Church of England.   He had previously been
the chaplain of a North Carolina regiment.   During the Stamp
Act discussion in Virginia the violence of Ford's denunciations
of the British government and his incitements to armed rebellion had caused him to be suspected as an *agent provocateur* in
the pay of the government he was attacking.   Finally on January 7, 1779, Patrick Henry, then Governor of Virginia, addressing the legislature and referring to Ford, put on record his
" assurance that the most essential interests of America will be
betrayed by this man." [1]   The legislature sent this denunciation
in the form of a resolution to Congress, but Lee obstinately refused to part with his secretary.   Ford finally disappeared, going, it is supposed, to England with stolen papers.

II

On August 6 of this same year, William Carmichael, American chargé at Madrid, wrote to Congress that " the loss of Mr.
Lee's papers at Berlin gave such a clue to the English court, that
the commissioners could not have conceived the operations at
that time commenced, unless in the midst of them they had
changed their whole arrangement, which was impossible.   From
this unfortunate circumstance arose the necessity of selling our

[1] Wharton's *Diplomatic Correspondence of the United States.*

frigate in Holland and many other obstacles to the transportation of our clothing from Europe." [2]

Lee, before coming to Paris, had been the American envoy in Berlin. There certain papers had been stolen from him and turned over to Elliott, the British ambassador, resulting in the loss to John Paul Jones of the command of the new frigate *Indien*, later the *South Carolina*, as previously described.

However, it was probably not this fact which caused Jones's fierce assault on Ford, but rather his well-founded suspicions that it was Ford who had been at work among the *Ranger's* homesick crew, inducing them, under promise of procuring their speedy return home, to sign a petition against Jones and in favor of the sheep-headed Simpson to whom had been promised the command of the *Ranger* in the expectation that Jones would take over the *Indien*. Seventy-eight of the crew signed the petition following the refusal of the commissioners to honor Jones's draft, after his triumphant return to Brest. Included were Cato and Scipio, Jones's former slave boys, a fact which stabbed Jones in the heart, though he realized that they had been merely misled.

III

Ford's predecessor as Lee's secretary was Major Thornton, formerly of the British army but later a professed American patriot. In the archives of the British foreign office is this letter dated March 6, 1778, from George III, King of England, to his prime minister, Lord North:

" The intelligence from Mr. Thornton of the discontents among the leaders in America, if authentic, will not only greatly facilitate the bringing that deluded country to some reasonable ideas, but will make France reconsider whether she ought to enter into a war when America may leave her in the lurch."

The same archives reveal the deposit on August 7, 1782, of

[2] *Idem.*

copies of a number of letters received from Thornton which belonged to the diplomatic correspondence between Lee, Franklin, Deane; Count de Vergennes, the French foreign minister; Florida-Blanca, the Spanish foreign minister; and the American Congress during the critical years of 1777 and 1778.

But the egocentric Lee could never be induced to admit that he had been a piece of puffed-up wax in the hands of these spying secretaries, and as long as he remained in France they continued to incite his megalomaniac mind against Deane, whose recall they caused; against Franklin, who barely escaped the same fate; and against John Paul Jones, whom they harassed with a thousand devices and plots, until Jones, realizing Lee's utter fatuity and malevolence, began to use his fists on them.

IV

Jones's second charge on the spying fraternity was at Nantes. Patrons of a coffee house there were confounded one day to see the American captain enter grimly, walk up to a fellow countryman named Stephen Sayre, who had gained a local reputation as a bully and boaster, and slap his face. Sayre sprang up and began to struggle with Jones, who seized a bystander's cane and began to use it on Sayre's head. The combatants were parted by police, who then felt bound to ask the captain's parole that he would thenceforth create no further disturbances in public.

Sayre was a hanger-on of Arthur Lee's, but there is no proof that he was a spy. More likely he was a simple mixture of Bottom, Bumble and Alfred Jingle, gripped with delusions of grandeur. He was one of those individuals who must needs inject themselves into any situation which promises publicity and reflected importance; they always know conspicuous people by their first names; and like to hint at dark secrets confided to them by the great or gained by amateur sleuthing. In pursuit of their queer aims, they recognize no closed door and are impervious to any hint short of a kick. Their mission is to provide the relief of solemn comedy in the midst of serious situations, and within limits are endured by the busiest.

Sayre, who was of Long Island birth, went from Virginia, where he was a tobacco speculator, to England in 1774 and joined the train of the agitating John Wilkes, the bitter enemy of George III's government.[3] He shared Wilkes's successes and with William Lee, brother of Arthur Lee, was elected one of the sheriffs of London. He was later sent to the Tower, charged with treason in publishing certain " surreptitiously obtained " letters, but obtained his release through Wilkes. During the war he was successively in Paris, Berlin, Copenhagen, Amsterdam and Stockholm, at each place holding conferences, chiefly in restaurants and cafés, with an air of mysterious importance. He wrote Benjamin Franklin: " I look upon myself as a modern Don Quixote, going about to protect and relieve the virtuous in distress." [4] In 1780 he turned up in St. Petersburg where Sir James Harris, the British ambassador to the Court of Catherine the Great, set secret agents to watch him and in alarm reported him to his government as an " American Agent, Spy & Speculator." Later Sayre came to Franklin with a luminous suggestion. It was that to settle the quarrel between Captain Jones and Captain Landais — of which more will follow — he, Sayre, should be made captain of the disputed ship, the *Alliance*. In 1782 he gave Franklin one more opportunity; he proposed that the island of Porto Rico be taken and that he, Sayre, be appointed governor of it. Having thus done what he could to save the commonwealth, Sayre deserted the European diplomatic field in disgust and returned home, lived for some time near Bordentown, New Jersey, and finally died in

[3] Cf. description of the " Hell Fire Club " in the author's book: *Benjamin Franklin, the First Civilized American*.
[4] Wharton's *Diplomatic Correspondence*.

Virginia, long after John Paul Jones's death, at the end of a respected old age.

v

Other spies and suspects who had some connection with Arthur Lee were Thomas and George Digges, of Maryland, and John Berkenhout, of England. Wharton says the former pair suggested to Lee that Franklin and the latter's secret agent, Dr. Edward Bancroft, were engaged in stock speculations, and Lee afterward made this charge against Bancroft, increasing the fury of John Paul Jones, who was Bancroft's close friend. Wharton also reports that Thomas Digges once "sent to Adams English informations (no doubt of a decoy character inspired by the British government) in a letter dated May 12, 1780." While employed in the relief of American prisoners suffering starvation in English jails, Digges was accused by Franklin of drawing excessive sums and embezzling the relief funds. His career was halted in an Irish jail.

Berkenhout, who had been a fellow medical student of Lee at Edinburgh and Leyden, was probably unfortunate rather than guilty. He was a scientist and writer on medicine, botany and natural history. He was first an officer in the Prussian army and then in the British one. In 1778 he came to Philadelphia with a British commission to discuss the exchange of prisoners. He remained there some time before being jailed on suspicion, as a correspondent of Lee.

Accounting for the easy victimization of Lee by hired spies and unattached informers would require the studies of a psychiatrist rather than the writings of a historian. A member of the famous Lee family of Virginia, and a brother of Richard Henry Lee, Arthur Lee may have been corrupted, as some writers suggest, by his association with the English faction of political adventurers headed by the cynical John Wilkes; and then in Paris his excitable brain was given a further twist by the tendency of Franklin, Deane, and the French court to proceed with arrangements without consulting him. His festering vanity led him to obstruct where he was unable to assist, and he early fixed upon John Paul Jones as a member of a cabal which he was certain meant to injure both him and the American cause. The injuries he inflicted upon Jones are not now calculable, but there is no doubt that Jones's colossal disappointments and difficulties in France were due largely to the manipulations of Lee and the men whom Jones, at first ignorant of their skulduggery, referred to as " spies and bandits in guise of private secretaries and seaport agents."

CHAPTER XVII

A Strange Letter to the Countess of Selkirk

And the good south wind still blew behind,
But no sweet bird did follow,
Nor any day for food or play
Came to the mariners' hollo!

I

FROM aboard the Ranger at Brest Jones wrote two letters in conspicuous contrast. He liked to write letters, and his secretaries, at times, must have been more busy than his gunners. The first communication was to Lady Selkirk. It was a strange mixture of autobiography, pleading for sympathy, and poetized rhetoric. He had chosen to appoint this woman, whose house his men had just robbed, his mother confessor; and to her he described his history, his heart-wound, his viewpoint as a warrior, and his feelings as an occasional sentimentalist. Your man of action is capable of overawing the hardiest of his fellows, but when he is finished with making faces, he will creep to a woman's knees like a child. The letter follows in full:

" Madam, — It cannot be too much lamented, that, in the profession of arms, the officer of fine feelings and real sensibility should be under the necessity of winking at any action of persons under his command, which his heart cannot approve; but the reflection is doubly severe, when he finds himself obliged, in appearance, to countenance such actions by his authority. This hard case was mine, when, on the 23d of April last, I landed on St. Mary's Isle. Knowing Lord Selkirk's interest with his King, and esteeming as I do his private character, I wished to make him the happy instrument of alleviating the horrors of hopeless captivity, when the brave are overpowered and made prisoners of war. It was perhaps fortunate for you, Madam, that he was from home; for it was my intention to have taken him on board the *Ranger,* and detained him until, through his means, a general and fair exchange of prisoners, as well in Europe as in America, had been effected.

" When I was informed, by some men whom I met at landing, that his Lordship was absent, I walked back to my boat, determined to leave the island. By the way, however, some officers who were with me, could not forbear expressing their discontent, observing that in America no delicacy was shown by the English who took away all sorts of movable property, setting fire not only to towns and to the houses of the rich, without distinction, but not even sparing the wretched hamlets and milch-cows of the poor and helpless, at the approach of an inclement winter. That party had been with me that same morning at Whitehaven; some complaisance, therefore, was their due. I had but a moment to think how I might gratify them, and at the same time do your Ladyship the least injury. I charged the officers to permit none of the seamen to enter the house, or to hurt any thing about it; to treat you, Madam, with the utmost respect; to accept of the plate which was offered, and to come away without making a search, or demanding any thing else. I am induced to believe that I was punctually obeyed, since I am informed that the plate which they brought away is far short of the quantity expressed in the inventory which accompanied it. I have gratified my men; and when the plate is sold, I shall become the purchaser, and will gratify my own feelings, by restoring it to you by such conveyance as you shall please to direct.

" Had the Earl been on board the *Ranger* the following evening, he would have seen the awful pomp and dreadful carnage of a sea engagement; both affording ample subject for the pencil, as well as melancholy reflection for the contemplative mind. Humanity starts back from such scenes of horror, and cannot sufficiently execrate the vile promoters of this detestable war.

" ' Had they, 't was they unsheathed the ruthless blade,
And Heaven shall ask the havoc it has made.'

[111]

"The British ship of war *Drake*, mounting twenty guns, with more than her full complement of officers and men, was our opponent. The ships met, and the advantage was disputed with great fortitude on each side for an hour and four minutes, when the gallant commander of the *Drake* fell, and victory declared in favor of the *Ranger*. The amiable lieutenant lay mortally wounded, besides near forty of the inferior officers and crew killed and wounded; a melancholy demonstration of the uncertainty of human prospects, and of the sad reverses of fortune, which an hour can produce. I buried them in a spacious grave, with the honors due to the memory of the brave.

"Though I have drawn my sword in the present generous struggle for the rights of man, yet I am not in arms as an American, nor am I in pursuit of riches. My fortune is liberal enough, having no wife nor family, and having lived long enough to know that riches cannot secure happiness. I profess myself a citizen of the world, totally unfettered by the little mean distinctions of climate or of country, which diminish the benevolence of the heart and set bounds to philanthropy. Before this war was begun, I had, at an early time of life, withdrawn from sea service in favor of ' calm contemplation and poetic ease.' I have sacrificed not only my favorite scheme of life, but the softer affections of the heart, and my prospects of domestic happiness, and I am ready to sacrifice my life also with cheerfulness, if that forfeiture could restore peace among mankind.

"As the feelings of your gentle bosom cannot but be congenial with mine, let me entreat you, Madam, to use your persuasive art with your husband, to endeavour to stop this cruel and destructive war, in which Britain can never succeed. Heaven can never countenance the barbarous and unmanly practice of the Britons in America, which savages would blush at, and which, if not discontinued, will soon be retaliated on Britain by a justly enraged people. Should you fail in this, and I am persuaded you will attempt it, (and who can resist the power of such an advocate?) your endeavours to effect a general exchange of prisoners will be an act of humanity, which will afford you golden feelings on your death-bed.

"I hope this cruel contest will soon be closed; but, should

[112]

it continue, I wage no war with the fair. I acknowledge their force, and bend before it with submission. Let not, therefore, the amiable Countess of Selkirk regard me as an enemy; I am ambitious of her esteem and friendship, and would do any thing, consistent with my duty, to merit it. The honor of a line from your hand, in answer to this, will lay me under a singular obligation; and if I can render you any acceptable service in France or elsewhere, I hope you see into my character so far as to command me, without the least grain of reserve. I wish to know the exact behavior of my people, as I am determined to punish them if they have exceeded their liberty."

Jones's elaborate explanations as to why he permitted the plate to be carried away from the Selkirk castle are scarcely satisfying. It is more likely that his subconscious motive was to provoke some kind of statement from the Earl of Selkirk which would clear up the facts regarding his own birth. But the earl's reply contained no light on this point. The earl's letter was finally received through the Postmaster-General, Lord le Despencer, former high priest of the " Hell Fire Club," of which John Wilkes and the Earl of Sandwich were members, and former close friend of Benjamin Franklin. His lordship informed the earl that he had his doubts regarding " the propriety " of his forwarding a letter to " such a Rascal and Rebel as this Jones " ; and the earl agreed that " you would see by his strange ridiculous bombast letter that he is altogether an exotick character," and " said to be a most cruel fellow, to have committed no less than three murders, and that in absconding from the West Indies after the last one, he fled to America."

However, the earl's reply to Jones was coolly polite: " You are entitled to the praise of having your men under good discipline, but it was also fortunate for you, Sir, that your officers and men behaved well, for had any of my family suffered outrage, murder or violence, no quarter of the globe should have secured you nor even some of those under whose commission you act, from my vengeance." The letter concluded with the statement that the return of the plate would not be accepted. However, it was; after Jones had bought it back from that " pig of a Schweighauser." It is evident that Jones was compelled to relinquish whatever notions he had entertained regarding his blood-relationship to the Selkirks, for when in Holland in 1780 he declared to the Baron van der Capellen that " he had no obligation to Lord Selkirk, except his good opinion, and that neither himself nor his immediate family were known to the earl except by reputation."

II

Jones's other letter was considerably sharper and more direct, having not a trace of the rhodomontade which had astonished Lady Selkirk. It was addressed to the American commissioners, Franklin, John Adams, and Arthur Lee, who had refused to meet his draft for 24,000 livres placed with the French agent, M. Bersolle. It declared, " My officers, as well as men, want clothes, and the prizes are precluded from being sold before farther orders arrive from the minister. I will ask you, gentlemen, if I have deserved all this." It went on: " To make me completely wretched, M. Bersolle has told me that he now stops his hand, not only of the necessary articles to refit the ship, but also of the daily provisions. I know not where to find tomorrow's dinner for the great number of mouths that depend on me for food. Are then the Continental ships of war to depend on the sale of their prizes for a daily dinner for their men? ' Publish it not in Gath! ' "

It was no great surprise to Jones that Arthur Lee should have inflicted this humiliation on him, or that John Adams should have agreed with Lee; but that Franklin had assented to their action was a grievous hurt. Even today Franklin's part in this incident is not explainable, except on the ground that he was already hard-pressed to meet the countless bills that at times almost overwhelmed him, and that, further, Jones's draft was for what was then an exceedingly high amount. It is likely that later he so informed Jones, who then wrote to the commissioners:

" I frankly ask your pardon for the undue liberty I took when I ventured to sign a draft upon you for the purpose of supplying the people under my command with necessary clothing, etc.; and I promise never to be guilty of the like offence again."

He reminded them, however, that he had already advanced £1500 out of his own pocket for public expenses and that so far he had received no wages whatever.

Meantime Jones had forgiven Lieutenant Simpson as having been " the victim of Arthur Lee's harpies " and allowed him to take the *Ranger* home with its crew of homesick, time-expired sailors. Twenty-seven of them remained behind to follow their captain's fortunes. Among them was Anthony Jeremiah, who craved one more battle. Jones was pleased. He wrote: " My little red Indian is not homesick. Maybe he had no home to yearn for. But I prefer to explain his choice to stay with me on other grounds." " Jerry " in due time got his second battle. No little red Indian had ever fought in one like it before, and none has since.

For one month Jones, by what means he could, had to care for more than 200 prisoners, feed and clothe his loyal seamen, repair his vessels, and support himself. Help then came from a source which not even his imaginative mind could have foreseen.

CHAPTER XVIII

The New Ship

There passed a weary time. Each throat
Was parched, and glazed each eye.
A weary time! A weary time!
How glazed each weary eye,
When looking westward, I beheld
A something in the sky.

I

AS soon as Jones gained the time to go up to Paris, he found himself the centre of an admiring circle. That an English ship of war should be defeated by an inferior vessel was extraordinary enough, but that it should be captured and taken intact into port as a prize — that was a sensation indeed. "The taking of the *Drake* was universally regarded here as an unequalled exploit," Jones proudly wrote to Hewes, " and it opened the eyes of the French to a fact they had considered out of the question, namely, that an English man-of-war could be forced to strike to a ship of inferior force."

Jones now began to meet influential people, chiefly at Franklin's home. Among them was the Duke of Chartres, and, what was more important to his later career — the Duchess.

" The Duc de Chartres has shown me sundry attentions," wrote Jones joyfully to Franklin, " and expressed his inclination to facilitate my obtaining the ship built at Amsterdam." About the same time Jones wrote in his *Journal* that " by his personal credit with Count d'Orvilliers, the Duc de Chartres, and his Intendant of Brest, he fed his people and prisoners cured his wounded, and refitted both the *Ranger* and *Drake* for sea."

The Duke of Chartres was France's "Sailor Prince," and as such had recently been made an honorary High Admiral. He was also the heir-apparent to the estate of the House of Orleans, which has ever since supplied Pretenders to the French throne. But history remembers this prince chiefly in connection with other events. He was later the famous "Philippe Égalité" of the French revolution, the only nobleman who endorsed the slogan of "Liberté, Égalité, Fraternité." On a chilly morning in 1793 he was guillotined, saying to the executioner, "Come; let us make haste." He was an eccentric personality of liberal views, but in his day, owing to his family and position, a power.

His wife was one of the great Frenchwomen of her time, of whom Count Keyserling has said: "The type that I refer to reached its perfection in the eighteenth century. Is a mode of life conceivable more empty than that of the great ladies of those days? Real love was unknown to them, they had no serious interests of any kind; the whole of their lives was spent in tittle-tattle. And yet many among them were profound." [1]

But the Duchess of Chartres was not exactly a fair idler. She spent much of her time in beneficence, and so greatly was she honored for her good deeds, she was permitted to remain safely in Paris during the Revolution, long after the other women of her class had fled or been beheaded; and this despite the fact that she was a Bourbon, belonging to that hated family of which Napoleon said: "They learn nothing and forget nothing." Before her marriage to the Duke — who astonished the attendants by hopping over her long train during the march to the altar — she was Mary Adelaide de Bourbon-Penthièvre, granddaughter of the Admiral Count de Toulouse, and daughter of the Admiral the Duke de Bourbon-Penthièvre. Having sea tra-

[1] *Travel Diary of a Philosopher.*

[117]

ditions in her family history, it was natural for her to become interested in the new naval hero from America. She not only became John Paul Jones's firm ally at the court of Louis XVI, but she lent him money " for the cause " and refused repayment. We have seen how the lonely young John Paul Jones, who had cut off relations with his own family, addressed Benjamin Franklin as a foster-son. In the Duchess of Chartres — " that Divine woman " — as he called her, he now found a mother. Her eldest son, Louis Philippe, afterwards King of the French, once wrote:

" In all my chequered life I have never known so beautiful a relation between woman and man as that of my mother and Paul Jones."

But there was another reason why the interest of this powerful Duke and Duchess in John Paul Jones should have been so particular; and here we come upon a phase of American history hitherto not brought to light.

The influence of Freemasonry upon the selection of the American leaders in the war against England has already been noted. Washington, Putnam, Montgomery, Anthony Wayne, Sullivan, Warren, Paul Revere, Thomas Paine, Lafayette, Kosciusko, Baron De Kalb, Count Pulaski, and Benedict Arnold were all Masons, and so were many colonial statesmen, including Jones's friends on the Marine Committee — Joseph Hewes and Robert Morris. In Paris at this very moment Franklin was a luminary at the Lodge of the Nine Sisters, which included among its members Voltaire, Helvetius the philosopher, and Houdon the sculptor. At this lodge Jones was a frequent visitor, and it was here that Houdon conceived the idea of making the bust of Jones which is deemed to be the best likeness of the captain that remains today.

The Grand Master over all the Masonic lodges in France was the Duke of Chartres, while the Duchess was a leader in an " adoptive " lodge of women Freemasons affiliated with the

Lodge of Candour. On March 25, 1775 this lodge "gave a *fête d'adoption* when the Duchess of Chartres, wife of the Grand Master of the Grand Orient was present." [2] At the subsequent installation of the Duchess of Bourbon as Grand Mistress "nearly a thousand persons, the élite of French society, are said to have assisted." [3] At the head of another feminine lodge was Madame Helvetius, Franklin's friend and hostess. Many ladies of the court were proud to be *franc-maçonnes*, including the Princess de Lamballe, Madame Campan, and the Countess Polignac, of Queen Marie Antoinette's own circle. It may be imagined how delighted these ladies, doubtless bored with much court routine, were to welcome a genuine hero from an exotic land as a fellow member, this being the young man who had once joined the humble lodge at Kirkcudbright, Scotland, as plain John Paul, mariner. But they did more for Jones than surround him with admiration; they furnished him with a very practical form of assistance, as will be later disclosed.

Mrs. John Adams in her letters to her New England friends gives us a picture of the women of the period as follows:

" The dress of the French ladies is, like their manners, light, airy and genteel. They are easy in their deportment, eloquent in their speech, their voices soft and musical, and their attitude pleasing. Habituate to frequent the theatres from their earliest age, they become perfect mistresses of the art of insinuation and the powers of persuasion. Intelligence is common to every feature of the face and to every limb of the body, so that it may be said, every man of this nation is an actor, and every woman an actress."

The first Masonic lodge of women was formed, legend says, as the result of a sin not unlike Eve's. A lady whose husband belonged to one of the first Masonic circles, was filled with

[2] Dudley Wright, *Women and Freemasonry*, London 1922.   [3] *Idem.*

[119]

alarm, mingled with dark suspicions, because of his absence
from the hearth on a certain night each week. On his return
from such absences she was unable to draw from him aught
but vague statements of the most unsatisfying character.
He maintained that his activities during these mysterious nights
were of the most harmless nature — were, in fact, productive
of much good. She could not avoid noticing, however, that
following one of his unexplained seances, he was frequently
seized with fits of profound abstraction, alternating with periods of chuckles and barely suppressed laughter. Her forebodings gave her no peace, and at length she traced her husband's nocturnal visits to a house whose door always closed
quickly behind him. Curious to the point of distraction, she
engaged a room in the adjoining house and had a hole bored
through its wall. To this hole she applied an unsatiated eye,
and saw her husband, in company with other men known to her,
going through curious rites of a solemn but — to her —
meaningless character. She did not care to remain to the end,
because she had satisfied herself that no women belonged to
the company. She went away appeased, but kept her own
counsel. Later, however, her secret escaped her and she disclosed her low deed to her husband. He was filled with con-
sternation, and after rebuking her, hurried to report to his
fellows that a woman, in defiance of laws and regulations, had
become possessed of Masonic secrets. To protect itself, the
lodge thought it best to admit the female offender as a member,
and for this purpose organized an auxiliary or "adoptive"
lodge which other restive wives were permitted to join. This,
it is recounted, was the foundation of female Freemasonry,
which has since, at certain times, spread far. Thus goes the
legend, which has certain plausible elements, though not at all
authentic historically.

II

It was well for Jones that he was thus soothed by the attentions of the great, for during a period stretching over several desolate months he was compelled to endure that which his electric temperament most hated — inactivity. The *Ranger* was no longer at hand, having sailed home under the command of the treacherous Lieutenant Simpson, who had unceremoniously dumped his late commander's belongings on shore. The American commissioners were divided among themselves, were short of money, and had other things to think of than a ship for a hungry captain. The French several times promised him a command, and as often disappointed him. He refused to serve under any French officer of the same or less rank. They then offered to outfit him with a privateer, but this Jones flatly declined. He unburdened himself, among many other supporters, to Hewes. " My object is not that of private gain," he wrote contemptuously. He complained that by a royal ordinance French warships could be commanded only by officers of noble birth, and they, he added, were jealous of him. " I am sure," he concluded, " that I will succeed in the end, though not quite as quickly as I would like or perhaps not on such a large scale. But I will succeed."

He relapsed into idle brooding at Brest, for days addressing no one, and then arousing himself to write interminable letters to Franklin, to the Duke de Rochefoucault, to Jonathan Williams, to Dr. Bancroft, and to de Sartine, the French minister of marine, who, he said, " shuffles all the time with one excuse or another." His only companion was a young officer and interpreter supplied to him by the French, Lieutenant Peter Amiel. After weeks of constant association, they scraped upon each others' nerves and soon were quarreling. Jones learned that Amiel had written a letter to his wife criticising his superior for

being, among other things, "taciturn." After their break,
Jones wrote to Amiel:

" You acknowledged to me yesterday that you six months ago
had taken liberties with my character *in writing*, particularly be-
stowing on me the reproachful epithets of " Proud and Con-
ceited, etc."

He demanded a retraction. Amiel gave it, admitting that he
had called Jones " taciturn," but denying that he had called him
either " a Fool or a Puppy."

III

After five months of this wretched existence, Jones resolved
to carry his case up to persons on high. He addressed to his fellow Freemasons, the Duke and Duchess of Chartres, two long
letters. To the Duke he wrote a passionate review of his position. To the Duchess he addressed an even more feeling letter.
" To my inexpressible mortification having no command here,"
he said, " I am considered everywhere as an Officer in Disgrace. . . . I am not an adventurer in search of Fortune, on
the contrary I laid aside my enjoyments in Private Life and
drew my sword at the Commencement of this War only in support of the Dignity and Violated Rights of Human Nature."
He concluded by requesting her to lay his case before the king,
Louis XVI. He added: " I should be supremely happy to
succeed through the influence of so amiable a Princess and
so powerful an advocate — whom I perfectly esteem and
respect."

In his letter to the Duchess he enclosed an appeal to be laid
before the king. It said: " As your Majesty by espousing the
cause of America hath become ' the protector of the Rights of
Human Nature,' I am persuaded that you will not disregard
my situation nor suffer me to remain any longer in this insup-
portable Disgrace. I am with perfect gratitude and profound

respect, Sire, your Majesties Very Obliged, Very Obedient, and very Humble Servant."

To Louis XVI, who so far from protecting the rights of human nature, or any other rights, was passing most of his time hunting, or making locks in his private smithy, this letter might have been, had it reached him, very flattering. But Franklin, to whom Jones first submitted it for approval, stopped it as being bad politics.

IV

The appeal to the Duchess, however, did not fail to obtain results. On December 17, 1778, occurred one of the captain's great moments — he was summoned to Versailles by the king, with whom he spent an hour. Meantime Jones had been inspecting at Lorient an old but serviceable forty-gun ship in the East India service named the *Duras,* and had begged Franklin's friend, M. le Ray de Chaumont, of the marine ministry, to obtain her for him. Chaumont had temporized, but events now began to happen. On February 4, 1779, M. de Sartine informed Jones that the King had ordered the *Duras* to be placed under his command, that it was to be refitted for him, and that he was to be permitted to levy French volunteers to fill up his crew.

In his transports at being released from the inaction of seven months, Jones hurried with bounding steps to the Duchess of Chartres. "Armed at last with such authority," says his *Journal,* " and with rays of hope once more lighting up the prospect, my first *devoir* was at the Palais Royal to thank the more than royal — the Divine — woman to whose grace I felt I owed all." To her he poured out " impassioned sentiments of gratitude." But the Duchess dismissed him with a " *bon voyage.*" She added, " *Ne m'oubliez pas* — do not forget me," and mentioned that a certain sum would be found for his use in the office of M. Gourlade at Lorient. (Her son, Louis Philippe, after-

ward declared this sum was no less than 10,000 louis d'ors —
about $47,500.)

"Madame," cried the glowing Jones, "I shall lay an English
frigate at your feet!"

And he did, too, in a manner which will shortly be related.
John Paul Jones had his little weaknesses, but failure to keep
promises was not among them.

V

Before proceeding with the arming of the *Duras*, Jones renamed her the *Bon Homme Richard*, in compliment to Benjamin Franklin, in whose *Poor Richard's Almanac* he had read
this maxim: "If you would have your business done, go yourself; if not, send."

He found that his new ship was not much better than a tub,
being well worn after twelve years afloat as an armed transport.
But he was in no position to be finicky, and he at once set to work
to alter her into a fighting ship. He discarded the six-pounders
of her old battery, and gave her forty-two bigger but doubtful
guns borrowed from the French. He gave her new spars and
rigging, and though he knew she was not meant for smart
handling, he considered her, when completed, fairly equal to a
thirty-two-gun English frigate. He was busy on these repairs
from the end of February to June 1.

In the midst of these exertions, Jones, worn by disappointment, lack of sleep, and worry, suddenly collapsed and took to
his bed with a severe illness.

VI

About this time Jones made his confession to Franklin concerning the thing that had never ceased to drag like darkened

lead at the ordinarily swift feet of his imagination — his un-intentional killing of the sailor at Tobago.

It was one of the two events in his life from which he never entirely recovered, the other being his supersession in rank at the hands of Commodore Hopkins and John Hancock. Of the two misfortunes, the sailor's death caused him by far the most woeful affliction. His inability to forget it, or to give it its due proportions in his memory of his past, is another sign of the tender-mindedness, the excessively acute sensibility, which observers were so often surprised to find in a man who had a reputation for rough exploits and rougher manners. It also indicates that Jones's soaring imagination had its edge of morbidity. The exaggerations added to the story of the incident and the frequency with which it recurred all but un-manned him. The spectre of the dead sailor lingered at his elbow. It obtruded itself between him and his Virginia sweet-heart. It looked out from the face of the clock in his cabin. It rustled the papers over which he burned midnight oil. It sat on the foot of his bed during sleepless nights. Its voice was heard in the tolling of the ship's bell. It whispered to him, threatened him, mocked him, and haunted him during his long periods of solitary brooding, his sudden fits of silence. It is significant that he strove for twelve months even to speak to Franklin about it, and then when at last a casual and un-suspecting reference in a letter from Franklin to a certain "mystery" awoke every suffering nerve, he believed himself compelled to enter the confessional. The dead sailor was a blacker raven than ever haunted Poe, a heavier albatross than ever hung about the neck of Coleridge's Ancient Mariner.

The correspondence with Franklin concerning this buried secret is of late discovery. Jones's written version of the incident lay for years among Franklin's papers, no one detecting what it was because Jones, in his anguish, found himself un-able to describe the killing in the first person but alluded to himself anonymously simply as "the Master of a West India ship from London." And this in a heavily written postscript.

But Franklin's perspicacious mind was not deceived by Jones's third-person narrative. The sage showed, however, by his brief dismissal of the case as being one "merely *se defendendo*," that he attached little importance to the incident, and sought to let the cleansing wind of laughter into Jones's morbidly sensitive mind by narrating a characteristically waggish story about a fancied attack, with improper intent, on an old woman, Jones himself being the alleged attacker.

If Jones, with his preparations for outfitting the *Bon Homme Richard*, was at that moment at all capable of a smile, Franklin's letter must have given him one and by that much lightened his mind. Jones's letter on this occasion is, from an autobiographical standpoint, one of the most valuable he ever wrote. It throws a revealing light not only on the state of his own mind, with its harassments, suspicions, generosities, and plaguing memories, but on the character and doings of some of his associates. His tribute to Franklin upon his appointment as supreme plenipotentiary at Versailles is in a characteristically whole-souled vein, while his reference to one Alexander — probably Captain Charles Alexander, of the U. S. Ship *Delaware*, one of the commanders who had been given a superior place on John Hancock's list — is no less characteristic in its resentment of fancied criticism.

The Mrs. Amiel mentioned was probably the wife of Lieutenant Peter Amiel, Jones's French aide and interpreter, a lady who seems to have had a dangerous tongue.

Jones's statement that at the time of his appointment to the navy he had heard no whisper of the "doctrine of Independence" is worth attention. It reveals that at the beginning of the war with England, there was little thought, among the colonies as a whole, of complete separation from Britain; but it somewhat disagrees from his other, oft-repeated statements that at the beginning of the war he had drawn his sword " in defense of the rights of man."

Jones's labored, sometimes incoherent explanation to Franklin of the mystery which he supposed the sage had discovered, and Franklin's humorous reply, follow as written:

JOHN PAUL JONES TO BENJAMIN FRANKLIN

L'Orient — March 6th, 1779.

Honored and Dear Sir,

The mystery which you so delicately mention in your much esteemed favor of the 24th. Ult. — it has been my intention for more than Twelve Months past to communicate to you; which however I have put off from time to time on reflecting that the account must give you more pain than pleasure: — yet had I not, on my sudden departure from hence for Paris, inadvertently neglected to take with me the Original Paper wherof the inclosed is a Copy, I certainly should then have put it into your hands. — The subject at the beginning of the War was communicated to Sundry members of Congress among whom I may mention Mr. Hewes of North Carolina and Mr. Morris of Philadelphia; and to various other persons in America before and since. — It was the advice of my friends, Governor Young among many others, when that great Misfortune of my Life happened, that I should retire Incog to the continent of America, and remain there until an Admiralty Commission should arrive in the Island, and then return. — I had waited that event Eighteen Months before Swords were drawn and the Ports of the Continent were Shut. It had been my intention from the time of my misfortune to quit the Sea Service altogether, and, after Standing Trial, as I had the means, to purchase some small tracts of Land on the Continent, which had been my favorite Country from the age of thirteen, when I first saw it. — I had settled my future plan of retirement in " calm contemplation and Poetic ease." — But the revolution in America deranged every thing — and the person with whom I had in Trust left a considerable part of my Effects in the West Indies, had, while the ports were open shewn very little inclination to make me proper Remittances. — Many of my friends had expressed their fears that he meant to abuse my confidence and take advantage of my situation. Among these I can mention a person whom I very much esteem, and who has always expressed great Obligation to you. I mean Doctor John K. Read of Goochland County Virginia. I was not however Undeceived until after the Ports were shut.

I had made the art of War by Sea in some degree my Study, and been fond of a Navy from my boyish days up. — Knowing the perfidy and ingratitude of Dunmore, as soon as an expedition was adopted against him from Philadelphia by Sea, I had the honor to be appointed Senior Lieutenant in the Navy of the Colonies which was then established under Hopkins. — I need not observe that as I had not then heard the doctrine of Independence even in a whisper, and as the Pamphlet called common Sense did not appear till a considerable time afterwards, I could have no Views of protection from a new Government, and therefore as I adhered to my first resolution of returning to West Indies, to Stand Trial, and to Settle my affairs there as soon as peace should be restored to the Continent it was the advice of my friends that I should till that wish'd event might be brought about, remain Incog. — Within a few Months after my first appointment as a proof of the public approbation of my conduct, I had the honor to receive a Captain's Commission, without my having either said or written a single word in my own favor to any person either in or out of Congress. — In the Character of an American Officer, I think you are convinced that Gain had not been the object of my pursuit. — I shall say nothing either of my Abilities (if I have any) or of my Services. — I have received no pecuniary gratification whatsoever, not even the expenses of my daily Dinner, from the publick Funds. — On the contrary I have disbursed for the publick Service, when our prospects were at the worst, considerable Sums of my private fortune, which has never yet been repaid. — But I have always acknowledged that Congress have far more than rewarded my poor endeavours; by the generous and Unsolicited attentions, and by the Confidential preferences which I have so often had the honor to experience in their appointments; and I hope, at least, never to tarnish the honour of the American Flag.

It may be said that I have been Unfortunate — but it cannot be made appear that I have ever, even in the weakest Moment of my Life been capable of a Base or a Mean Action. — Nature has kindly given me a Heart that is highly susceptible of the finer feelings — and I have endeavoured to watch over the happiness of my poor Relations Unseen. — For that purpose I sent several little remittances (Bills) from America in Trust to a very worthy friend of mine Captain Plaince of Cork, to be applied for their Use without their having the pain of knowing from whence: — But to my great Sorrow I find they have all miscarried — the letters that contained them some of them having been Sunk, the rest taken on the passage. — I brought no funds with me to Europe and since my Arrival in it you know that my hands have been Tied. — My Will, now in the hands of Mr. Morris, will evince that I have not been Unmindful of the duties which I owe to Nature — and, were it equally in my power, I think Pope himself could not have taken more pleasure than I should "to Rock the Cradle of declining Age" —.

In short, however chequered my fortune may have been, I feel no Sentiment in my Breast that can ever make me wish to conceal any event of my Life from persons of Candor and Ingenuity — therefore you are at perfect liberty to communicate my Story to whom you think proper, and particularly to Doctor Bancroft. — I am, and shall be always, ready to give you every explanation that you can require.

With respect to Lord Selkirk's plate, it is my wish to restore it to the Lady from whom it was taken. — When I wrote to her I expected that the plate had been of far more Value than it really is — But since you agree to restore the One half in the Name of the Continent — and as I feel myself above the Idea of receiving any profit from such a Pillage — I hope Lord Selkirk will gratify me so far as to suffer the Plate to be restored. — I claim no merit in this, nor has it been my intention to attract his notice either by my history or otherwise, except only as far as he might have been concerned in my Scheme of bringing about an Exchange of Prisoners. — If however his delicacy will not suffer him to receive what he thinks an Obligation from me — it will be no difficult matter to point out to him, if he should be at a loss, how to discharge that Obligation. — How Lord Selkirk came to renew his correspondence with Mr. Alexander, and on that particular Subject too, appears to me rather Surprising. — While I was at Passy in the Summer, Mr. Alexander asked me several questions about the landing on St. Mary's Isle — to gratify him I showed him a Copy of my letter to the Countess. — He invited me to dine with him and said "he would keep the Copy among the Papers which he most esteemed" — I remember also that in the course of the day he complained that Lord Selkirk had taken great offence at some freedom of Sentiment which had marked his letters, and that in consequence they had not corresponded for a great while past. — I remember too that he has frequently, by appearing to disclose his own Plans in some Measure, endeavoured to fish out mine. — Mrs. Amiel has told me often that he is my Enemy. — Yet, why he should be so I cannot imagine, as I never gave him Cause. — But this I know, that let them place round me as many Spies as they please — as I have no Confidants near me, and as I do not keep my intentions by me in Writing, they cannot betray my Councils — and I may yet appear in a quarter of the Globe which they little imagine.

The inclosed little correspondence between Mr. Schweighauser and myself on the Subject of the Plate I send you to show that he makes difficulties where there are none. — You will perhaps see fit to send him Orders of my claim to the Prizes which have been in his hands.

Mr. Williams did me the honor to show me the first paragraph of your letter to him on the Subject of your Appointment as sole American Ambassador at the Court of Versailles. — I believe that appointment to have been Unsolicited on your part, and I am sure that you are Above writing any thing that could tend either to Magnify the Merit of your own Services or to diminish that of others. — In the fullness of my heart I congratulate you on your well merited appointment, and I trust you will believe me that I do now and ever shall rejoice in every circumstance that tends to the honor or happiness of a great and good Man, who has taught me as well as his country to regard him with a Veneration and Affection which proceeds directly from the Heart, and that is due only to the best of Friends.

The outfit of the Poor Richard has engaged my whole attention since I returned here. — I received this day 33 Seamen from Brest, and Volunteers for Soldiers enlist with me daily to Serve for three years or during the War. — I have found several, and hope soon to have a full set of Brave and deserving Men, for Officers. — their Names and ca. I will send up to you. — I find myself under the necessity of taking a Journey to Bordeaux to give directions about the set of Cannon that are to be made there for the Poor Richard. — I shall set out after to Morrow, and as I return immediately, may I hope to be favored with a letter from you to meet me at Nantes on my way Back.

I hope nothing will prevent Doctor Bancroft from going to England on the Exchange of Prisoners.

I am with greatful and real Affection and respect

Honored and dear Sir,

Your very Obliged

very Obedient

very humble Servant

Jno. P. Jones.

The Master of a West India Ship from London had occasion to ship sundry Seamen at the Island where he Loaded — One of whom in particular behaved himself very ill — He was a principal in Embezzling the Masters Liquors — He got frequently Drunk — He neglected and even refused his duty with much insolence. — He stirred up the rest of the Crew to act in the same manner and was their avowed Ringleader.

As the Masters engagements were of such a Nature that his all depended upon despatch, he gave his Crew every reasonable Encouragement. — They had plenty of good Provision and were in other respects well Used. — Notwithstanding of which one forenoon when the Master came on Board that the Crew had formed or were then forming a plot to desert the Ship. — As the Master was walking aft the Ringleader rushed up from the Steerage and stopped with the grossest abuse that Vulgarism could dictate because, as he pretended, the Master had sailed his ship fourteen Months without paying wages. — The fellow having some time before complained that he wanted Cloaths, the Master now gave him Frocks and Trowsers telling him to go about his duty and to inform himself better — for that what he had said was not so. — But mildness had no good effect, for while the Master was distributing Cloathing to some of the rest who were also in want, the first conveyed his things into the Boat and another of the Crew was following his example, till observing that the Master had an Eye upon their proceedings, they Sneaked back into the Ship. — They remained quiet for a short space — But the Ringleader soon broke out again with Oaths and insisted on having the Boat and quitting the Ship. — This the Master Refused, but offered to give up his agreement if a Man could be found to serve in his Room. The disturber swore with horrid imprecations that he would take away the Boat by force! — and for that purpose actually rushed over the Gangway, bidding the Master the most contemptuous defiance! — Upon the Master stepping up to prevent this, the Man (having thrice his strength) leapt into the Ship and forced him into the Cabin. Using at the time language and attitudes too indecent to be mentioned, and charging him not to Shew his Nose upon Deck again till the Boat was gone at his utmost Peril. — The Master searched the Cabin for a Stick, but not finding one, and his Sword, by chance being on the Table, he took it up in hopes that the sight of it would intimidate the Man into Submission. — The Man had by this time descended the Gangway within a Step of the Boat, so that it would have been impossible to prevent his Elopement had he persisted. — But he now reentered the Ship breathing Vengeance, and, totally regardless of the Sword, tho within its reach, turned his back towards the Master, ran on the Main Deck, Armed himself there with a Bludgeon, with which he returned to the quarter Deck and attacked the Master. — The Master was thunder struck with surprise, for he had considered the Man's ravings as the natural effect of disappointed Rage which would soon subside of itself. — But now his sole expedient was to prevent bad consequences by returning again to the Cabin; —

and this he endeavoured to do as fast as possible by retiring backwards in a posture of defence. — But alas! What is human foresight. — The after Hatchway was Uncovered and lay in a direct line between the Master's back and the Cabin door, but the Momentary duration of the attack did not admit of his recollecting that circumstance before his heel came in contact with the Hatchway, which obliged him to make a Sudden Stop. — Unhappily at that instant the Assailants Arm being high raised, he threw his Body forward to reach the Master's head with the descending Blow, the fatal and Unavoidable consequence of which was his rushing Upon the Swords Point.

After this Melancholy accident the Master went Publicly to a Justice of the Peace and Offered to Surrender as his Prisoner. — The Justice, who called himself the Masters friend, persuaded him to withdraw and said it was unnecessary to Surrender before the day of Trial. — and the rest of the Masters friends who were present forced him to Mount his Horse.

Two weeks before this the Chief Mate had been for the first time in his Life advanced to that Station — and yet unworthy as his conduct had been in it he now openly arrogated his Unblushing pretentions to the Command, and to attain it associated with the Crew. The Testimony of such a combination may easily be imagined, conscious as they were of having embezzled the Masters property they were not likely to dwell on any circumstance that Manifested their own dastardly and Undutiful Conduct. — And as the Second Mate, a young Gentleman of worth lay sick as well as all the inferior Officers and best disposed of the Crew, in all human probability the Truth could not escape the grossest perversion. — Besides the nature of the Case Subjected it to the cognizance of a Court Martial — and there was no Admiralty Commission then in the Government. — For these obvious reasons the Masters friends constrained him for a time to leave the Country.

NB. The foregoing has been written in great haste to save the Post.

BENJAMIN FRANKLIN TO JONES

Passy, March 14, 1779.

Dear Sir

I yesterday rec'd your favour of the 6th inst. I did not understand from M. Alexander that Lord Selkirk had any particular Objection to receiving the Plate from You. It was general, that tho' he might not refuse it if offer'd him by a public Body, as the Congress, he cou'd not accept it from any private Person whatever. I know nothing of M. Alexander's having any Enmity to you, nor can I imagine any Reason for it. But on the whole it seems to me not worth your while to give yourself any farther Trouble about Lord Selkirk. You have now the Disposal of what belongs to the Congress; and may give it with your own Share, if you think fit, in little Encouragements to your men on particular Occasions.

I thank you for your kind Congratulations on my particular Appointment. It will give me more Satisfaction if it enables me to be more useful.

We cou'd not obtain a Passport for Dr. Bancroft. We were told it was needless, as the Cartel Ship was actually sail'd for Plymouth to take in the first 100 Americans to be brought to Nantes or l'Orient. Inclos'd is a Copy of a Letter from the Board to M. Hartley. I wish they may be arriv'd and that you may obtain such of them as you think proper. Possibly the Alliance which wants Hands may endeavour to engage some. Mr. Adams goes over in her; and I must not interfere, but leave you to scramble for the Men. I think, however, that if the Cartel comes to l'Orient you will have the best Chance.

I have look'd over the copy of my Letter to you of Feby. 24, not being able to imagine what Part of it could give you the Idea that I hinted at an Affair I never knew. Not finding anything in the Letter, I suppose it must have been the Postscript of which I have no Copy, and which I know now that you could not understand — tho' I did not when I wrote it. The story I alluded to is this: L'Abbé Rochon had just been telling me and Madame Chaumont that the old Gardiner and his Wife had complained to the Curate, of your having attack'd her in the Garden about 7 o'clock the evening before your Departure, and attempted to ravish her relating all the Circumstances, some of which are not fit for me to write. The serious Part of it was yt three of her Sons were determin'd to kill you, if you had not gone off; the Rest occasioned some Laughing; for the old Woman being one of the grossest, coarsest, dirtiest and ugliest that we may find in a thousand, Madame Chaumont said it gave a high Idea of the Strength of Appetite and Courage of the Americans. A Day or two after, I learnt yt it was the femme de Chambre of Mademoiselle Chaumont who had disguis'd herself in a Suit, I think, of your Cloaths, to divert herself under that Masquerade, as is customary the last evening of Carnival: and that meeting the old Woman in the Garden, she took it into her Head to try her Chastity, which it seems was found Proof.

As to the unhappy Affair of which you give me an Acct, there is no Doubt but the Facts being as you state 'em, the Person must have been acquitted if he had been tried, it being merely se defendendo.

I wish you all imaginable Success in your present Undertaking, being ever with sincere Esteem, etc.

B. Franklin

VII

In April there arrived from America a beautiful new frigate named the *Alliance*, and Jones asked that she be added to his squadron. She brought back as a passenger the Marquis de Lafayette, who, hearing that Jones was planning another daring raid on the English coast, immediately conceived a scheme, which was never carried out, to join him in an expedition which would carry a considerable land force. "Be certain, my dear sir," wrote Lafayette, "that I shall be happy to divide with you whatever share of glory may await us, and that my esteem and affection for you is truly felt, and will last forever."

Franklin endorsed the project in a letter which thrilled Jones to his sea-boots. "The letter I received from you today," he replied, "together with your liberal and noble-minded instructions, would make a coward brave. You have called up every sentiment of public virtue in my breast."

But Jones's delight would perhaps have been somewhat diminished had he regarded the lowering countenance of the *Alliance's* captain. This was Pierre Landais, a discredited officer of the French navy, who had been able to obtain no other employment than ferrying Beaumarchais's supplies to the American army. On his reaching the United States, a sentimental Congress had made him an officer in the American navy, and given him the finest and newest ship at its disposal. The forlorn Landais looked at the beaming, perfectly dressed Jones, aglow with anticipation and backed by his own country's highest personages, and he hated him in his heart.

With enormous exertions Jones collected a crew of three hundred and seventy-five, composed chiefly of British prisoners, Portuguese sailors, and French marines, and with the *Alliance*, the small French frigate *Pallas*, and the brig *Vengeance*, sailed from Lorient in the *Bon Homme Richard* on June 19, 1779. On the second day out Jones suddenly ordered the squadron to return to port. The *Alliance* had fouled him, severely damaging both ships.

CAPTAIN JONES REPLIES TO AN ENEMY'S BROADSIDE WITH A
SINGLE DERISIVE MUSKET SHOT.

CHAPTER XIX

Preparations and Plagues

And some in dreams assured were
Of the Spirit that plagued us so;
Nine fathom deep he had followed us
From the land of mist and snow.

I

THE repairs to the two ships caused more delay, during which further complications developed. It was found that the English prisoners, while at sea, had formed a plot to seize the *Bon Homme Richard,* and it was suspected that this had been connived at by Landais, who had disregarded Jones's signals, thus causing the collision. A court-martial placed the blame on two quartermasters. They were staked out on deck and severely flogged, and the navigating officer of the *Bon Homme Richard* was tried and broken.

Jones then put to sea again and convoyed some merchant ships to Bordeaux. On the return voyage the *Alliance* and the *Pallas* lost themselves in a fog, and the *Vengeance* fled into port from a gale. Thus left alone in the *Bon Homme Richard,* Jones suddenly encountered two British frigates. He called his officers into council and asked if they were ready for a battle. They answered yes, and Jones then tacked and bore down on the two ships, but to his chagrin, they outsailed and escaped him. This incident proved to Jones that in the *Bon Homme Richard* he had a very dull ship. " I would have taken them both together," he declared doughtily, " if I had been able to get between them," a remark which indicates that all his disappointments had not been able to shake his self-confidence.

About this time Jones sent to his family in Scotland a remittance of £30. His letter accompanying it was addressed not to his mother, but to his oldest sister. He subsequently learned from another sister, Mrs. Taylor, that his mother and older sister were dead. His letter to her indicated that his breach with his relatives had never been healed. "The loss of those dear friends," he wrote, "is the more affecting to me, as they never received the remittances I intended for them, and as they had not, perhaps, a true idea of my affection."

II

On returning to the roadstead of Groix Jones decided that the *Bon Homme Richard* must be further equipped, and that a new and better crew must be found. Permission was obtained, but further delays occurred, during which Jones remarked that he "half killed himself" by his exertions. Repeatedly he complained of the interference of M. le Ray de Chaumont, commissary of the French Ministry of Marine. It is possible that Jones, in his highly excited state of mind, either saw a plot where none existed, or there was some other reason for de Chaumont's actions.

De Chaumont, who was a warm friend of Franklin and had lent him part of the Hotel Valentinois in Passy to be used as a residence and office without pay, had at first been an admirer of Jones and had frequently entertained him at dinner. Not less admiring was Madame de Chaumont, a bright and agreeable woman with whom Jones sometimes corresponded. There is on record a letter which Jones sent her about this time.

"I am on the point again," he wrote, "of proving the uncertain fortunes of war. If I survive, I hope to return with laurels. I hope this, I say, because I am sure to take with me your good wishes, and because I know that my success would afford you pleasure. To support the cause of human nature, I sacrifice all the soft emotions of the heart, at a time too, when love is my duty."

Whether M. de Chaumont was a little uneasy regarding this friendship between the gallant American sailor and his wife there is no means of judging, but at any rate a coolness spread itself between the two men, and Jones accused the other of malfeasances in terms which drew down upon him the strong rebuke of Franklin.

III

The new repairs to the lumbering *Bon Homme Richard* extended over six weeks, during which time Jones combed all the ports for a better and more reliable quality of men and officers. Since only a few Americans were available, he was obliged to recruit his crew from the English prisoners confined in the French prison of Denan. To assist him in keeping order on board the ship, Lafayette procured him the loan of two French officers, Lieutenant Colonel Chamillard and Colonel Weibert, at the head of a force of French marines. The French ministry also allowed him to hire one hundred and thirty-seven Portuguese, Maltese and Malay sailors who had just arrived at Lorient. Laboriously he added men to his crew, sometimes one at a time. Nathaniel Fanning says he would walk the quay for hours, persuading single seamen to sign articles.

It was during this exciting period that one of those dinners was given by Captain Jones at the Café *Epée Royale* as described by John Adams in a previous chapter. Adams mentions those present as follows: " Amiel, Mr. Dick, Dr. Brooks, officers of the *Poor Richard*, Captain Cazneau, Captain Young, Mr. Ingraham, Mr. Blodgett, Mr. Glover, Mr. Conant, Messrs. Mayland, Mease, Nesbit, Cummings, and Mr. Taylor, with Captain Landais, myself and my son." Mr. Adams adds: " We practised the old American custom of drinking to each other, which I confess is always agreeable to me."

While these shore pleasantries were being exchanged between officers and their guests, there was turmoil aboard the *Bon Homme Richard*. Alexander Dick, who had come all the way from Virginia with Dr. Brooke to volunteer for service with Jones, one day wrote to the captain, who was in Paris, about an outburst of super-patriotism as follows:

" It is with the utmost uneasiness I acquaint you that discord is crept into our little society, that ungenerous hatred which some of our illiterate countrymen bear the French nation too much influences our present commanding officer; the sailors and volunteers have been in continual broils since your departure. I have used my utmost endeavour to preserve quiet, and counsel the inhabitants (who loudly complain) that you will not allow the French to be ill treated. Variety of orders is so confusing that they can't possibly do their duty."

IV

And then came relief in the form of a cartel of exchanged American prisoners who had been starving in British naval jails, while the British prisoners taken from the *Drake* had been suffering equal tortures aboard a French prison ship at Brest. At Nantes Jones selected one hundred and nineteen of these men and at the same port picked up about fifteen more stranded American seamen. From a total of about one hundred and fifty Americans, Jones selected his officers. Richard Dale, a youth of twenty-three, who had been two years in prison — " My good old Dick," as Jones learned to call him — was made first lieutenant. Henry and Cutting Lunt were made respectively lieutenant and master. The midshipmen were Nathaniel Fanning, John Mayrant, Thomas Potter, Benjamin Stubbs, Reuben Chase, Robert Coram, and John W. Linthwaite. " Old Jack " Robinson was the bo'sun.[1] Dr. Brooke was surgeon, and Mat-

---

[1] According to the narrative of John Kilby of Virginia, a survivor of the *Bon Homme Richard's* crew, Kilby was at one time a prisoner in Portsea jail.

thew Mease, a visiting Philadelphia merchant, who insisted on joining up, was made the purser. The French orderly to the captain was Pierre Gerard. A few Scotchmen, Swedes, Norwegians, Danes, French peasants who had never seen a fight, and several volunteer French soldiers were added to the crew — he was forbidden to recruit French sailors — and all were cheerfully welcomed by Anthony Jeremiah, the red Indian, who by now was a veteran. To complete this Noah's ark of nationalities nothing was needed except a few wild Irishmen. Three of them duly appeared — Lieutenants Stack, McCarty, and O'Kelly, volunteers from Walsh's Irish regiment belonging to the King. The marines, not all of whom had ever been at sea, were Frenchmen from the Royal Dockyard. There were about one hundred and thirty-seven of them. Their commandant was Colonel Weibert, whom we know best from this record of a conversation in John Adams's diary:

" We fell upon the subject of swearing: I asked him if the French sailors swore. He said, *chaque instant,* every instant — *ventre Saint Gris,* literally heavy grey belly. I asked him if this originally alluded to the *Vierge*. He believed not."

The rest of the crew, comprising three hundred and eighty men and boys, consisted of Englishmen who had agreed, with or without mental reservations, to make war on their own country. It was with this unholy aggregation of Americans, Englishmen, Frenchmen, Irishmen, Portuguese, Maltese, Malays, Scandinavians and one red Indian, that John Paul Jones proposed to undertake the most dangerous of all his ventures — to circle the British Isles and lay Liverpool and Leith under contribution. The latter town, be it noted, was the birthplace of John Paul's father. Franklin helped him prepare the terms of

---

There he met Robinson, who had broken out of the jail, together with Fanning, Mayrant, and Potter, stolen a barge, and rowed to Nantes, just in time to meet Kilby, who had been exchanged, and with him joined Jones's expedition. (*Scribner's Magazine,* vol. xxxviii, 1905.)

capitulation for Leith, whose treasury was to pay a levy of £200,000. His eventual destination was to be the Texel, Holland. The news of his impending departure promptly leaked into England. Jones blamed Chaumont's tendency to gabble, but more likely the heralds were the spies around Arthur Lee.

While awaiting final orders, Jones busied himself hammering his new crew into shape. He instructed his midshipmen in French; he showed his apprentices how to knot a rope; he taught his raw seamen to walk like blue-water sailors. " He was in everybody's watch and everybody's mess all the time," wrote Henry Gardner, who added: " I sailed in my time with many captains, but with only one Paul Jones. He was the captain of captains."

V

Meantime the rest of his squadron was also getting ready. Included were the *Alliance,* Captain Landais; the *Pallas,* Captain Cottineau; the *Vengeance,* Captain Ricot; and the cutter *Cerf,* Captain Varage. At the last moment the squadron was joined by two French privateers, the *Monsieur* and the *Grandville.* The former was a splendid vessel of forty guns, and Jones made a special request that she be allowed to join him. Wherein lay his special interest in this ship?

According to Jones's biographer, A. C. Buell,[2] the *Monsieur* was " a new ship built for an East Indian, but purchased by an association of ladies of Marie Antoinette's court, of whom the leading spirit and principal contributor was Marie Adelaide, Duchess de Chartres."

There can be no doubt that this " association of ladies " was the " adoptive lodge " of feminine Freemasons, led by the wonderful Duchess whose interest in the brilliant captain has already been described, and of whose contributions to this, the greatest of Jones's expeditions, history has so far been ignorant.

[2] *Scribner's Magazine,* vol. xxxviii, 1905.

This Masonic ship was commanded by a regular officer of the French navy, Captain Philippe G. de Roberdeau. At the first opportunity he made it plain to Jones that he disliked and distrusted Landais, and that he did not intend to soil his uniform by associating with him. Landais afterwards heard of this and challenged de Roberdeau to a duel, but the latter declined to meet him on the ground that Landais was not a gentleman.

One more hitch occurred before anchors were weighed. De Chaumont appeared and induced Jones to sign a " Concordat " by which each captain was authorized to act virtually on his own authority, obeying Jones only at discretion. It also provided that prizes should be sent only to de Chaumont's agents and that prize-money should be distributed only at his direction. It is possible that Jones, in his eagerness to be off, did not realize the full implications of this crippling document, for afterwards he had reason upon reason to repent it. He sent a letter of farewell to Franklin and another to Joseph Hewes, the last that faithful supporter ever received, for before Jones was able to write again, Hewes was in his grave at Christ Church, Philadelphia. A parting present came from the Duchess of Chartres. It was a watch, cunningly contrived, which had belonged to one of her sailor ancestors.

At last the little squadron of seven was clear of the unending tangles of shore politics, and on August 14, 1779, it sailed on its momentous cruise, its elephantic flagship commanded by a romantic egotist, its second ship in charge of a hysterical neurotic, its other units captained by timid opportunists, and all rife with forebodings, national and racial rancours, and treachery. Nothing but the soaring, blind, and heedless self-confidence of John Paul Jones ever could have induced him to lead such an expedition, on its face so ridiculous, so grandly into the unknown.

CHAPTER XX

More Treachery

And now the storm-blast came, and he
Was tyrannous and strong:
He struck with his o'ertaking wings
And chased us south along.

I

JONES shaped his course northwest across the mouth of the English Channel toward the western shore of Ireland. "Unfortunately," says his *Journal*, written in the third person, "there was neither secrecy nor subordination. Captain Jones saw his danger, but his reputation being at stake, he put all to the hazard."

Trouble began to occur at once. Captain de Roberdeau informed Jones that he could not endure the presence of Landais; but he remained in the squadron long enough to assist in the capture of a Dutch ship which had been taken as a prize by the British. De Roberdeau tried to send her as his own prize to Ostend, but being overruled by Jones, he took what he needed out of the ship during the night, gradually dropped behind the squadron, and finally disappeared with the splendid ship which the lady Freemasons of France had so trustfully contributed to Jones's expedition.

The squadron, now reduced to six sail, took a brigantine. Two days later, off Cape Clear, Ireland, while another ship was being overtaken, Jones ordered some of his British sailors to get into a barge and tow the *Bon Homme Richard* so as to avoid the rocks called the Shallocks. While Jones was busy watching the boats pursuing the new prize, the Englishmen cut the tow rope and made off with the captain's barge. Cutting Lunt pursued the deserters with four soldiers, but, becoming lost in a fog, landed and was captured.

Then appeared over the rail of the *Bon Homme Richard* the contorted face of Landais. Announcing that he was " the only American in the squadron," he accused Jones of being responsible for the loss of the barge, and lugubriously predicted the British would yet get the whole squadron. Colonel Chamillard, who witnessed the dispute and who described Jones as *doux, honnête, très indulgent,* says Jones treated Landais very calmly. For a man so choleric as Jones, this is surprising. He would have been justified in arresting Landais and taking his ship away from him; but perhaps he felt himself bound to obey the terms of Chaumont's " Concordat."

He ordered the *Cerf* to look for the missing boats. Her captain seized the opportunity to return to France. That left five sail. On the 26th the *Grandville* took a prize and likewise disappeared. Four vessels now remained in the squadron.

Jones had intended to remain several days off the Irish coast, to intercept homeward-bound ships from India, but Landais objected. He reminded Jones that he was not bound to obey his orders, and as proof sailed away on his own tack. He reappeared on the 31st with a captured privateer, the *Betsey*. Jones on the same day took the Quebec-bound *Union,* laden with valuable supplies intended for the British ships on the Great Lakes.

Jones now ordered a council of officers to assemble on the flagship and map out their future course. Landais refused to attend. Purser Mease, Captain Cottineau, and Colonel Chamillard pleaded with Landais in vain. He said he would meet Jones on shore " when they must kill one or the other." By now it should have been apparent to Jones that he had either a crazy or a dangerously obstinate man to deal with, but for some inexplicable reason he held his hand. A gale then coming up, Landais followed the other deserters over the horizon. He disobeyed Jones's order and sent his prizes to Bergen, and Denmark returned them to the British, setting up a dispute which lasted for years. Three sail were now left to Jones.

He called his remaining captains into consultation and proposed they make a descent on the English coast. They objected, considering their position already dangerous. Jones then proposed a raid on Leith, informing them of the enormous levy to be raised there. To this they agreed, and all shaped their course to the Firth of Forth. On the way Jones picked up a boat containing a pilot, who, finding all the officers in British uniform, readily gave the news.

" That rebel Paul Jones is expected to land every day," said the pilot. " He is the greatest pirate that ever was, and ought to be hanged."

" And where would you hang me? " asked Jones.

The pilot, suddenly sensing the truth, dropped to his knees and begged for his life.

" Get up," said Jones. " I won't hurt you. We've got a better use for you."

II

On September 15, the American squadron was seen from Edinburgh as it sailed into the Firth. Visiting in the town was a lad who witnessed the fright of the inhabitants. In later years he was known as Sir Walter Scott. A new panic had seized Scotland, and Whitehaven was now certain it would not survive a second raid. The London *Gazetteer and New Daily Advertiser* remarked:

" We hear that Dr. ——, with about a dozen half-starved Scotch physicians from Glasgow and Edinburgh is shortly to go to Whitehaven to restore the inhabitants to their senses; but should those gentlemen not succeed, it is determined that a Scotch architect be employed to build there a madhouse." [1]

And the Earl of Sandwich, the English Admiralty's " Jemmy Twitcher," dashed this note off to Captain Francis Reynolds: " For God's sake get to sea instantly . . . if you can take Paul Jones you will be as high in the estimation of the public as if you had beat the combined fleets."

III

But a gale arose, against which the little ship beat in vain and which sank one of Jones's prizes. His associate captains took alarm. They pointed out that the whole country was now aroused, they were laden with prisoners, and they must get back to their prizes. Jones yielded and in disgust shaped his course southward for the Texel. He steered directly for Flamborough Head, which had been given as a rendezvous to the *Alliance* and *Cerf*. This headland projects far out from the east coast of England. On its north side rests the port and town of Scarborough, which did not again see an enemy squadron until a German one bombarded it in the course of the World War in 1916.

Jones's ships chased and took several prizes, and then on a quiet afternoon they sighted a large fleet of merchantmen coming from the Baltic. These fled, disclosing a heavy ship of war and an armed sloop. Jones at once made for the large ship and drove the *Bon Homme Richard* between her and the land. It was evident there was going to be a battle, and crowds hurried to the shore to see it. In this northern latitude the dusk fell slowly and the evening was clear, lucent, and tranquil.

[1] Don Seitz, *Paul Jones, His Exploits in English Seas.*

CHAPTER XXI

The Battle in the Moonlight

From the sails the dew did drip —
Till clomb above the eastern bar
The Hornéd Moon, with one bright star
Within the nether tip.

I

THE ships came together very slowly, neither, in the gathering twilight, being yet certain of the other's nationality. On the men of the *Bon Homme Richard* fell a profound silence. Few of them had anything to gain by a battle, and no small part of them were Englishmen looking desolately across the six miles of blue water to " England, home and beauty."

The moon rose and in its light Jones called Richard Dale and Pierre Gerard, his French orderly, to his side. Through their telescopes they studied the big ship approaching on an opposite tack. About seven o'clock they made her out to be the British ship *Serapis,* forty-four guns, but actually carrying fifty. Her crew was smaller, but she threw a much superior weight of metal. She was a new ship; her yellow sides and brasses gleamed in the moonlight. The sound of her name ran swiftly from mouth to mouth of the *Richard's* crew. The Americans were not sure, says John Kilby, how her name should be pronounced. They knew nothing about the Egyptian goddesses for which the more classical English loved to name their ships.

" Look out, men," bawled a voice, " here comes the Sea Raper."

That broke the leaden spell of silence. A raucous chorus of

[148]

jeers and guffaws rose from the decks of the *Richard*. It was a tonic sound. It made everybody feel better. The afflicting silence and the awe which many of the crew felt, having never before seen a British ship-of-war at close range, had been rapidly spreading a nervous uneasiness. A narrative by the surgeon of the *Serapis* says there was a like scare on that ship. Her commander, Captain Pearson, at first thought the broad black stranger might be a French " fifty." This bears out Napoleon's observation that at the beginning of a battle both sides are afraid of each other.

At last the English captain lowered his glass.

" It is probably Paul Jones. If so, there's work ahead."

II

Meantime Jones had been sending his men to their posts. His battery of twelve-pounders, on which he placed chief reliance, he gave to Lieutenant Richard Dale and Colonel Weibert, with a mixed crew of Americans and French. The steerage battery of decrepit eighteen-pounders he assigned to John Mayrant, who had come over from South Carolina in the hope of joining Commodore Gillon in the *Indien*. On the high poop deck Jones stationed Colonel Chamillard and his French marines. In the tops he placed his best marksmen under Lieutenant Stack, the Versailles Irishman, and Nathaniel Fanning, "the fighting Puritan." Being short of officers, he was compelled to assign the quarter-deck guns to Matthew Mease, the acting purser and former Philadelphia merchant. Under him was Henry Gardner, of New Hampshire, and Arthur Randall, an English prisoner. The newly-taken English prisoners were shut up below decks under John Burbank, acting master. Dr. Brooke, the humorous Virginia surgeon, prepared the cockpit for the wounded, but came out on the quarter-deck and remained there so long, smoking quietly, that Jones had to order him below. " Red Cherry," the Narragansett Indian, at the prospect of action began a wild chant. He had his slow-matches ready to touch off his gun, which was No. 2 in the forward starboard, an exposed position.

III

Both ships now maneuvered for position, the *Bon Homme Richard* being much the slower. Tacking gradually brought the ships side by side, both pointing in a northwesterly direction, a pistol shot apart. Silence again fell upon each ship and upon the crowds at Scarborough Fort and Flamborough Head. The *Serapis* hailed:

" What ship is that? "

From the *Richard* came the reply:

" I can't hear what you say."

" Answer at once," shouted Captain Pearson, " or I shall fire."

Jack Robinson, the *Richard's* bo'sun, leaned out of a port.

" Fire, and be damned to you."

The last entry in the log of the *Serapis* reads:

" Ships now fairly abeam, a cable's length apart on the same tack, wind abeam, southwest, light but steady. Sea smooth, moon full, sky clear, time 7.15 P.M. We hail second time, enemy answers with broadside."

IV

Gunners on both ships, stripped to the buff, began to work like eels in a pond, and broadside after broadside spurted through enormous black rolls of smoke which could be seen far inland.

In a moment a red streak of flame pierced the sky and the *Richard* rocked clumsily in the wash. Two of her old 18-pounders, cast off by the French but in desperation borrowed by Jones, had burst on the lower gun-deck, killing almost the entire crew, partly wrecking the main-deck above, and opening a gap in the hull. In the explosion acting Lieutenant Mayrant was hurt in the head and severely scorched. Dale ordered him to close the lower deck entirely and report with his men to the main-deck. This disaster left the *Richard* with but one tier of guns, while the *Serapis* increased her destructive fire from two decks, equipped with ten 18-pounders. The British ship also showed herself to be a much better sailer. In turn she nosed ahead and then dropped back, each time raking her opponent at close range, while the *Richard,* with her braces shot away, answered her helm only after laborious efforts. One after another of the American guns were silenced. Mease, the middle-aged merchant from Philadelphia, dropped to the floor with a hole in his head, and his gunners retreated from the terrible gases. He was carried below where Dr. Brooke was using raw knife and saw on the limbs of the quivering men. The surgeon trepanned his skull and Mease returned to his guns, where he found Jones himself serving one of the nine-pounders borrowed from the lee side of the ship. At the No. 2 gun nineteen men were killed in succession, and at last Anthony Jeremiah alone remained to serve it.

And now a new weakness appeared aboard the *Richard.* Colonel Chamillard fell wounded, and his marines on the poop-deck, under a hurricane fire which had virtually decimated them, were wavering. There was afterwards some disposition to criticize these men, but there is plenty of excuse for them. Few of them had ever been under fire before and not all of them had even been aboard a fighting ship, but the roster of the killed shows how valiantly these French marines stood their ground and how grievously they suffered. There was no protection for them on their high and open deck, and they fell in clusters. For an instant only they were shaken, and then John Paul Jones himself sprang among them.

" Frenchmen! " he shouted, " Will you give way under the eyes of the Americans and English? "

He seized a musket from the nearest and mounting the rail, fired it at the enemy. He discharged six muskets as fast as they could be handed to him. His example was infectious. The marines rallied with a cheer for the captain, and thereafter held the deck. But the *Richard's* position was serious, and might have become worse but for the quick and accurate fire from her tops whence French and American marksmen repeatedly swept the enemy's deck clean.

V

The quiet moon rose higher and the battle now entered a new phase. The *Serapis* luffed and advanced as if to cross the *Richard's* bows. But the wind was against Captain Pearson, and the men who tried to handle his sails were shot down from the *Richard's* tops. Eleven men in succession fell at his wheel. Jones was then directing the fire of one of his three remaining cannon against the enemy's mainmast. As both ships were afire and the *Richard*, pierced through and through, was leaking badly, Jones recognized that a critical moment had come. He put his helm over, and braced back his main and top sails. A lucky puff of wind caught the *Richard* and pulled her ahead. The *Serapis*, losing way, was struck on the larboard quarter, and Jones at once forced his jibboom well over the enemy's rail and into her mizzen rigging. This was what he wanted. Calling for boarders, he ordered the forecastle crew to grapple the enemy. Anthony Jeremiah, his gun having been dismounted, was the first to come running up with a pike in his hand, but the grappling irons failed to hold, and the *Serapis*, with a rattle and creak, fell off and lay almost in a line behind the *Richard*.

It was now clear to Jones what he must do. He was on a foundering ship with several feet of water in the hold. She no longer held her trim. His cannon were almost gone and half his gunners were dead or wounded. He hurried to Dale's deck.

"Dick," he cried, "his metal is too heavy for us. He is hammering us to pieces. We must close with him. Bring your men on the spar-deck and give them the small arms."

Again the wind helped the *Richard*. It filled her sails, which blanketed the *Serapis* and left her momentarily stationary. Gradually Jones wore ahead and began to round the enemy's bows. And then a chance shot broke his tiller. He managed to reeve on a spare tiller and continued his attempt to foul the *Serapis*, which was frantically backing her sails in the effort to get clear.

At this moment a ship appeared to windward. Through the glass she was made out to be the *Alliance*. Though she was captained by the deserting Landais, Jones was heartened. The arrival of this reinforcement would quickly end the battle. Captain Pearson afterwards reported he also thought it was now all up with him. The *Alliance* came up swiftly; the *Richard* hung out signals for her; but to the amazement of both the fighting crews and despite yells of warning, the crazy Landais fired a broadside into the stern of the *Bon Homme Richard* and followed this with a round of grapeshot. He then passed to leeward in the darkness.

VI

The *Richard* continued her slow maneuver. As she cut across the nose of the *Serapis*, the fluke of the latter's anchor hooked itself in the *Richard's* stays. The line held and the two ships settled side by side, gripping each other fast as they tore at each other's vitals.

In passing over a hawser, Samuel Stacy, the assistant master, discharged a sailor's oath. It gave John Paul Jones the opportunity to make one of those saintly remarks which school histories love to attribute to heroes:

" Don't swear, Mr. Stacy, we may at the next moment be in eternity, but let us do our duty."

This does not accord with Nathaniel Fanning's account. He says, Jones, in rallying the French marines, uttered " such imprecations upon the enemy as I never before or since heard in French or any other language."

VII

At that moment things were happening which could not have permitted Jones much time to pronounce rotund sentiments. Fire suddenly began to lick upward to the *Richard's* rigging, and she settled further in the water. The opposing gunners stepped to each other's decks to swab their cannon. Burbank, the acting master-at-arms, in panic, opened the hatch and released the English prisoners confined below, who came flooding up on deck, mad with fear. Jones snapped his pistol at Burbank, and when it missed fire, felled him with the butt. He then ordered the prisoners to man the pumps. One refused, and Gerard shot him through the head. This was the basis of a later canard to the effect that in the action Jones shot and killed a " Lieutenant Grub," of his own crew. Dale then came running up and with a pistol herded the prisoners to the pumps.

A shot now broke the *Richard's* flagstaff and the ensign trailed in the water astern. Randall, the gunner, yelling that the ship was sinking, called for quarter. The exultant cry, " They've surrendered! " swept through the *Serapis*. Captain Pearson came to the rail.

" Do I understand that you have struck? "

Here the school-book story differs from that of the survivors, including Jones himself. The tradition is that Jones replied:

" I have just begun to fight." This is somewhat in agreement with the memoir of Pierre Gerard, which makes Jones say:

"*Non! je vais à l'instant commencer le combat* (No! I am just now beginning the fight)."

Jones, however, in his report to Franklin, merely states that he answered Pearson "in the most determined negative," but in his *Journal* he expands his reply as follows:

"I have no intention of surrendering, but am resolved to make you ask quarter."

And then came up Landais for the second time. He crossed the *Richard's* bow and again fired on her, killing one man and wounding others.

VIII

The battle was renewed, Jones records, "with double fury." He adds: "I was advised to yield by officers of whose courage I had and still have a high opinion. But, having other objects in view, I declined the advice." Jones was capable of cool thinking at the hottest moments. He knew that a victory over an English line-ship would bring him renown, while to surrender would fetch him to an English hangman's gibbet as a pirate.

The English now changed their tactics. They began to hack at the lashings which bound them to the *Richard*, knowing that if only they could wrench their ship free, her heavy guns would soon finish the waterlogged enemy. But American and French marksmen picked off the axemen as fast as they appeared, and Jones himself took a hand in this sharp-shooting. He was, in truth, all over the ship. He was resolved either to win or sink.

The English, having detected the arming of boarders, then attempted a counter-charge at the gangway, and Jones dropped his musket to seize a pike and lead the defense. The attack was repelled, but in the rush Jones lost his hat. Midshipman West Linthwaite brought another.

[155]

" Never mind the hat, West," exclaimed the sweating captain, " I'll fight this out in my scalp."

Meantime John Mayrant had assembled twenty-five or thirty men under the break of the quarter-deck. Pikes being short, they had armed themselves chiefly with cutlasses and pistols. Most of them were former prisoners in Portsea jail.

" Are you ready, boarders? " shouted Jones.

" Ay, ay, sir."

" Then now is your time, John. Go in."

With his " fierce Huguenot blood boiling," writes Henry Gardner, Mayrant leaped the rail, followed by " Red Cherry," and charged into the waist of the *Serapis*. He was met by a sailor whose pike pierced his thigh. He shot the sailor dead.

IX

John Kilby's narrative relates Mayrant's exploit differently. Kilby says at the moment when Jones gave the order to the boarders, Mayrant was discovered in the main chains " on the opposite side of the ship from the enemy." An officer was about to run him through, when Mayrant ran across the deck " and was actually one of those who boarded the enemy at that very moment." It is thus that glory in war and fame in peace have not infrequently been won. Henry Gardner, however, describes Mayrant as earning the particular commendation of Jones, who afterwards wished to mention him in a report. Mayrant observed it would satisfy him if a private letter were written to his sister, Josephine. " Then my sister will communicate the contents of the letter to another young lady of South Carolina, whose good opinion I very much wish to enjoy."

The said young lady's name is given as Miss Florence Huger, of the South Carolina family still prominent in Charleston.

X

Meeting Jack Robinson, the bo'sun, hurrying about the deck, Jones, who was already scenting victory, gaily asked him whether they should surrender.

"No, sir," was the bo'sun's reply. "I think we've still got a shot in the locker."

That shot was now tried. The enemy's main hatch was partly open, and Jones directed Fanning to lie out on the yardarm of the maintop and try to drop grenades into it. Gardner carried him two buckets of grenades, and Fanning crept out on the arm with Jerry Evans of Nantucket and Peter Nolte, a Swede. At the third attempt Fanning's grenade went into the two-foot opening. It fell among the powder-monkeys and fired more than fifty cartridges, which blew up the hatchway and wrecked the starboard guns. More than fifty men were killed or crippled. Almost at the same time the weakened mainmast of the *Serapis* crashed overboard.

XI

Fanning's grenade and the boarders' charge ended the fight. Captain Pearson himself hauled his colors down. But the smoke of battle hid his movements, and his gunners continued to bombard the rumpled timbers of the careening *Richard*. Mayrant was compelled to come back to the rails and shout to Dale, who was trying to save the burning mainmast:

"He has struck. Stop firing, and come on over."

Dale sprang over and asked Captain Pearson to pass on board the *Richard*. At that moment the *Serapis's* first lieutenant appeared. Seeing the Americans, he asked:

"Has the enemy struck, sir?"

"No, sir, I have struck," was Captain Pearson's melancholy reply.

Dale hurried below to stop the cannonading while Pearson slowly crossed to the smoking *Richard* and offered his sword to Jones with a slight bow. Neither he nor his lieutenant spoke. Jones, with chin in air, received their swords and handed them to Midshipman Potter. He told Captain Pearson he had fought " heroically " and added:

" I hope your sovereign will suitably reward you."

Captain Pearson again bowed, but remained silent as he was escorted to Jones's cabin.

It was nearly midnight and the spectators on the shore went home. Captain Cottineau in the *Pallas* brought up the *Serapis's* companion, the *Countess of Scarborough,* which he had taken after a brief fight. Captain Ricot in the *Vengeance* had remained safely in the rear. The moon still shone clear and strong, and under its light Captain Jones prepared to get a full night's sleep for the first time since leaving Lorient. Since the beginning of the cruise he had had only from three to four hours' sleep a night, having suffered much from insomnia. But first the dramatic artist in him had its say. He wrote a little note for the Duchess of Chartres:

" The enemy surrendered at thirty-five minutes past ten P.M. by your watch, which I consult only to fix the moment of victory."

A LAST GLORIOUS MOMENT AT THE BURNING OF WHITE-
HAVEN ON THE ENGLISH COAST.

CHAPTER XXII

Aftermaths

The many men, so beautiful!
And they all dead did lie:
And a thousand thousand slimy things
Lived on; and so did I.

I

ON the *Richard*, beset by both fire and water, lay
sixty-seven dead and 106 wounded out of total effec-
tives of 340. On the smoking *Serapis* eighty-seven
were dead and 134 wounded, thirteen mortally. Only about
100 of Jones's men were fit for duty, with 211 prisoners to
guard and care for. It was a desperate night for Dr. Brooke
and Dr. Bannatyne, the two rival surgeons. The carpenters
tried to plug the holes in the *Richard*, but in vain, and the next
morning Jones ordered all the wounded British and Americans
transferred to the *Serapis* and prepared to follow himself.
Landais in the *Alliance* meantime sailed round and round the
two ships, but made no offer to help. The *Pallas* took off some
of the *Richard's* prisoners and Jones also permitted Captain
Pearson to go to the French ship. All the other British officers
made a common mess on the *Serapis* with their late enemies
until port was reached.

It was Jones's hope that somehow he could bring the *Richard*
into port, but the harder his men worked, the lower she sank.
Fire had missed her powder only by a few inches and the timbers of the lower deck aft were found to be too rotten to repair.
Her masts remained upright, but between decks daylight
yawned almost to the water's edge. At nine o'clock the next

morning her head began to dip and Jones had to abandon her hastily, losing the best part of his clothes, books and papers, including various souvenirs intended for lady friends. " A little after ten I saw with inexpressible grief," he wrote, " the last glimpse of the *Bon Homme Richard*."

Her departure, says Kilby, was stately and dramatic. " She went down head foremost with all sails set — studding sails, topgallant sails, royals, skyscrapers and every sail that could be put on a ship — the jack pennant and that beautiful ensign that she so gallantly wore while in action and when we conquered."

II

A gale bore down and Captain Jones rigged up jury masts on the *Serapis* and made sail for Dunkirk with 700 men crowding the crippled ship to the very rails.

" There were very few cots," writes Fanning, " and not even enough hammocks for the wounded, so that many of them had to lie on the hard decks, where they died in numbers night and day. . . . In the common danger enmity was forgotten and everyone who could walk worked with a will to save the ship and their own lives."

The *Alliance* and *Vengeance*, signalling that they were sailing for the Texel, left the *Serapis* to go it alone, and after a few days of storm, Jones anchored beside them in the Dutch harbor on the afternoon of October 3, 1779, both his and the British officers being exhausted. He dispatched his report to Paris by Colonel Chamillard, who promptly wrote from there as follows:

" I delivered your dispatches to M. de Sartine and to Franklin, who both appeared to me to be enchanted with your exploits. . . . Your combat of the 23rd places you in the ranks of the greatest men and immortalizes you."

These were the first appreciative words received from any of his associates in fifty days, and it is certain that to the thirty-three-year-old captain, who loved praise like life, they were an elixir. At Amsterdam enormous crowds gathered in the hope of seeing him, but Jones had not yet time to revel in this notice. Two disagreeable tasks pressed upon him. The first was to suspend Captain Landais and place Lieutenant Degge in command of the *Alliance*. The second was to prevent Sir Joseph Yorke, the British minister to Holland, from carrying out his threat to demand the surrender of Jones and his crew to George III as " rebels and pirates."

III

The political world was buzzing over Jones's exploit. The capture of a British warship on its own coast by an inferior vessel which was itself in a sinking condition was a novelty in naval history; and the Hollanders, who, recalling old wounds, had little love for the British navy, knew how to appreciate all the finer shades of the feat. England itself was in an uproar, which was not allayed by the bestowal of a knighthood on Captain Pearson. Caricatures of " Jones the Pirate " erupted into shop-windows throughout the island. They portrayed the young Scotchman, who was so famed elsewhere for his meticulous attire, with a whiskered face, high boots, and a dripping sword. Only one item of the captain's occasional dress did they depict correctly — they gave him a short apron of Masonic cut, but instead of the Masonic emblem, it bore a skull and crossbones.

In London, where the Whigs furiously assailed Lord Germain, the Earl of Sandwich (the " Jemmy Twitcher " of *The Beggar's Opera*), Lord North, and the other cabinet ministers in charge of the war, a song appeared as follows:

Of heroes and statesmen I'll just mention four
That cannot be matched if we trace the world o'er,
For none of such fame ever stept o'er the stones
As Germain, Jemmy Twitcher, Lord North and Paul Jones.

If success to our fleets be not quickly restored,
The leaders in office we'll shove from the board;
May they all fare alike and the Devil pick the bones
Of Germain, Jemmy Twitcher, Lord North and Paul Jones.

IV

Jones's order deposing Landais had been taken to the *Alliance* by Captain Cottineau. Landais angrily challenged him to a duel. Cottineau accepted and they fought on an island in the Texel. Each drew blood and their seconds then ended the affair. Landais removed his belongings from the *Alliance* and went to Amsterdam where he wrote insulting letters to Jones and ordered a fantastic amount of supplies from the agents there. Franklin, however, soon put a stop to this. Landais then sent Jones a challenge through the mails. Jones accepted and appointed as his seconds Lieutenants Henry Lunt and John Mayrant. They waited on the semi-lunatic and informed him that Jones, as the challenged party, had chosen pistols at ten paces. Landais held out for the rapier, but the Americans being firm, he dropped the subject and took a chaise for The Hague, where he found an order from Franklin summoning him to Paris.

V

On October 17, 1779, the *London Chronicle* published a dispatch from its Amsterdam correspondent describing the homage paid to Jones during his visit to the Exchange. " He was dressed in the American uniform, with a Scotch bonnet edged with gold; is of middling stature, stern countenance and swarthy complexion."

[162]

The Dutch street urchins were not the only persons who thus honored the stern captain. The ladies of Holland, bearing baskets of delicacies for the wounded, visited the wharfsides in numbers that became embarrassing.

There is preserved at Washington a curious letter from Jones written to Dr. Bancroft from the Texel about this time. After acknowledging a " warm and affectionate letter " from Franklin's secret agent, Jones proceeds:

" I have seen the ' fine lady ' of this Country which I came to Europe to Espouse. She is really a fine woman — yet I have seen also a second sister equally a Belle who will soon be fit for a man; and I should prefer this younger because one might prevent some little errors from taking root in her mind which the other seems to have contracted. It is a great pity that two such lovely ladies should be watched with so much jealousy; for they are not so comeatable as they are in France — I have left to me only Dr. Franklin's remedy, — Patience."

There is at present no means of accounting for the references in this letter. Jones's correspondence as preserved contains no previous hint of his intention to espouse a lady in Europe. The wound inflicted by Miss Dandridge's marriage to Patrick Henry had doubtless been healed and Barkis was perhaps again willin', but no further record exists as to this " fine lady " who had contracted certain mysterious errors. There is one possible clue, however, contained in the memoirs of Madame Vigée le Brun, the celebrated French portrait painter, who in the following note indicates that in Paris, at all events, Jones was on good terms with a certain pair of sisters who will be later referred to:

" I have often supped at Madame Thilarié's, Madame de Bonneuil's sister, with the celebrated sailor who accomplished such services for the American cause and so much harm to the English. . . ."

[163]

VI

The Dutch authorities were not at all delighted to have John Paul Jones as their guest. For his very presence instantly precipitated a political broil which Jones, probably instigated by Franklin, helped to promote. Its purpose was to induce Holland to break with England. The protest of Sir Joseph Yorke at first caused the States-General to forbid the American captain to land his prisoners, but an outcry from the politicians favorable to America caused a partial reversal of this order, and Jones was permitted to land his wounded prisoners and to obtain supplies. Meantime his status as a prisoner had been chafing Captain Pearson, and he now sent a letter to Jones complaining of the delay as " a breach of civility." Jones's reply was somewhat tart. " I wished to avoid any painful altercation with you on that subject," he wrote, " I was persuaded that you had been in the highest degree sensible that my behavior towards you had been far from ' a breach of civility.' This charge is not, Sir, a civil return for the polite hospitality and disinterested attentions which you have hitherto experienced." He concluded by intimating that until the American Captain Cunningham, then in Plymouth jail, was better treated, Captain Pearson could not expect superior consideration.

The Dutch admiralty authorities, known as their " High Mightinesses," finally promised Sir Joseph Yorke that Jones would be invited to depart at the earliest possible date. The British admiralty then posted a squadron at each entrance of the Texel, and the letters of Yorke to the Dutch government left little doubt as to what would happen to Jones should they catch him upon his exit.

VII

An infinity of complicated situations resulted, but in the midst of them Jones was consoled by a letter of praise from Franklin. " For some days after the arrival of your express," wrote the sage, " scarce anything was talked of at Paris and Versailles but your cool conduct and persevering bravery during that terrible conflict." He congratulated Jones upon his capturing sufficient prisoners to exchange for those long shut up in British prisons and directed him to forward the complete charges against Landais. He added this postscript: " I am sorry for your misunderstanding with M. de C. who has a great regard for you." This reference was to de Chaumont, to whom Jones had sent a bitter letter regarding the results of the " Concordat." De Chaumont had replied in the most friendly terms. " This action," he said, " will immortalize you. . . . M. de Chamillard made the hair rise from our heads when he drew us the picture of the fire which in turn devoured both vessels, which you had bound together to serve for your triumphal bridge." Jones, however aggrieved, was not the man to reject olive branches, and soon he was back at the dining table of M. and Mme. de Chaumont, exchanging jokes with Franklin, who had just contrived one of his famous newspaper hoaxes, this being a witty reply by Jones to Sir Joseph Yorke's charge that he was a pirate. It was not known for some years that the real author of this letter was Franklin himself.

Sir Joseph later encountered Jones by accident at the home of a Dutch official and was astonished to find him courteous and agreeable, though dignified. Sir Joseph, however, did not abate in the least his efforts to force Jones out of the Texel into the jaws of the British sea-dogs waiting there. In writing to Lafayette of his trials Jones remarked:

" I must sail from the Texel in course of next month, because ships cannot afterward remain here in this road. My destination or route from hence I know not; but I need not tell you that I wish to see your face."

VIII

While Jones, in the face of a thousand harassments, was trying to repair the *Serapis* so as to make her again fit for sea, there fell upon him another of those blows which, had he not been of stout heart, must have cracked him. At the request of de Sartine, he was suddenly ordered to give up the *Serapis,* in which he had expected, with banners flying, to return to France, and to take command of the *Alliance.*. His prize was to be taken over by the French government so as to remove diplomatic difficulties. Jones accepted the order with surprising quietude. " I am not sorry," he wrote to Robert Morris, " that my connexion with them (the French government) is at an end. In the course of that connexion I ran ten chances of ruin and dishonour for one of reputation; and all the honour or profit that France could bestow should not tempt me again to undertake the same service, with an armament equally ill composed and with powers equally limited."

The French ambassador, the Duc de la Vauguyon, tried to mitigate the blow by offering him a French letter-of-marque. Jones refused this with cold dignity. " They invite me," he wrote to Jonathan Williams, " to insult the Stars and Stripes, they are mistaken, the Stars of Freedom are but rising here — they are not rich enough to buy the ' Pirate Paul Jones.' "

Jones found the *Alliance* in a filthy condition. The officers were drunk and insubordinate. The crew was ailing, idle and quarreling, and the beautiful ship was full of dirty and broken equipment. With his spirits low in the water, Jones was setting about the repairs when there came a message from the new port admiral, de Reynst, belonging to the pro-British party of the

Prince of Orange. It was a peremptory command to clear out of the Texel, otherwise action would be taken.

"Tell your Admiral," said Jones to the messenger, "that of course he has force enough to sink me here. But a league off land I can sink any 40-gun ship he has in one hour, and would like in such case for him to be in command."

IX

Jones at once prepared to sail, and then came a new blow. He was ordered to turn over his prisoners to the French ships. To compel the British to release the American seamen herded as rebels in foul jails had been one of his chief ambitions. "I consented on this occasion," he wrote in his *Journal*, "to a greater sacrifice than was made by any other officer during the revolution."

The exchange of prisoners with the British was thus delayed several months, but one purpose of Jones's three months' stay in Holland had been gained. A rift had been opened between the Dutch and English; within a year they were at war, Holland thus becoming an ally of America.

While Jones waited for a favorable wind, he addressed to Congress at home a memorial containing his claims for reinstatement to his proper rank — a subject which had never been far from his broody mind; and then, two days after Christmas, a gale arose, blowing straight out to sea. It was exactly suited to his purpose of driving at full speed through the squadron of Admiral Hardy waiting outside. Steering straight out into the English Channel, he ordered the reefs out on the *Alliance's* topsails and hauled the topsail yards up taut. Lieutenant Degge became uneasy and suggested less canvas. Jones's reply was short.

"She'll either carry this sail or drag it."

It was an adventure such as he loved, and now that he was in a fast ship again, with some of his old companions around him, his spirits rose as the barometer fell, and by the time he sighted Ushant he was writing verses to a lady friend. They were addressed to Mlle. Dumas, daughter of the American agent in Holland, who had honored him with a poem of her own. The first verse follows:

> Were I, Paul Jones, dear maid, " the king of the sea,"
> I find such merit in thy virgin song,
>   A coral crown with bays I'd give to thee,
> A car which on the waves should smoothly glide along;
>   The Nereides all about thy side should wait,
> And gladly sing in triumph of thy state
>   " Vivat, vivat, the happy virgin muse!
> Of liberty the friend, who tyrant power pursues."

x

The *Alliance* deceived the British by doing the unexpected and sailing along their own coasts. Bellied full before the wind, she scudded along in plain sight of the Downs, passed the Isle of Wight, and fled lightly by Portsmouth and Spithead, where the enemy fleet lay suspecting nothing. The same storm the *Alliance* was riding so gaily had scattered her pursuers, and, describing a great arc curving southward, Jones was soon safe in the open sea, without having had so much as a brush with an enemy. He had many of his old *Richard* crew with him and these, headed by Jack Robinson, now came forward with an enthusiastic petition:

" We respectfully request you, sir, to lay us alongside any single-decked English ship to be found in these seas, or any double-decked ship under a fifty."

Greatly moved — " I could hardly control my feelings," wrote Jones — he granted their request and for two weeks cruised off the Spanish coast, while all hands eagerly watched the horizon for an enemy sail. But none appeared, and being short of water and victuals, Jones was forced to halt the cruise and put in at Corunna. Here the captain and all his merry men were greeted as heroes, and certain junior nuns in a convent so far forgot their vows as to yield to the spirit of worldly romance and glance sidelong at the brave young American midshipmen. Mayrant and Potter failed to sleep any more until the night before their departure. They then gravely saluted their captain as he stalked away to dine with the governor and disappeared into the darkness. At midnight the Corunna police heard sounds of laughter rising straight up to the moon from a cottage near the convent. They investigated and were instantly scandalized. The next morning the two junior officers were in the *calabozo* — whence the word " calaboose " — and the nuns were facing a frozen Mother Superior. Jones asked that he be permitted to punish his guilty officers with appropriate frightfulness, and this the governor thought was best. Mayrant and Potter were court-martialed, deprived of their rank, and otherwise punished. The finding was copied by Jones himself, who sent it to the governor in charge of Lieutenant Stack, supported by Linthwaite and Fanning. " His Excellency expressed complete satisfaction," the account says, and the *Alliance* sailed away. The next day the case was reviewed by Captain Jones, who set the finding aside " on the ground that the punishment was inadequate to the offense." But the guilty parties of course did not hear the last of " Spanish love " for many a windy day and fair.

How shines a naughty deed in a goody world! How dismal do wars and politics and diplomacy, and the other stodgy pursuits of men, appear beside a bit of bracing foolishness!

XI

The *Alliance* dropped her anchor with a splashy thud in the harbor of Lorient, where the *Serapis* already lay at anchor, on February 10, 1780. Jones walked ashore with a hacking cough in his lungs and with eyes painfully inflamed, supposedly from the action of sea water. But his young officers were high in health and spirits. French merchants were waiting for them with open arms and commissions, and soon Mayrant, Potter and Chase sailed away as Commander, First Lieutenant and Second Lieutenant of a French ship significantly named *La Bonne Aventure*, and Fanning and Gardner were made Commander and First Lieutenant of the *Eclipse*. " Their cruises," their late captain proudly wrote, " were among the most daring and successful in the annals of French privateering."

The sight of the *Serapis* inspired new hopes, to which Franklin lent some encouragement, and Jones wrote to Dr. Bancroft:

" If I get the *Serapis*, of which my advices from Dr. Franklin and M. de Genet lead me to be hopeful, I shall miss sadly my gallant boys, Fanning and Mayrant, and the 128 Yankee sea-tigers they took with them in the privateers."

The de Genêt mentioned here was the " Citizen Genêt," who afterwards, as minister to the United States, raised one of the biggest storms known to early American political history. His daughter was Madame Campan, companion to Queen Marie Antoinette, and one of those feminine Freemasons who had done much to help Jones obtain the ships which made possible the successful cruise led by the *Bon Homme Richard*.

CHAPTER XXIII

The Warrior's Reward

Sometimes a-dropping from the sky
I heard the skylark sing;
Sometimes all little birds that are,
How they seemed to fill the sea and air
With their sweet jargoning.

I

"WOMAN," wrote Friedrich Nietzsche, "is the relaxation of the warrior." She is also, he might have added, sometimes his commissary department and chief source of supply. One may be sure that, as soon as he could untangle his feet from the anchor chains, John Paul Jones hurried to Paris to pay homage and give thanks to his chief backer and most faithful supporter, the Duchess of Chartres, and to those Masonic sisters who had shown their faith in him by contributing a ship to his squadron. In gratitude he wrote in his *Journal*:

"The men of France I esteem, respect and honor. They are brave, generous and faithful. But the women of France! what words can I find to express my homage, my worship, my devotion! They have been in these years of toil and storm and battle my guardian angels; they have saved me from despair; and they have inspired me to conquer. Their approving smiles and tender praise have been to me more than the applause of statesmen and even more than the favor of royalty itself."

To face the applause whose murmur had already come to his ears, he dressed himself with that care which made him conspicuous even in the exacting Paris of Louis Seize.

[171]

" Excuse the liberty I take," he once wrote to Hector Mc-
Neill from Portsmouth, N. H., " of enclosing a guinea which
I pray you to invest in a good hair powder and ship it to my
address. *Entre nous,* there is none of that luxury to be had
here; except such as is imprenated (*sic*) with Luxurious Mites."

His formerly loose dark hair he now wore in crisp powdered
rolls above his ears, possibly in imitation of Lafayette, whose
elegance he much admired. To his cornered hat, cocked with
a rosette, he added a white and fluted edging. To his shoulders
he attached a pair of heavy gold epaulets, and admired the effect
so much that he sent a duplicate pair home to General Washington. The facings of his navy blue coat were buff, edged with
a brilliant scarlet.

The impression he thus made upon Paris thrilled his very
arteries, every channel of which was instinct with vanity.
France was waking from the long stupor of feudalism. The
doctrines of Rousseau, preaching simplicity and democracy, had
penetrated even to the boudoirs of Marie Antoinette at Versailles, where silken ladies daily went forth to pat nature on
the head as if it were a new-born lamb. Diderot had summed
up the store of human knowledge in his Encyclopedia, setting
up a sudden cult for objective science. Voltaire, though two
years dead, was finding an increasing audience for his mockings
at Church and State. The popular Franklin had become a
French Confucius. Novelty, of whatever kind, was not only
welcome; it was a craze. Into this atmosphere suddenly strides
a handsomely dressed young sea captain from exotic America,
bold; conquering; daring with voice, pen and sword; freshly
laureled; lady-loving. . . .

II

Louis XVI bestowed on him a gold-hilted sword of fine
workmanship inscribed: *Vendicati maris Ludovicus XVI re-*

munerator strenuo vindici — " Reward of Louis XVI to a strenuous defender of the rights of the sea "; thus introducing to the American vocabulary two new terms: " strenuous " and " rights of the sea," of which the world has since heard not a little. Jones was fairly overcome by this gift, and refrained with difficulty from referring to it in all his subsequent letters. It was a symbol of unquestionable success; it was tangible evidence that he had won his life's ambition — undiluted, openly acknowledged distinction.

The King also awarded him the medal of Military Merit and the right to use the title Chevalier. Jones signed himself " Chevalier " in only a few letters to America, only one of which has been preserved; and then he heard from the patriots back home. To the sword and the medal they made no objection, but to parade himself as a Chevalier was going a little too far. It savored of proud monarchies and corrupt courts; it was, besides, foreign. It must be stopped; and Jones stopped it.

Marie Antoinette was curious to see the hero and had him presented at one of the levees given at Versailles for Franklin and the other American commissioners. She afterwards had him brought to her box at the opera and presented to him a fob chain and seal. The Commodore's opinion of her is on record. He thought her a " sweet girl."

The Duchess of Chartres installed him as her guest at her apartments in the old Palais Royal, an unprecedented honor to a commoner, and gave a banquet to which both the eminent and the curious flocked. At a suitable moment Jones recalled his promise to lay at her feet an English frigate. He explained that he had indeed brought one to France, but could sail it no closer than Lorient. However, he was keeping his word as well as circumstances would permit. And then he arose and with a bow placed in her hands the sword of Captain Richard Pearson, defeated commander of the *Serapis*.

Followed much gay talk, during which the Duchess asked

him what gave him the courage to fight on, when his ship was sinking under him. The gallant Jones's reply was as ready as if it had been rehearsed:

" May it please your Royal Highness, I could not be the first to lower the flag that I had been the first to raise in Europe; moreover, surrender must have postponed the rapture of seeing you again."

Whereupon the Duchess, who had a fondness for nicknames — she called Franklin " Monsieur the Sage " and Jefferson " Monsieur the Clever " — declared that whereas he had been previously " The Untitled Knight of the Sea," he should now be known as " The Bayard Afloat."

III

The feminine Freemasons having first had their turn, the sterner ones then invited him to come and be eulogized at a meeting of the Lodge of the Nine Sisters, in the rue Pot de Fer near the church of Saint Sulpice. Bachaumont's memoirs give us some of the details. The panegyric was pronounced by M. de la Dixmerie, who " reviewed the origins of Masonry, tracing it back to the institution of Chivalry, which in turn derived its origin from the ancient mystics." Explaining that their guest had " served Apollo before he enrolled himself under the banners of Mars," the eulogist then closed with a complimentary quatrain of which the English translation reads:

> Jones resourceful in battle when met,
> Acts toward enemies, so 'tis said,
> As acts toward us a clever coquette;
> One thinks to take her and is taken instead.

Soon after this, the sculptor Houdon, whose busts of his fellow Masons, Washington, Franklin, and Voltaire, are celebrated, began, at the order of the lodge, work on his head of the new American hero. Jones was very proud of this bust and had several copies made for friends in America. One was dug up years later in the basement of the Pennsylvania Academy of Fine Arts, Philadelphia, where no one recognized it. Houdon in his sculpture leaned strongly toward the Romanesque, hence he gave his subject features which from the front appear somewhat stern, but the poise of the lean head is, seen from the profile, youthful, winning and immensely proud. It is by far the most convincing portrait of John Paul Jones which has come down to us. That General Washington admired Houdon's bust of Jones no less than that of himself done by the same hand is evidenced by this letter to him from the Commodore written in 1787:

" Your determination to ' *place my bust with your own* ' confers on me a greater honor than I ever before received. An honor which I shall ever be ambitious to merit."

IV

Franklin, who took a great pride in " our commodore," frequently had him to dinner at his Passy home and introduced him to the great ladies who were then so enthusiastic for American liberty. Among them was the Countess d'Houdetot, the friend of Rousseau, who gave a *fête champêtre* in honor of Jones at her country home at Montmorency; Madame la Presidente d'Ormoy, also a friend of Rousseau, who caused demoiselles to greet the conqueror of the *Serapis* with verses celebrating the victory; and Madame de Saint Julien, the friend of Voltaire, one of whose letters to Jones has been preserved. It reproaches him for having " less reliability than courage," apparently as a result of a broken appointment to dinner, and concludes: " You should love better those who love you, my dear captain."

Among the influential men who entertained Jones during

this glorious period was de Genêt, then secretary to the Foreign Minister, Count Vergennes; and one whom Bachaumont calls the Marshal de Biron, possibly meaning the Duke de Biron, afterwards a general in the French revolutionary army and as such guillotined in 1793. De Biron is said to have commented upon Captain Pearson's elevation to knighthood by George III.

"I hope, Monsieur" — Bachaumont thus quotes Jones — "that I may one day make a lord of him."

This is the origin of the anecdote which is still being told in the schoolbooks. Jones in his *Journal* of 1791, however, remarks that it was "a story that annoyed me excessively." He corrected it at a subsequent luncheon given to him by the Duchess of Chartres. He told her that, "as rewards were then going in the British Navy, knighthood alone was hardly a suitable reward for such conduct as Captain Pearson had exhibited; that he ought to have been fully ennobled, and comparatively to services for which other officers were being knighted then, a dukedom would not have been extravagant for Captain Pearson." Jones also relates that he denounced the story to other persons, including Captain Ralph Willett Miller, a native New Yorker who had remained a royalist, as exhibiting him "in the character of a buffoon, than which nothing could be more foreign to my aspirations."

V

"I love women, I admit," Jones once wrote to Potemkin, commander-in-chief of the forces of Catherine the Great in Russia; hence it is not surprising that the Commodore's period of relaxation should have been marked with more than one flirtation. A visitor at the home of the de Genêts at that time was Miss Caroline Edes, a young Englishwoman.

"The famous Paul Jones dines and sups here often," she wrote home. "He is a smart man of thirty-six, speaks but little French, appears to be an extraordinary genius, a poet as well as a hero. A few days ago he wrote some verses extempore of which I send you a copy. He is greatly admired here, especially by the ladies, who are all wild for love of him, but he adores Lady (the Countess Lavendal) who has honored him with every mark of politeness and attention."

The lady who at the moment had captured the gallant seaman's somewhat roving eye was the Countess de Lowendahl, a daughter of Joseph de Bourbon Condé, and the wife of Count François Xavier de Lowendahl. Her husband was a former army officer with mild ambitions and still milder initiative. The Countess's opinion of him is thus recorded:

"Alas! My poor husband; he is so good and withal so dull!"

She is described as an amateur artist, "possessed of youth, beauty and wit and every other female accomplishment." Jones's admiration for her was ardent, and in her company he passed many hours, in the course of which she drew his portrait. "You have made me," he wrote, "in love with my own picture because you have condescended to draw it." One evening before he was about to sail away he visited her at Versailles and on returning to Nantes wrote her a long letter.

"Nothing," he said, "short of my duty to the Glorious Cause of Freedom in which I have the honor to be engaged, could have induced me to leave Versailles a little hour after I parted from you, while my Heart urged me to stay that I might have the happiness to see you the next morning."

He enclosed a cipher "for a key to our future correspondence, so that you will be able to write to me freely and without risk," also a lock of hair. "I am sorry it is now eighteen inches shorter than it was three months ago. If I could send you my heart itself or anything else that could afford you pleasure it would be my happiness to do it."

The Countess's reply would have caused a chill beneath any

waistcoat less romantic than Jones's. She informed him that evidently his packet had been misdirected. She concluded by introducing him to her husband, then visiting at Lorient, and asking his help in promoting the Count's ambitions. Jones's next letter disclosed the shock he had received; he put a brave face upon it, but still he could not believe that her admiration for a victorious captain was less than his own.

" I . . . cannot conceive," he wrote, " what part of the letter itself could have occasioned your imagining I had mistaken the address. As for the little packet it contained perhaps it might better have been omitted, if so it is easily destroyed."

He added that he would esteem himself " very happy " to have the coöperation of her husband in a project for a joint expedition by land and sea which had been laid before the King, and then in his infatuation risked another rejection. Referring to the King's gift of a sword, he said:

" I hold the sword in too high estimation to risk its being taken by the enemy; and therefore propose to deposit it in the care of a friend. None can be more worthy of that sacred deposit than you, Madam, and if you will do me the honour to be its guardian I shall esteem myself under an additional obligation to deserve your ribbon, and to prove myself worthy of the title of your Knight."

But the lady was not in need of a knight and in her reply she made this plain. She made it still plainer that the price of her future friendship with him would be some advancement for her husband, a statement in which the latter had evidently connived. With the door thus firmly closed in his face, Jones could only retreat in good order and march away.

" I was honored," he wrote, " with the very polite letter that your Ladyship condescended to write me the 5th of last month. I am sorry that you found it necessary to refuse me the honor of accepting the deposit mentioned in my last, but I am determined to follow your advice and be myself its guardian "; and no doubt he again recalled the worn but serviceable maxim of Benjamin Franklin which had been useful to him in obtaining the good ship *Bon Homme Richard.*

VI

There was another charmer whose letters to Jones during the same period leave no doubt that in similar circumstances he would have received from her far different treatment. This was she who appears in Jones's paper simply as " Delia," and to whom the commodore was " adorable Jones." Her letters, still preserving the stains of tears and despair after one hundred and forty-seven years, are sufficient proof that one should never write impassioned letters to a famous man who keeps an efficient and orderly correspondence file, indexed with impersonal alphabetics. Her impulsive missives to Jones show that in a society trained to subdue all disruptive emotions and frequently prosecuting cool business purposes under the mask of *amour,* she was warm-hearted, a little hysterical, sincere, and a little foolish.

" Dear and too adorable friend! What would I not give if you were free to remain in France. O God! I am dying to rejoin you, never again to separate from you. But no! I feel by the anguish of my soul, which seems to whisper it to me, that I shall never see you again. Heavens! Jones will forget me. He may cease to love me. No, his noble heart is incapable of such cruelty and I trust him as I would in heaven itself."

Whatever her weaknesses, " Delia " at least had the merit of generosity. That she was no cold schemer like the Countess de Lowendahl appears from the following:

" I am told that neither you nor your people have yet been paid. In the name of all the love which is consuming me, command me if I can be of service to you. I have diamonds and possessions of all sorts and could easily realize the amount. Command your mistress, give me this happiness! ''

Further evidence of Jones's attacks of ill health during this period appear in letters from this lady: " I am suffering the cruelest anxiety in regard to your health, my only love. . . . You ask me what you can do to make me happy. Take care of your health, love me and think of a way which will enable us to pass our lives together. . . . I have your letter of the 16th. The state of your health alarms me."

She complains that the absence of news from him distresses her beyond telling. She describes " the awful despair to which the fear of losing you has reduced me," but tries to reassure herself. " The charming and tender Jones is as faithful a lover as he is a valiant and zealous patriot. . . . Pardon my fears, too cherished friend. I will force myself to be calm."

This tumultuous lady actually tried to convert into cash her little fortune of 80,000 livres for the purpose of following Jones, but he sailed away to America before she was able to do so. The brevity of a sailor's love is notorious. He had been in America a year when he wrote her from Portsmouth, New Hampshire, a letter which was no more flamelike than a glass of water:

" I wrote my most lovely Delia various letters from Philadelphia, the last of which was dated the 20th of June (six months before). On the 26th of that month I was unanimously elected by Congress to command the *America* of 74 guns on the stocks at Portsmouth in Hampshire . . . Providence all good and just has given thee a soul worthy in all respects to animate nature's fairest work. I rest therefore sure that absence will not diminish but refine the pure and spotless friendship that binds our souls together and will ever," etc, etc.

History for a century or more professed not to know the identity of " Delia," as if to give time an opportunity to hide her indiscretions beneath a heap of faded years; but at last it was revealed. She was the Countess de Nicolson, wife of Count William Murray de Nicolson, a Scotch politician who sometimes acted as a secret agent for the French government. Her brother, the Chevalier William Nicolson, was captain of marines on Jones's ship the *Ariel*, which succeeded the *Alliance*.

Jones once wrote her a poem which is still preserved. It consists of five long stanzas written in the classical style which in the eighteenth century was deemed to be highly elevated, referring to " Jove," " Juno," and other names from Greek mythology in the fashion set by the commodore's favorite bard, James Thomson. Jones's frequent efforts to be poetical were manful, but little more can be said about them. In his attempts to sound a lofty note, he barely escaped being dismal.

VII

The list of Jones's feminine friends is a long one and has not yet come to an end. The mystery of the two sisters he encountered in Holland remains to be cleared up. Madame Vigée le Brun's reference to Jones's frequent hostess, Madame Thilarié, and her sister, Madame de Bonneuil, would seem to indicate that the former was the " Madame T." often mentioned in Jones's correspondence. Madame Thilarié became a widow in 1783 and then married Jean Jacques Duval d'Esprémenil, the enemy of Louis XVI and Marie Antoinette. He was guillotined in 1794 and the former Mme. Thilarié followed him on the scaffold a few weeks later.

But there was another " Madame T." in Jones's life and she likewise had a sister of whom little is known. So concerned was the commodore about this " Madame T." that when absent from France he more than once asked Thomas Jefferson, who succeeded Franklin at the court in France, to look after her welfare.

[181]

" I shall now tell you in confidence," he wrote to Jefferson in 1787, " that she is a daughter of the late King, and a lady of quality, on whom his Majesty bestowed a large fortune on his daughter's account . . . I feel the greatest concern for the situation of this worthy lady."

Jones's description of this lady as " worthy " perhaps left Jefferson unprepared for the sight of a red-haired young woman in her early twenties. This was the woman to whom Jones, in his fashion, was faithful for fourteen years, whom he protected, to whom he constantly sent money, and who long survived him. She was Aimée de Tellison, daughter of Louis XV and a lady known as Madame de Bonneval, later married to an official, a widower named de Tellison. Aimée had been well educated under the provision of Louis XV, who had also bestowed an annuity on her mother. Louis XVI renewed the payments from the royal treasury to the daughter, and after her case had been brought to his attention, received her in audience. In this Jones told Jefferson he had been " instrumental," perhaps through the agency of the Duchess of Chartres, who as a Bourbon knew her way so well about courts.

Mlle. de Tellison is described as " petite, extremely vivacious and possessed of all the polite accomplishments," though " without fortune." Before she received the grant from Louis XVI, Jones mentions that she was ignored by her mother and " was long the silent victim of injustice." Her fortunes being low, someone, perhaps either the Duchess of Chartres or one of the other influential women of the court, brought her to the attention of Jones, who on arriving in France knew little of the language, and she assisted him as an interpreter and translator of official papers, thus bearing out Benjamin Franklin's roguish adage, " The best master of languages is a mistress." To what extent this relationship ripened cannot be said, but Jones in one of his letters to her from America declares, " The last French packet brought no letter to me from the person whose happiness is dearer to me than anything else. I have been on the rack of fear and apprehension. . . ."

In the letter to her sent from New York through Jefferson he mentions that he is short of money; "it is impossible for me to transmit you a supply under my present circumstances. . . . You will see how disgracefully I have been detained here by the Board of Treasury." He laments the recent death of a certain "friend and protectress." He goes on: "She was a tried friend and more than a mother to you. She would have been a mother to me also had she lived. We have lost her. Let us cherish her memory and send up grateful thanks to the Almighty, that we once had such a friend."

The identity of this protectress is not known. The Edinburgh biography of Jones supposes it was the Princess de Marsan, governess to the royal children; but as she survived till after the French Revolution, it was probably one of the ladies of the court who benevolently watched over this love-affair between a daughter of Louis XV and the young American sailor.

Jones's letter to Aimée continues:

"Present my best respects to your sister. You did not mention her in your letter, but I persuade myself she will continue her share of her sweet godson and that you will cover him all over with kisses from me. They come warm to you *both* from my heart."

Buell thinks this does not necessarily indicate a close tie between the young Frenchwoman and the Commodore, but Mrs. de Koven believes "it is impossible to come to any other conclusion than that the 'sweet godson,' whom Jones wished Madame T. to 'cover all over with kisses from him,' was his son."

CHAPTER XXIV

Further Intrigues

The very deep did rot; O Christ!
That ever this should be!
Yea, slimy things did crawl with legs
Upon a slimy sea.

I

WHILE the air about his powdered head was thus scented with *amour*, a heavier undercurrent of intrigue was playing about Jones's legs in a new endeavor to trip him.

Soon after his return to port, he tried to induce Franklin to find the money to repair the *Alliance* and to buy the *Serapis*. The harassed doctor replied, in what was for him an unusually testy letter, that the French government would be unlikely to consent to either proposal:

" The whole expense would therefore fall on me and I am ill provided to bear it, having so many unexpected calls for me from all quarters. I, therefore, beg you would have mercy upon me, put me to as little charge as possible, and take nothing which you can do without. . . . I have no money if I had authority and no authority if I had money. The purchase of the *Serapis* is in the same predicament. For God's sake, be sparing! unless you mean to make me a bankrupt, or have your drafts disregarded for want of money in my hands to pay them."

Jones replied with a gesture of filial obedience: " As I have not hitherto been among the most extravagant servants of

America, so you may depend upon it, my regard for you will make me particularly nice in my present situation."

Franklin urged him to repair the *Alliance* as soon as possible, so as to carry to America 15,000 stand of arms and 120 bales of clothing, for which General Washington was already waiting. The *Alliance*, too, was wanted for the defence of Charleston, and Franklin added that Jones was to take with him several passengers, including John Ross and Ralph Izard, the American agents, and — of all people! — Arthur Lee.

Jones, having little money and the expected settlements of prize awards being repeatedly delayed by the de Sartine ministry, was compelled to put his own crew to work repairing the *Alliance*. They went about it slowly and sullenly. They were improperly clothed; they had received neither wages nor prize money; and part of them began to entertain dark-green suspicions of Jones. They saw him, gaily dressed, flitting up to Paris and Versailles and entertaining laughing dames and chevaliers on his ship, while they were cold, bored, and homesick. They were roused to fury by the sight of the *Serapis* and the *Countess of Scarborough* being dismantled before their eyes, and they began to accuse both Jones and the French.

Jones was aware of their condition and wrote indignantly to Franklin and the French ministry about it, but with his romantic disposition and self-centred ambitions, he failed to understand their viewpoint. He accused them of " self-interest." The American soldiers and sailors of the early days of the Revolutionary War were a canny lot. Their hard-headed practicality frequently aroused even Washington to angry objurgations. They went into the war as they would have gone into farming or whaling — for regular day-wages and for strictly limited periods. War-makers have since then learned a better technique: they provide the rank and file with fair pay and, what is scarcely less important, an emotional slogan. But the American soldiers and sailors of the Revolution for a long time had neither.

This rift between Jones, who had his diversions, and his men, who had none at all, left an opening through which the twisted, saturnine tongues of Arthur Lee and Peter Landais began to lick.

II

Landais, who had been ordered home to face an inquiry, now had the effrontery to ask for the command of the *Alliance* on her return home. Franklin's reply was blunt:

" I think you so imprudent, so litigious and quarrelsome a man, even with your best friends, that peace and good order and consequently the quiet and regular subordination so necessary to success, are where you preside impossible. . . . If, therefore, I had twenty ships-of-war in my disposition, I should not give one of them to Captain Landais."

Meantime General Washington was anxiously writing for his supplies. This lent encouragement to Landais and at last, " by the advice of Mr. Lee and Commodore Gillon," Franklin says, Landais seized the *Alliance*, locked up those members of the crew who remained loyal to Jones, sent Dale and other officers ashore, and threw Jones's baggage off. Jones was then in Paris, trying to get the pay promised him by de Chaumont and laying before the French court plans for new expeditions. He was also, it must be said, probably philandering.

III

It is odd that Jones should have permitted Landais to retain possession of the *Alliance*. Some of his former officers and men smuggled out to him pathetic letters begging him to free them from Landais; but others sent to Franklin a document calling Landais their " legal " commander. This was based on

a signed opinion by Lee, who thus meant to fling one more defiance in the hated face of Franklin.

Weeks of charges and counter-charges followed, during
which Jones vainly tried to have Landais removed from the
Alliance. The French offered either to arrest Landais or if he
tried to sail, to sink the ship, but Franklin, probably wishing to
give Lee a chance to hang himself with finality, would not give
a definite order. It seems clear that Jones did not greatly care
to retain command of the *Alliance;* he believed that he could
persuade the French, in the face of numerous cold receptions,
to give him a new squadron with which he could further harass
British commerce; and finally the *Alliance* got away, under
a neurotic captain conveying a megalomaniac chief-passen-
ger.

What a homeward voyage was that! In a few days the two
semi-lunatics, Landais and Lee, were fighting like cats from
Kilkenny, and Lieutenant Degge, who had signed the round-
robin against Jones, was not speaking to his captain. The ship
veered and wallowed, and the passengers, afraid of imminent
death and yet equally afraid they would live, kept to their
cabins. And then one day Landais went to pieces and flew into
hysterics. It was because the passengers, during a calm, had
fished over the side without his permission.

That was enough for the passengers. They formed themselves into an emergency committee, and Arthur Lee, by virtue
of his authority as a former medical man, pronounced Landais
unfit to command the ship. Landais was ordered confined to
his quarters and Lieutenant Degge was made acting captain.
But in Degge's feeble hands the ship progressed little better,
and then the passengers' committee, in a panic, gave the navigation of the straining *Alliance* to James Pratt, the bo'sun. Pratt
was hard-boiled as to temperament and knotty as to hands, but
he sailed the ship home. A few leagues out from Boston, Pratt
called Lieutenant Degge aside.

" It's all done except this last bit. You're the captain. Now you take the ship in."

And Degge, with a meek " Yes, sir," took her in.

Lee returned to Virginia politics, while Landais was tried, broken, and dismissed from the service. He survived for many years, living in New York on a small pension and every two years beseeching Congress for prize money he declared was still due him. Long after John Paul Jones's death he could be occasionally seen talking to himself as he walked up lower Broadway, dressed in his old Continental uniform, with red clocks on his yellow stockings. He was buried in Old St. Patrick's Churchyard, Mott and Prince Streets, New York, under a stone inscribed in French which merely stated that he had " *disparut* " — disappeared.

THE CRITICAL INSTANT IN THE FIGHT BETWEEN THE *Serapis* AND THE *Bon Homme Richard.*

CHAPTER XXV

Farewell to France

With sloping masts and dipping prow,
As who pursued with yell and blow
Still treads the shadow of his foe,
And forward bends his head,
The ship drove fast, loud roared the blast,
And southward aye we fled.

I

THE *Alliance* was scarcely out of sight before Jones made another attempt to obtain the *Serapis*, but perceiving no results, he next tried to induce the French to give him the great frigate *Terpsichore*. He wrote letter after letter to officials, sought interviews, and buttonholed persons of influence at Versailles. But the French ministers were either cold or dilatory; he could not obtain even a hint regarding prize money from the unbusinesslike de Chaumont. His correspondence at this time mirrors his fretful bewilderment. His complete absorption in his craving for a new and more glorious expedition to the English coast, where he hoped to complete the destruction of the British Baltic fleet, which had escaped him off Flamborough Head, made him blind to the apparent fact that the French court in presenting him with a sword, a decoration, and a knighthood, considered it had done enough for him. France was preoccupied with its own part in the war against England, and had scarcely enough ships for its own waiting captains. Moreover, de Sartine himself, the Minister of Marine, had belonged to the party headed by Turgot, Minister of Finance, which had from the first opposed

France's war-alliance with America, and he did as little as he could to further Jones's ambitious plans. Even after Jones's resounding triumph over the *Serapis,* when Franklin brought the Commodore to him for congratulations, de Sartine " gave us," wrote Jones, " a reception as cold as ice, did not say to me a civil word, nor even ask me if my health had not suffered from my wounds, and the uncommon fatigue I had undergone."

Jones, conscious of his ability and of his superiority to most of the captains he had encountered abroad, could not let go his dreams of further exploits at sea. He knew he must return to America soon, but was determined to come back to France and prove to all the world that his victories over the *Drake* and the *Serapis* had been but auguries of yet grander achievements to come. He wrote to Madame Tellison from Lorient:

" My sole business at court was to obtain the free sale of the prizes, which I effected . . . I know that soon after my arrival in America, Congress will render me impartial justice. I will then have the happiness to furnish you with the account I promised, and the circumstances will be supported by the fullest evidence. I dare promise that it will then appear that I have only been to blame for having returned here from Paris, without having insisted absolutely on the previous payment of my men. Money is essential in war: in love, you will tell me, perhaps the case may be otherwise. I have still in contemplation to return to France soon after I arrive in America, for I have the most ardent desire to give the court, the nation, and my friends farther proofs of my gratitude, by my services in the glorious cause of freedom that France has so nobly espoused in concert with America."

Meantime the French government had offered Jones, at Franklin's request, the loan of the small ship *Ariel,* for the purpose of sending over supplies to General Washington's half-naked armies. Jones accepted the command, but repairs delayed his sailing, and weeks went by while he continued to bombard Franklin and the French ministers with schemes for attacks on

England and her shipping. Most of these were perfectly practical and might well have shortened the war; but responsible officials would take no action, and de Sartine finally refused to answer any more of Jones's imploring letters. Jones then tried to bring pressure to bear through influential friends, writing to the Chevalier de Baudoine that he " would rather be shot to death than suffered to pine in idleness while our glorious cause is undetermined." Even Franklin became testy under the flood of letters, saying:

" I am perfectly bewildered with the different schemes that have been proposed to me by Mr. Williams, Mr. Ross, yourself, and M. de Chaumont. Mr. Williams was for purchasing ships. I told him I had no money, but he still urges it. You and Mr. Ross proposed borrowing the *Ariel*. . . . We obtained her. Now you find her insufficient. I think therefore that it will be best that you take as much into the *Ariel* as you can and depart with her. . . . That is my present opinion and when I have once got rid of this business no consideration shall tempt me again to meddle in such matters."

Privately Franklin confessed to Williams that he was " plagued to death with the passions, vagaries, and ill-humour and madnesses of other people."

The truth of the situation was that the French government, though willing to assist America in every way that would damage England, was not in the least concerned to strengthen a navy that might, in time, rival her own. The canny Franklin was well aware of this policy, and no doubt had made up his mind he would ride a willing horse no farther.

II

Revealing the exacerbation of his nerves at this time, and also his ideas of discipline, Jones got into a quarrel with Captain Thomas Truxton, afterwards the famous Commodore, who had arrived at Lorient in the *Independence* from Philadelphia and pitched his anchor without saluting the colors on Jones's ship. Jones sent two armed boats to force him to lower his pennant and rebuked him in a searing letter.

" The government of the United States of North America," he wrote, " requires all her citizens to pay respect to her flag and commission, which is particularly due in foreign ports. Now, Sir, you have been wanting in this respect. You passed some time ago . . . close under the stern of the continental ship *Ariel*, under my command, in the Road of Groix, and you then showed no mark of respect to the continental flag commission, but went on with the long pendant flying and without lowering any sail or color and without showing any mark of politeness."

After describing how his boat's crew " had been menaced by your people " who said they " had your orders to treat with contempt and disobey any order or request to haul down the pennant," Jones remarked:

" I hope I have said enough to show you your error . . . I shall receive no more letters from you on this subject. It is not me you have offended. You have offended the United States of America."

This letter is further evidence of the extraordinary manner in which Jones was often treated by other officers in the United States navy. The open dislike they so frequently exhibited toward Jones was due partly to his own haughty attitude of superiority — maintained as a defence mask; partly to jealousy; partly to his " foreignness " ; and partly to sheer early-Yankee bumptiousness.

III

The *Ariel* being at last put in condition, Jones prepared to sail, but before he did so he consoled himself by giving his French friends an elaborate farewell entertainment on board

[192]

the ship. It took place at Lorient on September 2, 1780. It is significant that Jones staged for his guests a sham sea fight by moonlight, representing in part his battle with the *Serapis*. It symbolized his parting message to France, to England, and to America. It was also an expression from Jones, the artist. Nathaniel Fanning, who, with Richard Dale, had remained loyal to Jones, has left an account of the spectacle, in which the " fighting Puritan's " distaste is evident.

Among the guests were " one prince of the royal blood [probably the Duke of Chartres] and three French admirals with some ladies of the first quality." The quarter-deck had " the appearance of a lady of qualitie's drawing room." The sides of canvas, " lined with pink colored silk," were hung with " a great variety of pictures and looking glasses. Some of the first had been drawn by one of the most finished artists in France and some of which were quite indecent especially to meet the eyes of a virtuous woman."

And then the Puritan's sense of justice intervenes: " However in these days they made a part of French etiquette." He continues:

" A French lady (who was said to be a great connoisseur in the art of cookery and in hanging and arranging pictures in a room where the first company went to dine) was gallanted on board by Capt. Jones." The day " was ushered in by thirteen guns and the dressing of the ship with thirteen stripes and the colors of all nations that were friendly to the United States. Capt. Jones and his officers were all dressed in uniform with their best bib and band on, and we were directed by Capt. Jones to conduct ourselves with propriety and to pay implicit obedience to my lady superintendent of the ceremony."

This " lady superintendent " was probably Mme. Gerard, mother of Pierre Gerard, Jones's French orderly on the *Bon Homme Richard*. She was long his landlady at Lorient and later his housekeeper in Paris.

[193]

" At a quarter before 3 o'clock in the afternoon the ships boats (three in number each having a midshipman who acted for this time as coxswain and the men who rowed the boats were all neatly dressed in blue with the American or French cockades in their hats) were dispatched on shore to bring on board the company. Jones received them as they came up the ships side and conducted them to their seats on the quarterdeck with a great deal of ease, politeness and good nature. The company was superbly dressed and the Prince was distinguished from the rest by a brilliant star which he wore upon his left breast. Dinner was served up at half past 3 P.M. The company did not rise from table until a little after sunset, when Capt. Jones ordered his first lieutenant to cause all hands to be called to quarters which was done just as the moon was rising."

The sham fight then began, the action taking place chiefly in the fighting tops. " Such a cracking of great guns, swivels, cow horns, blunderbusses . . . such a hissing and popping of hand grenades, stink-pots, powder flasks." The male guests enjoyed this, but the ladies stopped their ears.

" The fight would have been continued longer had it not been that some of them entreated Capt. Jones to command the firing to cease. The fight over, a band of music . . . now played their part and all was glee and harmony."

IV

Writing letters of farewell occupied Jones several days. To Dr. Bancroft he wrote: " I must take leave of you. No man loves and esteems you with more tender heart-felt affection than your own Paul Jones." To Madame la Presidente d'Ormoy he addressed one of his characteristically dramatic requests:

" My particular thanks are due to you, Madam, for the personal proofs I have received of your esteem and friendship, and for the happiness you have procured me in the society of the charming countess, and other ladies and gentlemen of your

[194]

circle. But I have a favour to ask of you, Madam, which I hope you will grant me. You tell me in your letter that the inkstand I had the honor to present to you, as a small token of my esteem, shall be reserved for the purpose of writing what concerns me; now I wish you to see my idea in a more expanded light, and would have you make use of that inkstand to instruct mankind, and support the dignity and rights of human nature."

From the Countess de Nicolson came a despairing note:

" Your letter . . . tears my heart and augments my despair. With the grief of a desolate child, I kissed the dear marks of your tears, while those that fell from my eyes were the cruelest, the bitterest of my life. . . . Be calm now. Take courage and believe that a kind heaven will reunite us and watch over the fate of two beings who love each other dearly and whose faithful hearts deserve to be happy. Take care of your precious life and know that mine is wrapt up in yours. I shall ceaselessly address my prayers to heaven for your safe arrival in America. If you are satisfied in your service to that country, you will continue it. Otherwise you must abandon it and regain her who loves you so faithfully. . . ."

In a farewell letter to Aimée de Tellison Jones expressed his resigned acceptance of his defeated dreams:

" In bidding adieu to you, dear Madame, for how long a time I cannot now determine, but which I hope may not be protracted beyond the coming spring, I bid adieu also to the beloved nation of France, where, though I have met with some difficulties, I have found many reasons to be satisfied. . . . If in official and public pursuits I have met with disappointments here and there, it may be the fault of my ambitions and an excess of hope beyond the reasonable power of even King and Ministers to gratify."

v

On Oct. 8, 1780, he sailed, carrying as passenger Samuel Wharton, head of the Philadelphia mercantile family which has continued in business ever since. Jones had behind him a fair breeze, but in the night the weather changed, and the next day there blew up a furious gale which drove him almost onto Penmark Rocks. The *Ariel* began to leak, and soon was helpless and waterlogged. For three days and nights the little ship fought for her life. In moments of crisis Jones always rose to the best that was in him. He now proved to the full his capacity as a seaman and captain.

To save the ship from the rocks, he cast anchor. But the toiling *Ariel* could not get her head into the wind, and Jones cut away the foremast. This eased the ship, but a new danger arose; the mainmast worked loose and threatened to wreck the hull. Jones cut this away too, and overboard it went, carrying away the mizzenmast and the quarter gallery. The ship was now entirely without masts, but her anchor held and eventually she rode out the storm. When it had abated, Jones rigged up jury-masts, cut his cable, and slowly worked the *Ariel* back into Lorient.

" Never saw I," wrote Richard Dale, " such coolness and readiness in such circumstances as Paul Jones showed in the days and nights when we lay off the Penmarque Rocks, expecting every moment to be our last." Wharton, in a letter to Franklin, was equally enthusiastic in praise of the " matchless skill and cool and unshaken intrepidity of our Captain, who truly ' rode in the whirlwind and directed the storm.' "

Repairs to the *Ariel* occupied two more months, during which a new hope arose. The Marquis de Castries succeeded the slow de Sartine at the marine ministry, and Jones at once besieged him to authorize a new expedition against England, with himself in command, but de Castries, though polite, merely answered that the King would await his return from America before he would lend him any ships. Sadly Jones once more locked up his hopes, and once more wrote letters of farewell. In a final letter to Mme. d'Ormoy he said:

[196]

"It is certain that till the night of the 8th I did not fully conceive the awful majesty of tempest and shipwreck . . . I am extremely sorry that the young English lady you mention should have imbibed the national hatred against me. I have had proofs that many of the first and finest ladies of that nation are my friends. . . . The English may hate me, but I will force them to esteem me too . . . I have returned without laurels and, what is worse, without having been able to render service to the glorious cause of liberty."

Once more he begged de Castries to settle the claims of his men to prize money. "I have already suffered many reflections on their account," he wrote, "and I beseech your excellency to order them immediate payment."

But all he could learn was that the King had not yet approved the payments, and once more he was compelled to weigh anchor and leave France empty-handed. On December 18, 1780, he caught a fair wind, and having on board supplies which must not be captured, he sailed out of Lorient and pointed his ship southward.

The usual conspiracy was uncovered as soon as the *Ariel* struck the heavy swells of the sea. It was among the English prisoners who formed part of the crew. Twenty of them were put in irons, arms were distributed to the passengers, and a guard was posted night and day with fixed bayonets.

Jones was soon close to the West Indies, and here a trick was played upon him which caused him no little chagrin. It was of the kind which he himself loved to perpetrate, but on this occasion he failed to see the humor of it. An enemy frigate hove in sight and at once pursued him. Jones kept out of range until nightfall when he shortened sail and cleared for action, doubtless expecting to repeat his moonlight triumph over the *Serapis*. The frigate, which proved to be very fast, was discovered to be a captured American privateer, formerly commanded by the son of Jones's late enemy, Commodore Ezek

Hopkins. She had been renamed the *Triumph*. Jones promptly engaged her, and in ten minutes the opposing captain, John Pindar, an American Tory, was begging for quarter. The *Ariel's* crew deserted their guns to cheer for their victory. The English ship then suddenly filled its sails, got on the *Ariel's* weatherbow, and was off in the wind before the Americans could collect themselves.

" The English captain may properly be called a knave," wrote Jones indignantly, " because, after he surrendered his ship, begged for and obtained quarter, he basely ran away, contrary to the laws of naval war and the practice of civilized nations."

VI

He dropped anchor at Philadelphia on Feb. 18, 1781, three years and three months from the time when he had pointed the nose of the little *Ranger* towards France. His first action was to go ashore and borrow money for himself and his men.

The country itself was in not much better state. Charleston had been taken by the British. South Carolina and Georgia had been overrun, and Cornwallis and Tarleton seemed to be succeeding in their attempt to cut off the South. Benedict Arnold had turned traitor. Pennsylvania, New Jersey, and Connecticut troops had mutinied for the same reason that Jones's seamen had turned against him — lack of pay. The Continental currency had depreciated until forty paper dollars were worth only one in specie. Washington, watching his troops starving and freezing at West Point, was telling the French to expect the worst unless they could give him instant military and naval assistance. Lafayette was paying out of his own pockets for shirts and shoes to clothe his troops in Virginia. New York was corruptly content in the hands of the British. Desertion to the enemy was common. The prestige of Congress had declined so greatly that America was divided virtually into thirteen governments instead of one. The people at large were grumbling because of high taxation and ceaseless military requisitions.

" In a word," wrote George Washington to Henry Laurens in France, " we are at the end of our tether, and now or never our deliverance must come."

Not a very dainty dish to lay before a victorious young naval commander, fresh from the drawing rooms of Paris and Versailles, but with not a penny of pay in his pocket, with his prize earnings still withheld, and with his proper rank still in question.

CHAPTER XXVI

The Tenth Renunciation

Nor dim nor red, like God's own head,
The glorious Sun uprist:
Then all averred, I had killed the bird
That brought the fog and mist.
'Twas right, said they, such birds to slay,
That bring the fog and mist.

I

SCARCELY had he straightened his sea legs when Jones learned he was to be investigated by Congress, according to a practice which that body has maintained ever since, particularly when the usual reaction has set in against excessive hero-worship. A scandal had been worked up about the delay in forwarding the supplies from France long needed by General Washington's miserably armed and worse clothed soldiers, and both Jones and Franklin had been made the targets of loose charges.

Jones soon learned who his enemies were. They included Samuel Adams, of Massachusetts, who disliked Jones on general principles; Commodore Gillon, who declared that Jones had improperly issued commissions to captains of " an amphibious squadron of French privateers " ; and, of course, Arthur Lee, now a member of Congress. A list of forty-seven questions was submitted to Jones by John Brown, secretary of a newly formed board of admiralty. These questions required answers covering Jones's whole term overseas, from the time of his sailing in the *Ranger* to the date of his return.

[200]

"The first thing I could perceive," wrote Jones, "on reading these interrogatories, if I had not known the fact before, was that Arthur Lee must have reached America some time ahead of me. Many of the questions were clearly drawn either from his express dictation or by his own hand, because they involved presumptive versions, by implication, of certain events which no one but he could have taken the view of indicated by their wording."

Though Jones was convinced the board was packed against him, and so declared, he wrote his answers to the absurdly long list of questions — some of them silly and others merely malicious — in the same spirit in which he had weathered storms and won battles; he was cool, resourceful and determined to master the situation, though he did not completely suppress an occasional vein of irony. For example, this was Question No. 35:

"When and why did Capt. Landais resume command of the *Alliance* at l'Orient? Why did you acquiesce in the same? What passengers and what and whose private property were brought to the United States in the *Alliance?*"

Jones at once perceived the trap that lay hidden in this question. Prior to the *Alliance's* departure Lee had tried to take on board her, as baggage, two *Louis Seize* horse-carriages, some furniture, and assorted bric-à-brac, although every inch of space was needed for munitions and clothing. On Jones's protesting to Franklin, Lee had transferred this private cargo to another ship. It was Lee's evident purpose to lead Jones, by means of this important question, into charges which could be easily refuted. But Jones promptly picked up the burden and placed it back on the shoulders of Lee himself, as follows:

"Captain Landais repossessed himself of the *Alliance* the 13th of June. Mr. Arthur Lee and the rest of his counsellors can best answer why he sailed contrary to my orders as well as contrary to the orders of Dr. Franklin. The passengers he had on board, to the best of my knowledge, were Mr. Lee, his two nephews, Mr. M. Livingstone, Major Frazer, Mr. Brown, and three officers now with the Marquis de Lafayette. I heard of no others. I cannot answer as to what or whose private property might have been on board the *Alliance* at the time she left France."

Jones's answers were laid before Congress, which appointed a committee of three to deal with them. This committee summoned the Commodore before them and for three days grilled him at length. Jones had been careful to preserve copies of all his orders, letters, and other documents, and he brought a mass of them with which he answered all oral queries in detail. By the time he had finished his story, the committee was his.

" I confess," wrote James M. Varnum, of Rhode Island, one of three inquisitors, " there was a magic about his way and manner that I had never before seen. Whatever he said carried conviction with it. From his beginning no one thought of disputing with him. Toward the end we seldom ventured to ask him any questions. He made himself master of the situation throughout. At the end the committee felt honored by having had the privilege of listening to him."

II

Meantime Jones's friends, among whom was Robert Morris, had been active, and even before the answers to the questionnaire were completed, they pushed through Congress resolutions expressing " a high sense of the distinguished bravery and military conduct of John Paul Jones, esq., captain in the navy of the United States," and concluding with the statement that Louis XVI's " offer of adorning Captain Jones with a cross of military merit is highly acceptable to Congress."

Two days later, on March 1, 1781, the Articles of Confederation of the United States of America were adopted unanimously after a three years' delay in ratification by Maryland. They expressly forbade any officer of the United States to " accept any present, emolument, office or title of any kind whatever from any king, prince or foreign state " ; so Jones's position as a decorated Chevalier of France was and remained unique.

Having received the admiralty board's report, which cleared both Jones and Franklin of all blame for the delay in forwarding the much-discussed supplies from France, Congress then passed formal resolutions of thanks to Jones for his " zeal, prudence and intrepidity," and at Jones's own request, added a paragraph extending these thanks " to the officers and men who have faithfully served under him from time to time."

Jones promptly wrote to General Washington offering him a copy of his vindication, and adding:

" Our navy has been badly conducted: it has ever been without a head, and is now almost entirely lost; though its operations have done little for the cause and less for the flag. I have pointed out many desirable operations that promised success and would have taught the barbarous Britons humanity; but my voice has been a cry in the desert."

He appended a melancholy reminder that he was then " unemployed in actual service " and begged for Washington's influence so that he " could be instrumental to put the naval force that remains on a more useful and honorable footing."

In all his life Jones never wrote a letter with more pathetic implications than this. At the very moment when the country which he had ardently served most needed proven talent and ability, it permitted him to wander idly about the streets of Philadelphia with the medal of a foreign prince on his chest but with scarcely a pound in his pockets.

Even Robert Morris, who had been appointed head of the Marine Committee, was compelled to confess that " the present state of our affairs " would not permit him to employ Jones and expressed his " great concern that there was so little probability that he (Jones) would be able to render his talents useful to that country which he had already so faithfully served and with so great disinterestedness."

In his horror of idleness Jones entertained the desperate thought of finding active service on land where he could not on sea, and asked that he be permitted to join Lafayette's forces operating against Cornwallis in Virginia; but even here he could not obtain a definite decision from the distracted heads of government.

Two incidents brought him a little cheer. One was a reply from General Washington which said:

" Whether our naval affairs, in general, have been well or ill conducted it would be presumptuous for me to determine. Instances of bravery and good conduct in several of our officers have not, however, been wanting. Delicacy forbids me to mention that *particular one*, which has attracted the admiration of all the world, and which has influenced a most illustrious monarch to confer a mark of his favor which can only be obtained by a long and honorable service, or by the performance of some brilliant action."

Jones now again tried to obtain his restoration to the proper rank of which John Hancock's easy-going methods had deprived him. A committee examined his claims, and reported that with regard to his appointment as captain, he should stand fifth on the seniority list; or with regard to his lieutenant's appointment, he should be second. But rival captains, on hearing of this, pulled political wires so successfully that Congress pigeon-holed the report, marked " not to be acted upon."

III

Six months passed, and then Congress ordered a ballot to choose a commander for the first American ship-of-the-line, supposed to be ready for launching at Portsmouth, New Hampshire. Her name was the *America,* and in size and equipment she was in those days regarded as a perfect Dreadnaught. Several captains hoped to walk her quarter-deck. Jones's victory was immense. He was elected unanimously, and it was a day's sensation when it became known that even Arthur Lee had voted for him. Moreover, John Adams suspended his enmity long enough to write from The Hague:

" Indeed, if I could see a prospect of half a dozen line of battle ships under the American flag, commanded by Commodore Paul Jones, engaged with an equal British force, I apprehend the event would be so glorious for the United States, and lay so sure a foundation for their prosperity, that it would be a rich compensation for the continuance of the war."

Jones was so pleased that he promptly put all his grievances out of mind and even forbore to press the matter of his due rank. " Thus," says his *Journal,* " Congress took a delicate method to avoid cabal and to do justice. It was more agreeable to Captain Jones to be so honorably elected captain of the line than to have been, as was proposed by the committee, raised at once to the rank of rear admiral, because Congress had not then the means of giving a command suitable to that rank."

He then asked Congress to settle his long-delayed accounts. He had received some advances on prize-money, but of pay not a shilling. His accounts were approved, but no allowance was made for expenses or for interest on loans he had made to the government. Despite Congress's approval, no cash arrived, and Morris had to advance the defender of the rights of the sea enough to pay his fare to Portsmouth.

IV

But once more high of heart, Jones bounded off to New Hampshire, already seeing in his mind's eye a picture of himself leading an all-American squadron against the English, with himself on the quarter-deck of a magnificent seventy-four, 1982 tons burden, complement 626 officers and men. However, he found her not even fully planked, with rigging and sails wanting, and with not even sufficient iron at hand for making fastenings. Only twenty-four carpenters were at work, and few of these knew how to make the calculations on so large a ship.

"The task of inspecting the construction of the *America*," he wrote, "was the most lingering and disagreeable service I was charged with during the whole period of the Revolution," but he adhered to it with his usual steadfastness, and on November 29, 1781, joined heartily in the celebration with which Portsmouth vented its joy at the surrender of Cornwallis, in October, to General Washington and Count Rochambeau at Yorktown. Almost a year elapsed before the *America*, greatly altered according to his own designs, was ready for launching, but meantime Jones was made happy by the presence of such stout assistants as Henry Gardner, and Elijah Hall, and by the enthusiastic enlistment of nearly 100 men from his old *Ranger* and *Richard* crews.

His relatively peaceful life at Portsmouth, where he constantly received the social attentions that never failed to please him, again inclined him toward dreams of domesticity, and he seems to have had designs on a "fair daughter of Liberty," who was to be won with the aid of John Brown, secretary of the admiralty board, then staying at Boston. One day he wrote to Brown:

"There is one delicate subject of a private nature on which you remain silent, though, as I wrote you to Boston, I expected to hear much from you on that head. Your silence, I fear, carries with it a disagreeable meaning. Present, if you please, my respects to my fair friends, as I have done yours here."

Brown's silence did indeed prove to carry a disagreeable meaning, and nothing more was said about this delicate subject. The Commodore continued to send remittances to his Aimée in Paris.

V

In August, 1782, the *America* was almost completed, and Jones was joyfully selecting his officers, including the well-tried Richard Dale, Nathaniel Fanning, John Mayrant, Edward Stack, and Hall and Gardner, when the *Magnifique*, a seventy-four belonging to the fleet of the French Admiral, the Marquis de Vaudreuil, was wrecked at Boston harbor. This fleet was part of a vast Franco-Spanish armada which was to assemble under Count d'Estaing and Admiral Don Solano in the West Indies and there destroy the British fleet under Admirals Hood and Pigott. On hearing this news, Jones wrote to Gouverneur Morris, assistant secretary of finance:

" Your kind letter, my dear Morris, of the 13th ult. and the public one of the same date, are as welcome favors and as necessary to me as fresh air and the saving hand of friendship to a drowning man. I know your ability and am convinced your friendship will manifest itself so effectually that we may avail of the loss of the *Magnifique* at Boston . . . I can take no delight in the effusion of human blood, but if this war should continue, I wish to have the most active part in it."

This letter, signed J. Paul Jones, was dated Sept. 2, 1782. The next day Congress voted to give the *America* to the King of France, to replace, it was announced, the lost *Magnifique*, but Robert Morris afterwards confessed it was because he had no money to complete her with; and Jones was ordered to turn his beautiful ship over to the French commander, the Chevalier de Martigne.

It was the tenth promising command of which Jones, through no fault of his own, had been deprived.

[207]

CHAPTER XXVII

The Evils of Peace

Down dropt the breeze, the sails dropt down,
'Twas sad as sad could be;
And we did speak only to break
The silence of the sea.

I

IT would be interesting to know upon what ideal John Paul Jones, during his formative years, had fixed his gaze. That it was a lofty one is certain, for at such moments as this he rose to it with a true eighteenth century grandeur. He surrendered his cherished *America* to the French with a generous bow, and whatever bitterness he felt was withheld from his letter of renunciation to Robert Morris, who replied:

" I have read your letter of the 22nd of last month. The sentiments contained in it will always reflect the highest honor upon your character. They have made so strong an impression on my mind that I immediately transmitted an extract of your letter to Congress."

With these thanks in his pocket but little else there, Jones left the little colonial town and once more found himself in Philadelphia among the unemployed. It is tragic to have to record that his gesture of abnegation bestowed no benefit on anyone. The French could not get the *America* ready in time, and sailed to the West Indies without her. She did not fire a shot against the enemy during the war. She did not reach France until peace had been declared, and the only consolation Jones could have drawn from the episode was to learn that the French, in compliment to his friend, the renowned Doctor who could borrow money from them with an ability equalled only by the French commissioners to Washington in 1917–1918, had renamed her the *Franklin*.

II

Meantime the war went on, English hopes having been freshly stimulated by the thumping victory of Admiral Rodney over the majestic fleet of Count de Grasse at Martinique — a victory which well-nigh destroyed the sea power of France and insured British domination over the routes through the Caribbean Sea.

Robert Morris then held out a dim hope by assuring Jones that he would try to obtain the *South Carolina,* the renamed *Indien,* for him, but the legal snarls into which the unhappy Commodore Gillon fell, due to the suit begun by the Chevalier de Luxembourg, prevented this, and Jones was again without so much as a prospect.

At that time the American navy consisted of exactly three seaworthy fighting ships — the *Alliance,* the *America,* and the *Deane,* a little sloop of thirty guns. The *Alliance* had been given to John Barry; the *America* had been presented to France; and the *Deane* was scarcely worthy of a captain of the line. Morris, busy with his own and the nation's finances, could think of nothing; so Jones, whose pride would not permit him to remain looking out of the window of his Philadelphia boarding house, asked that he be permitted to join the departing fleet of the Marquis de Vaudreuil as a volunteer, to gain " military marine knowledge in order to better serve my country when America should increase her navy."

Congress, with many laudations, but no cash on account, readily gave Jones this permission, and at Boston he boarded the French flagship, *Triomphante,* to be received there with hearty greetings by sixty officers of Rochambeau's former army at Newport, now on their way to attack the island of Jamaica under the Baron de Viomesnil. Among these Frenchmen were vigorous and talented young fellows who had been drawn to America by the romantic example of Lafayette, and they afterwards played their part in the French Revolution which so quickly followed the American one.

The squadron sailed south on December 24, but the expedition, so gaily begun, ended in a fiasco. Storms separated the transports from the frigates, and the French ship *Bourgoyne*, striking a rock, foundered with enormous loss of life. Don Solano, the Spanish admiral, failed to keep his rendezvous, and the cruise was continued to the Venezuelan coast at Porto Cabello without accomplishing any object. Tropical heat and unhealthful food brought on illness. Among the victims was Jones, who was already sick from frustrated hopes.

Then arrived a French ship carrying a white flag at her masthead — symbol of the war's end on January 21, 1783. This news brought Jones out of his bed to join the other officers in cheers for American independence. He wrote letters of congratulation to Morris, to de Castries, to de Genêt, and to the Duc de la Rochefoucauld, and could not refrain from sending a note to the faithless Countess de Lowendahl announcing his hopes of returning to France.

He took a ship back to Philadelphia with letters of praise for his deportment from the Marquis de Vaudreuil and the Baron de Viomesnil, but suffering from a return of the intermittent fevers of which he had never been entirely free since his slave-trading days. To recuperate he went to Bethlehem, Pa., to enjoy the hospitality of the Moravian brethren who, throughout the Revolution, had maintained a rest home for sick and wounded officers of both the American and French armies. Entries regarding Jones's presence are still visible in the Moravian archives there.

In a letter to John Ross, evidently that of a tired and sick man, though Jones was then only thirty-six years old, he mentioned his desire to marry and settle down on a farm he hoped to purchase near the present site of Newark, N. J. He added that such property ought to become valuable, since it was near New York, which he was sure was destined to become a great and populous port.

III

Returning to Philadelphia, he again pleaded with Morris for restoration to his proper rank, this having again been called in question by the presentation to France of the *America*. He wrote:

" I have met with many humiliations in the service that I have borne in silence. I will just mention one of them. When the *America* was presented to His Most Christian Majesty, I presume it would not have been inconsistent with that act of my sovereign if it had mentioned my name. Such little attentions to the military pride of officers are always of use to a state and cost nothing."

Again he wrote:

" I hope I shall be pardoned in saying it will not be expected, after having fought and bled for the purpose of contributing to make millions happy and free, that I should remain miserable and dishonored by being superseded without any just cause assigned."

Besides the question of his rank, the failure of his men to obtain the prize-money due them from Europe had fretted him no little. He now asked Congress to appoint him agent empowered to go abroad and settle these claims as well as to gain further marine knowledge. A committee reported favorably, the last named signed being that of Arthur Lee. Jones, with official dispatches in his pocket for John Adams at The Hague, and Franklin at Paris, sailed from Philadelphia on the packet *Washington*. Among the passengers was Major l'Enfant, upon whose plans the city of Washington was laid out. The captain was Joshua Barney, one of the few American commanders whom Jones was always ready to praise. During the voyage Barney conversed with Jones often, but found him inclined to be reserved, his manner indicating that he had something on his mind about which he did not care to talk.

RECEIVED AS A CONQUERING HERO IN THE SALONS OF PARIS.

CHAPTER XXVIII

The Collection Agent

I pass, like night, from land to land;
I have strange power of speech;
That moment that his face I see,
I know the man that must hear me:
To him my tale I teach.

I

TO Barney's surprise, Jones insisted on being put ashore at Plymouth, though there was still some danger that he might be seized as the " pirate and renegade " which the English had always declared him to be. However, he was not molested when he took a post-chaise for London, and he was soon safe in the capital where a few months previous terrible things might have happened to him.

There is some evidence that Jones's haste to reach London was to establish connections for a commercial enterprise, through which he hoped to recoup himself for the personal losses he had sustained during the war and to fill the gap left in his bank account by the failure of Congress to pay him his due. Letters exist showing that soon after partly recovering his health at Bethlehem, he was obtaining cargoes of whale oil on credit and sending them on French merchant ships to France and Holland, where they were sold by the agents and bankers he had met when abroad. This oil, used for lighting, fetched high prices, and assisted by Dr. Bancroft, Jones in the course of a few months pocketed tidy sums which made him independent of a poverty-stricken Congress. There is no other way to account for his way of living, which was never penurious, during his months of unemployment ashore. For example, in a letter to Dr. Bancroft at London he asks him to obtain a partial settlement of an account of £5,175 due him and his associates from the famous John Ledyard, who had been an officer of Captain Cook in his celebrated voyage around the world.

Other documents indicated that in 1785 Jones and Ledyard had formed a scheme for trading in furs to be obtained from the Northwest Territory, then a promised land which Lewis and Clarke surveyed a quarter of a century later. The peltry was to be exchanged for " gold or other commodities " in Japan or China. It was calculated that a single voyage from France of a vessel of 250 tons would produce a profit of £36,250 — provided that 3,000 skins could be obtained on the northwest coast at the customary low figure and sold in China at the equivalent of " 10 Louis a-piece." Robert Morris promised to take a hand in it. This particular scheme, however, fell through, due to opposition from Spain. It was just such get-rich-quick speculations which eventually led to the ruin of Morris.

II

It was thus that the old trading instincts of John Paul, the quondam Scotch merchant captain, were revived. However, on reading London newspapers, he learned John Adams was there, and he at once reported to him with his dispatches. Adams, much amazed to find John Paul Jones, of all people, in the British capital, examined the papers and informed him they referred to the opening of commercial treaties with Holland. Such documents, he told Jones, must be referred to Franklin, and he advised the Commodore to go to Paris with them at once. Jones, cutting short his own errand, did so, and quickly found himself again in that city where so much of his own history, as well as that of numberless other restless human beings, was being made.

Franklin took charge of the dispatches and left Jones free once more to re-open his struggle with the French government for a settlement of his prize-claims. He soon renewed old friendships, but there was one call which he must have been slow in making, if we may judge by a forlorn note from the Countess de Nicolson. It bears this matter-of-fact endorsement in Jones's writing: "From her apartments in the Boulevard."

"Is it possible that you then are so near me and that I am deprived of the sight of a being who has constituted the misery of my life for four years? O most amiable and most ungrateful of men, come to your best friend, who burns with a desire of seeing you. You ought to know that it is but eight days since your Delia was at the brink of the grave. Come, in the name of heaven."

After this there falls a silence.

III

De Castries, who had always been friendly, now received Jones with cordiality and procured him a luncheon with Louis XVI, "a distinction," we are told, "that no naval officer under the rank of admiral had enjoyed in France since Louis XIV similarly entertained Jean Bart." At the same time Jones was also received by Marie Antoinette, who was disposed to be a little more friendly to the Americans, now that her lover, Count de Fersen, had safely returned from the wilds of Newport, Rhode Island, where he had been long and idly immured with the expedition of Rochambeau.

The King was gracious and promised Jones all due help; but as soon as the Commodore officially presented his claims before the *maître des requêtes*, or cashier's office, a thousand obstacles and vexatious delays arose. They continued for nearly two years. Those ministers who knew Jones and admired his achievements wished him to be promptly paid, but their sympathy was of little avail in face of the fact that the golden sands in the treasury of Louis XVI were fast running out. The dismissal of the great Turgot, who had labored for a pay-as-you-go policy, had left the field open to thimble-rigging financiers who were accumulating a weight of debt that eventually lent power to the axe which cleaved Louis's neck. Jones's demand for money simply came as an additional embarrassment to the shaky tower of financial toy-blocks which a few years later crashed in the dust of the French Revolution.

Another delay-making circumstance was the fact that de Chaumont's accounts for advances made to the *Bon Homme Richard* expedition were entangled with Jones's own; and the Commodore lost his temper when he found that de Chaumont had charged him with the unused services of the hospital for wounded at Paris, for repairs to prizes, and for feeding Jones's five hundred prisoners at the Texel. With dignity he wrote to de Castries:

" I will not now complain that the prisoners I took . . . were not exchanged for Americans. It was all the reward I asked for the anxious days and sleepless nights I passed . . . in the glad hope of giving them *all* their liberty."

Franklin, after making a protest in Jones's behalf, lost a portion of his serenity too, and sent a ruffled letter to the persistent Commodore, saying: " If I can once get rid of this business, nothing shall ever induce me to approach it again. I know nothing about it, I never did know anything about it, and I am too old to begin learning it." After assuring Jones he would " approve anything you may recommend," he concluded: " But I beg you to have mercy on me, and refrain from bothering me any more with masses of technical details, and even sea-lingo, which is worse than Greek to me altogether."

Jones's reply was humble: "If I have invaded your peace or disturbed your tranquillity I am sorry and beg your forgiveness. . . . I trust you will permit me to subscribe myself your most devoted and obedient foster son."

IV

In time the French government waived one counter-charge after another, but four months elapsed before the Marine Ministry approved the statement of liquidation, and it then deferred payment for another interval on the ground that Jones's credentials must be passed upon by Thomas Jefferson, the new American plenipotentiary. From July to September, 1785, Jones waited at Lorient for the money, and then suddenly the lump sum was paid into his hands. It amounted to 181,039 livres, nominally equivalent to the same number of shillings but actually worth much less. From this Jones was provisionally permitted to deduct 47,972 livres for his expenses over three years and for advances made to his officers. This left a balance of 157,483 livres for the officers and crews of the *Bon Homme Richard* and the *Alliance*, Jones refusing to diminish their dividend by making any charge for his time or trouble spent in the exhausting task of collection.

In high elation Jones carried the money to Jefferson at Paris, who calmly took possession of the whole sum, informing Jones that he could not even touch his share until the deduction had been approved by the Treasury officials at home! Unknown to Jones, Jefferson had been instructed by Samuel Osgood and Walter Livingstone, of the United States Board of Treasury, to place the money where he "might judge best, as it is destined for the express and sole object of paying the salaries of yourself and other ministers in Europe." Otherwise, they hinted, these diplomatic expenses could not be met. This meant that Jones and his men would not, after all, receive their money for a long time. And a long time it was. What the French, if they learned of it, thought of this disposition of the money, already so long withheld from American sailors and their families, is not recorded. As for John Paul Jones, he did not even have sufficient cash in hand to proceed to Denmark, whose treasury he was next due to assail.

v

He remained in Paris in the hope of interesting the French government in various business projects, and at one time was encouraged to believe he would be appointed the leader of an expedition against the pirates of Algiers, who had been making the Mediterranean unsafe for both French and American ships, but the distracting problems of peace left officials with but little time to listen to the schemes of an out-of-work naval officer, and nothing resulted.

In 1785 he was admitted to the Order of the Cincinnati, composed of French and American officers who had served under Washington, who was somewhat fancifully supposed to have been called to the supreme command from his Mount Vernon plough. Jones was inordinately proud of his membership in this association. At home, however, the order was almost at once bitterly attacked by factionalists who saw in it a subversive society subtly designed to introduce foreign ideas and monarchical institutions into free America.

Meantime something was going on around him of which Jones was at first unaware. On February 18, 1785, the Earl of Wemyss, a Scotsman then in Paris, wrote to an unidentified correspondent:

" My Lord: Since coming to Paris I have made the acquaintance of my compatriot the celebrated Commodore Paul Jones.

Your Highness knows that he distinguished himself in the last war and that he is brave as well as a great sailor; with that, he is an agreeable man full of all kinds of knowledge. I can see that he does not love an inactive life and without having spoken positively to him of the service, I think he would not be averse to it, though he is well off; if your Highness finds it advisable to write of him to the Russian court, if need be I will undertake to speak with him."

In March the Earl wrote that he had sounded Jones, and that he was sure if advantageous terms were offered him, " he would prefer the service of his Imperial Majesty to all others."

VI

The next year Jones completed and presented to Louis XVI his patiently prepared *Journal,* which was his *apologia pro vita sua.* Like Caesar, Napoleon, and U. S. Grant at other periods, Jones found that the deeds of the man of action must be supplemented by the work of the scribe if his achievements are to be appreciated. And like them, he found it best to be his own eye-witness and recorder. Jones had a sufficient appreciation of himself as an historical figure, and he meant that posterity should not forget him, though his contemporaries might. As a writer Jones expressed himself surprisingly well for a man whose academic education had been so meager; being intent on the content rather than the form of his narrative, he avoided the weaknesses to which the professional writer is prone, and composed his sentences with a sinewy vigor, directness, and egotism. He first submitted his manuscript for examination to the sagacious Malesherbes, the King's adviser, who returned it " quite intact," with this suave letter:

" I have read with great eagerness and pleasure your most interesting relation. My first impulse was to desire you to have it published, but after having read it more carefully I perceive

[219]

that you did not write it with a view to publication, because there are passages in it which are written to the King, for whose information alone they are intended. However, actions so memorable as yours ought to be made known to the world by an authentic journal published in your own name. I earnestly entreat you to work at it as soon as your affairs may permit; and in the meantime I believe the King will read this particular narrative with that attention which he owes to a relation of services rendered to him by a person so celebrated."

Jones accepted the hint and, assisted by secretaries who spread the oil of grammar over his wave-tossed English, prepared further journals in 1787, 1790 and 179   His collected writings would fill a ponderous volume.

VII

While preparing to go to Denmark to press for a settlement in the case of the three prizes which that country — illegally, he contended — had returned to England, Jones was again prostrated by a severe illness. Those who believe that illness frequently has its origin in mental or psychic no less than in physical states, would find considerable ground for their belief in the record of Jones's various maladies. At this stage of his career he was seldom in good health. His repeated vain attempts to break through the doughlike ring of inertia around him, added to long strain, exposures at sea, and cumulative disappointments, were fast breaking him down, although in years he was at the prime of life.

However, he recovered enough to go to London on his private affairs, crossing from Ostend on an English packet. " It was the first time," he noted, " since 1773 that I had trod an English deck with the King's colors flying. I own that for a moment the sensation was queer." In London he was hospitably received on the Underwriters Exchange at Lloyd's, an observer describing him as of " middle stature, slender build, has delicate features, a swarthy complextion, his attire is of the most faultless make-up, and his bearing martial and imposing to the last degree."

Returning to the Continent, he learned that his business affairs in New York were endangered, and it was also intimated to him by Jefferson that if he hoped to collect the prize-money due him, he had better apply to Congress in person. So he again took ship for America, arriving in New York July 2, 1787. He laid his representations before John Jay, then "Secretary for Foreign Affairs," and learned from him that the Board of Treasury had raised some question as to the correctness of his accounts. On investigating, Jones once more discovered the malignant spoor of Arthur Lee, who had recently been made a member of the board. Lee not only opposed Jones's claims but demanded that the Commodore furnish large security before proceeding to Denmark. Jones replied, flatly declining to give security as if he were " a common agent or messenger," and pointing out that his accounts had been approved both by Franklin and Jefferson.

Congress then voted Jones not the cash but a gold medal commemorating his services, and requested Jay to notify Louis XVI of this action by a letter to be delivered by Jones personally. At the same time the King was asked to permit Jones to embark with the French fleets of evolution for the purpose of acquiring greater naval knowledge.

The Board of Treasury then took up Jones's account " for deferred pay, advances, expenses, and special services from Dec. 1775, to Oct. 1787." Deducting the £400 advanced to Jones by Morris, Jones stated the balance was £5,013-18s-1d. The board, pleading poverty, offered 2000 guineas on account. But Jones scorned " any partial payment at a time when arrears are due to everyone who served our cause in all ranks," adding that he had in French, Belgian and Dutch banks

[221]

" a sum greater than the total of the account under consideration."

Whether this was a magniloquent falsehood told to save his
pride, or whether his European bank accounts were unavail-
able at the moment, there is no means of knowing; but it had
been only a few days since he had written to Aimée de Tellison, in care of Jefferson, " I am almost without money, and
much puzzled to obtain a supply. I have written Dr. Bancroft to endeavor to assist me."

Jones never received his pay from the United States, either
then or during his life. Congress did not settle the account
till 1848, fifty-six years after the patriotic Commodore's death,
when it paid $50,000 to the women who were his heirs. " The
people " who had bled and died with Jones were entirely forgotten.

Jones's four months' visit home, however, was replete with
social if not with pecuniary triumphs. He was a dinner-party
lion of high degree, but what pleased him more were visits of
respect paid to him by his comrades of the fighting deck, including Dale, Fanning, Lunt, Stacy, Hall, Gardner, Potter and
Mayrant. The last dinner given to him took place at the New
York home of John Jay on November 10, 1787. The next
day he sailed for Europe, never to return.

John Paul Jones had no mind for the whirlpools of politics,
or for the conditions which the froth of political brews concealed. If he had, he might have detected, almost from mid-
ocean, the gigantic clouds hanging over that Europe which
in his day had always been held so securely in the grasp of ruling princes. And he might have foreseen that these clouds
would break into a storm which would be bound to affect his
fortunes. Only a few weeks previous, Congress had addressed
Louis XVI, in Jones's behalf, as " Great and Beloved Friend."
But already Louis's own subjects were speaking of him in quite
different terms.

CHAPTER XXIX

The Call from the East

It raised my hair, it fanned my cheek
Like a meadow-gale of spring —
It mingled strangely with my fears,
Yet it felt like a welcoming.

I

JONES first delivered dispatches to Adams in London, vainly tried to raise some money through Bancroft, and then hastened to Paris, whence he had recently received no word from the person whose happiness, he wrote, was dearer to him " than anything else." In the course of the previous October he had written from New York to Madame Tellison that he had been " on the rack of fear and apprehension. . . . I have been honoured here beyond my expectations. But your silence makes even honours insipid."

On reaching Paris he sent a messenger to Jefferson with a mysterious note requesting him to call at his hotel, but instructing Jefferson not to ask for him by name but simply for " the gentleman just arrived." He added that he had " several strong reasons for desiring that no person should know of my being here until I have seen you and have been favoured with your advice as to the course I ought to pursue." Jefferson during their interview informed Jones that he had been in communication with M. Simolin, the Russian ambassador at Versailles, who had made known the desire of his sovereign, Catherine II, that Jones should enter her service to fight the Turks in the Black Sea. Jefferson recommended that the Commodore consider the invitation favorably. It appears from the diplomatic papers of the period that the Virginian thought Jones's presence in Russia might help to cement a trade treaty between that country and the United States, and might in any case make a friend for an infant nation which needed all the friends that could be gained for it. Jefferson had evidently advised Washington about the negotiations, for soon there arrived from Mount Vernon a note saying: " I am glad our Commodore Paul Jones has got employment."

In this expression of relief the General doubtless echoed the opinion of his late associates; for neither in the army, the navy, nor the government, did anyone ever quite know what to do with Commodore Jones.

II

Concerning the Russian invitation, Jones was at first skeptical, and in his *Journal* remarks that he " lost no time in setting the wits of Little Madame at work to trace out the mystery." This " Little Madame " was doubtless Aimée de Tellison. She found that the Empress Catherine had originally asked Louis XVI for the loan of an able French officer to organize and command the Black Sea navy. But the King's ministers had advised him against appearing to take sides with Russia against Turkey, so Louis had avoided this difficulty by suggesting the name of John Paul Jones. Through the same lady Jones also learned that Catherine had already engaged for the same purpose the services of the Prince of Nassau-Siegen, a Franco-German adventurer whom Jones had met at Amsterdam during the negotiations for the *Indien*, of sad memory. This plausible combination of Stephen Sayre and Baron Munchausen had once so impressed himself upon Arthur Lee at Paris that Lee had induced the other American commissioners, Deane and Franklin, to give him employment in Holland. There the Prince had " reported upon " the construction of the *Indien* and had graciously offered himself as a commander in one of Jones's proposed land-and-sea expeditions. He had at the court of Marie Antoinette an assured position, which had not been disturbed by his farcical failures as a French colonel in attacks on the island of Jersey and the fortress of Gibraltar. The European courts of the eighteenth century were full of such characters, who frequently had the ear of impressionable women, and through them pulled many concealed wires.

III

After several interviews with Simolin, Jones left Paris, at his own expense, for Copenhagen, arriving there ill and worn. He was in bed a week. The flattering reception given him by Count Bernsdorff, the Danish premier, however, helped to revive him, and when a few days later the French Minister, Baron de la Houze, presented him at court, he was well enough to feel the glow which never failed to suffuse his being when in the presence of the great.

" The Queen Dowager," he wrote, " conversed with me for some time and said the most civil things. . . . The Princess Royal is a charming person, and the graces are so much her own, that it is impossible to see and converse with her without paying her that honour which artless beauty and good nature will ever command. . . . His Majesty saluted me with great complaisance at first and as often afterwards as we met in the course of the evening. . . . The company at table, consisting of seventy ladies and gentlemen, including the royal family, the ministers of state, and foreign ambassadors, was very brilliant."

These social attentions, however, only served to soften the blow which Bernsdorff dealt to the Commodore when he informed him he could not deal with him any further because Jones lacked sufficient diplomatic powers. Jones's mission to Denmark was thus at an abrupt end, and since he was once more unemployed and without cash, there was no other path for him to take than that from which a hand had been extended — Russia.

On April 8, 1788, he wrote Jefferson a long letter tinged with melancholy. " I shall now set out for St. Petersburg," he announced. After hinting that it would help him in Russia if Congress would make him a Rear Admiral, he asked Jefferson " to justify to the United States the important step I now take," since he had not " forsaken the country that has had many disinterested and difficult proofs of my steady affection, and I can never renounce the glorious title of a citizen of the United States." He added that in accepting service under Catherine II, he regarded himself as obeying the wishes of Congress that he utilize all opportunities for improvement in his profession.

Meantime Simolin was writing from Paris to Potemkin: " I congratulate myself, My Lord, on having been the first means of securing this officer, who is one of those geniuses whom nature rarely produces." Simolin added this in a letter to Count Besborodko, his chief: " Mr. Jefferson, who knows the character of the said chevalier, pointed out that on great and dangerous missions this officer, who is as spirited as he is disinterested, will be better employed as chief than under the orders of a superior." Which reveals that Jefferson knew his man.

Potemkin replied, without enthusiasm, " I will do all in my power to place him comfortably and to advantage," and Catherine wrote to her Paris factotum, Baron de Grimm: " Friend Paul Jones will be well received and welcome . . . but have the kindness not to make a great noise about it, so that no one may prevent our getting him."

She ordered Potemkin to appoint Jones to the grade of Rear Admiral as soon as he should present himself. She also ordered a thousand Dutch ducats to be advanced to him for travelling expenses. She waited impatiently for a glimpse of her new acquisition.

IV

It was once believed by European gossips that Catherine, attracted by the fame and gallantry of John Paul Jones, sent for him with a view to adding him to her staff of lovers, and that she expected the bold Scotch-American to impart a new sensation to her somewhat worn emotions. To bolster up this theory, they cited the evident coolness of Potemkin, chiefest of her favorites, towards the importation of Jones. For this ingenious hypothesis there is little ground. Potemkin was already in the position of a past-master, or alumnus, of Catherine's boudoirs, and was content with his vast power as first adviser and commander-in-chief to the temperamental empress. Catherine herself was content at the moment with the lovers provided for her by the helpful Potemkin. There was abundant reason for the engagement of Jones on purely material grounds. Russia was once more reviving her historic attempts, continued by spasms up to the final effort, collapse and destruction of the imperial system in 1917, to force the Turk out of Europe, to capture Constantinople, and to get astride an ice-free sea at the Straits of Bosphorus. She also meant to hold off her defeated enemies, Sweden and Poland. To accomplish this, she needed a navy, adequately organized and competently commanded. Within her own borders she had little naval talent. Having tried commanders brought from the eastern ports of the Mediterranean with farcical results, Catherine obtained a few naval officers from England and Holland. To counterbalance these, she sought trained commanders from France. Failing to obtain Louis XVI's consent, she gladly accepted Jones, no doubt being stimulated by Simolin's suggestion that " if her Imperial Majesty should confide to Jones the chief command of her fleet in the Black Sea, with *carte blanche*, he would answer for it, that in less than a year Jones would make Constantinople tremble." Her interest in Jones may also have been heightened by the fact that he was a Freemason, she herself having become *tutrice* of the Masonic Lodge of Clio in Moscow.

V

Though Jones usually had scant interest in politics, holding that it was his sole " duty to obey those whose province it is to make and enforce laws," he ventured, before he left Western Europe, to send to Jefferson a memorandum of his observations on the adoption of the United States Constitution, the debates upon which he had witnessed before last leaving America. These remarks, whatever may be thought of their correctness, are clearly and thoughtfully expressed, and indicate that under other circumstances John Paul Jones might have been useful in the councils of statesmen. They disclose him as a Federalist and an upholder of a strong central authority; in which respect he differed from Jefferson and his other Virginia friends, who were unalterably tenacious of state and individual rights. Indeed, Jones mentioned a warm argument he had once had with Patrick Henry on this very subject. " I could not reason him out of the admission," wrote Jones, " that the absorption of power by any central government could mean anything but surrender of the rights of communities and the freedom of individuals."

The Commodore, who could be Democrat as well as Federalist, continued:

"This new constitution beyond question will create, when adopted by the necessary nine states, a firm and solid government. Its adoption is assured not only by nine at once, but by all eventually. There is but one clause in it that I would modify in any respect if I had the power. That is the one making the President commander-in-chief of the army and navy. This clause fails to draw in so many words the all-important distinction between civic and martial command."

This matter of the president's receiving so tremendous a power, a power still not possessed by any monarch in Europe, was a source of concern to Jones; he referred to it on at least three other occasions, notably in a letter to Lafayette:

" I hope, by the time the necessary nine states have adopted the new Constitution they will have provided in some way to divest the President of all actual and substantive military rank and command; for though General Washington might be safely trusted with such tempting power as the chief command of the fleet and the army, yet, depend on it, in some other hands it could not fail to overset the liberties of America."

VI

Having thus relieved his mind, Jones prepared to descend upon Russia — Holy Russia, at no time in history darker and more mysterious than then. Before his departure, he received news that the Danish king had bestowed on him a life grant of 1500 crowns annually " for the respect he had shown to the Danish flag while he commanded in the North Seas." This created a situation which Jones, as a claimant for prize-money, recognized as " embarrassing." He said nothing about it for three years, and then when circumstances made it necessary for him, with the approval of friends, to draw on this fund, he failed to collect a crown of it. It became another of those misfortunes which at times rose to mock him with an almost satanic malignancy. It was one of the penalties he paid for his naïve confidence in and admiration for the great and the highly placed.

He started for Russia with his usual impetuosity. He even

suppressed his misgiving when he learned he might have to divide his Black Sea command with the Prince of Nassau-Siegen. The project before him, he wrote, " opened up a vista of ambitious hopes and dreams of glory on a grand scale too powerful and vivid to be cast aside, and well worthy the most careful consideration and deepest meditation."

"Vista of ambitious hopes and dreams of glory " — he was never the man to resist such a cluster. Over innumerable seas he had chased rainbow after rainbow. At the end of this one he was certain he would find his pot of gold and glory.

Brest September 13th 1778

Honored Sir

I am not a mere adventurer of Fortune. — Stimulated by
principles of Reason and Philanthropy I laid aside my Enjoyments in Private Life and Embarked under the Flag of
America when it was first Displayed. —————

If I can furnish any projects or execute those —
already furnished so as to distress the common Enemy, it
will afford me the truest Satisfaction,

I am with great Esteem

Honored Sir

Your very obliged very obedient

very humble Servant

Jn P Jones

M. De Sartine.

LETTER, BELIEVED TO BE IN JONES'S OWN HANDWRITING, AD-
DRESSED TO M. DE SARTINE, THE FRENCH MINISTER
OF MARINE. AT THIS DATE THE CAPTAIN WAS
SIGNING HIMSELF "JNO. P. JONES."

CHAPTER XXX

Unholy Russia

Her lips were red, her looks were free,
Her locks were yellow as gold:
Her skin was as white as leprosy,
The Night-mare Life-in-Death was she,
Who thicks man's blood with cold.

I

FROM Copenhagen Jones set out through Sweden, and in his haste declined even to pause long enough in Stockholm to receive the social attentions of the court. On reaching the Gulf of Bothnia he found the sea blocked by ice. He decided to sail around it south through the Baltic sea. At Gresholm he chartered a thirty-foot boat, with a smaller one in tow, and without telling his plans to the boatmen, steered south along the coast of Sweden. At nightfall he headed across the open sea. A freezing gale blew them off their course and the boatmen began to grumble. When they proposed to turn back, Jones drew his pistol and ordered them to steer for the southern coast of the Gulf of Finland. The gale increased, but with demoniac fury Jones urged his men to push through the ice blocks and on through gusts of bitter wind clogged with snow. The small boat overturned and was lost, but Jones helped to rescue its frozen crew, and kept on, with one hand on the tiller, the other on his pistol, and his eyes fixed on the compass. To one in his weakened condition, such exposure was the reverse of good, but picturing the Empress as waiting, he permitted no sensible pause either for eating or sleeping. Too long had he been idle in counting houses and ante-rooms: he now had only one desire — to get into action again.

After four days and nights of furious labor, he grounded his boat at Reval, where his voyage was regarded as "a kind of miracle," as well it might be. Here he rewarded his men, stocked them with provisions, procured them a pilot, patted them on the back, and rushed on to St. Petersburg, where on May 2, 1788, he stood on the banks of the Neva and contemplated the palaces and ambitious buildings constructed by Peter the Great, who had meant to have an outpost of European culture there or burst.

In the city which the upheavals of history have since renamed Petrograd and re-renamed Leningrad, he was delighted to find the French ambassador, Count de Sègur, who had sailed with him in the squadron of the Marquis de Vaudreuil and who was friendly to Jones, as well as to all Americans. In three days the Count presented him to the Empress.

II

History has painted this self-made German woman, whom chance and revolution had placed on the throne of the world's vastest country, variously as a Messalina, a female Jack the Giant-Killer, a whiskerless Attila, a cheated and embittered mother, and a skirted Augustus Caesar. She was Roman, she was Oriental, she was Teutonic, she was both maternal and masculine, she was everything. Her unsated energy enabled her to fill all rôles, essay all tasks, meet all situations. In a burst of admiration, Voltaire changed "Catherine the Second" into "Catherine the Great." She cared for no man long — save the one-eyed Potemkin, whom she had picked out of the streets as an obscure cavalry subaltern and with whom she alternated in ruling Russia. Potemkin was her hairy lover, her Prince Charming, her spoiled Newfoundland puppy, her fractious child who would not wash behind his ears, her grand opera basso. By turns he bossed her and kowtowed to her, he yelled at her and kissed her hand, he ignored her and called her babyish and insinuating names, he puzzled her and frightened her. She knew him, she loved him, and she was afraid of him.

Catherine could be a fish-cold despot; she could also be gracious and dazzling. She proceeded to dazzle John Paul Jones. It was easy; she was a woman, a monarch, the mistress of an effulgent court. He was not proof against any one of these, let alone the combined trio. He wrote giddily to Lafayette:

" The empress received me with a distinction the most flattering that perhaps any stranger can boast of. I was detained against my will [under the circumstances a pardonable falsehood] and continually feasted at court and in the best society. . . . For the empress fame has never yet done her justice. I am sure that no stranger who has not known that illustrious character ever conceived how much her majesty is made to reign over a great empire; to make people happy, and to attach grateful and susceptible minds."

For a fortnight Jones was feasted, petted, and massaged by the unctuous hands of flattery. The most pretentious nobles, the most seasoned veterans of war and diplomacy, called on him and treated him as an equal and a saviour. His cool Scotch head began to swim. His Caledonian caution melted in the warm, scented currents of Tsarskoe-Seloe. " *Je me laissai séduire* — I let myself be seduced," he confessed; so much so that he forgot the stipulations he had laid before Baron Krudener, the Russian envoy at Copenhagen, regarding the rumored joint command to which he was to be invited:

" You will discover, I presume, that my talents have been considerable; but that, loving glory, I am perhaps too much attached to honours, though personal interest is an idol to which

I have never bowed the knee. The unbounded admiration and profound respect which I have long felt for the glorious character of her Imperial Majesty forbids the idea that a sovereign so magnanimous should sanction any arrangement that may give pain at the outset to the man she designs to honour with her notice, and who wishes to devote himself entirely to her service. A conjoined command is hurtful, and often fatal in military operations. There is no military man who is so entirely master of his passions as to keep free of jealousy and its consequences in such circumstances."

He forgot this now, and in his exhilaration he again wrote to Lafayette: " You would be charmed with Prince Potemkin. He is a most amiable man, and none can be more noble-minded " ; and so in the intoxicating presence of Catherine he waived all reservations, making only one request, that he " should never be condemned unheard." He made this last stipulation, not because in these aureoled surroundings he anticipated either disaster or criticism, but because already it had come to his ears that envious persons were talking. They had whispered that in America it was known that he " had killed his own nephew."

Thus, at this distance, did the ghost of the dead sailor at Tobago rise in this guise to haunt him. Was he never to be rid of the weight of this body of death?

III

In 1788 Russia was engaged in one of her immemorial wars with Turkey, which, though driven back from Vienna, still held most of the territory now covered by the Balkan States, including Serbia, Bulgaria, Greece, and Rumania. In a previous struggle the Russian army under Potemkin had wrested the Taurida, or Crimea, from the Turks, winning for him the right to be called — in French, which was the court language — by the sonorous title of the Prince Marshal de Potemkin-

Tauridien and Grand Admiral of the Euxine. Turkey, however, still divided with Russia the command of the Black Sea, and it was Potemkin's intention by the present war, which he himself had provoked, to clear it entirely of Turkish ships and convert it into a Russian lake. Comic attempts to do this by a Russian fleet under Alexiano, a Greek but a Turkish subject, had failed, the Turkish navy under the sturdy Captain Pasha, the Ghazi Hassan of Algiers, having been too diligent and aggressive. Potemkin then suspended operations and awaited the arrival of Jones.

On May 7, seated in a *tarantass* provided by the Empress, Admiral Jones, as he was now called, started for Kherson, over 1000 miles distant. Bearing a letter from Catherine, he drove night and day, with his customary reckless disregard for his body, until he tired of the vehicle and resorted to relays of horses. He had become used to horseback-riding in Virginia, and he now pushed ahead at the rate of ninety miles every twenty-four hours. He stopped for rest only at Moscow, Tula, Khursk, and Ekaterinoslav. At the last place he faced Potemkin for the first time in an official interview. Potemkin pushed aside his usual late breakfast of smoked goose, washed down with wine, to receive the celebrated Scotch-American.

IV

To read of the performances of this fantastic Cyclops is to realize the essential truth of the unbelievable characters who stalk through the pages of Tolstoi, Gogol, Dostoievski, and Chekhov. Potemkin was not only a creature of his period; he was Russia itself — barbarous, unholy Russia of the eighteenth century. He was part loafer, part actor, part genius, and part obscene priest. He was at one moment a man of assumed learning and an affable courtier; at another he received nobles and bishops in his shirttail, with his hairy legs bare of drawers.

[235]

One day he would surround himself with women, to whom he addressed insults; on the next he would sigh to be a monk and chant orisons in a desert solitude. He was capable of passing hours in a moorose silence, making diagrams with diamonds which he owned by quarts, or of frightening ambassadors with impassioned tirades. He built a palace in the Crimea and tired of it before it was finished. He conceived grandiose military projects, gave the orders for them, and countermanded them when almost completed. He donned gorgeous uniforms and walked away without his boots on. He caused men to die in hecatombs and wept when he heard the sound of the cannon which he believed were sending unredeemed souls to hell. He sent for generals and let them stand stiffly at attention while he dreamily ate raw turnips. He cowered at the thought of danger, but when it arrived exulted in it, singing savage songs. He remembered everything he had seen or heard, but daily forgot to comb his hair. He was in turn filthy, commanding, saintlike, treacherous, faithful, gluttonous, ascetic, childishly happy or introspectively gloomy. He despised the human race, but treated his successors in Catherine's favors as if they were his brothers; he even helped to select and discharge them. He put on military and naval shows which delighted Catherine's mogul heart, and from the midst of exacting campaigns sent her little presents which transported her. He was her dog, master, *concierge*, next friend, and Dutch uncle. In her position as mistress of all the Russias, he worshipped her, but as a woman he often despised her, treating her dearest wishes as mere whims. And one of these, he thought, was John Paul Jones.

v

Potemkin first assigned Jones to the Sevastopol fleet, to co-operate with the Russian army defending Crimea, but on receiving word that the Turkish Pasha had come to the rescue of the besieged fortress of Oczakoff with 120 armed vessels, he ordered Jones instead to report to Admiral Mordvinoff at Kherson and take command of the Russian squadron in the Liman, an arm of the Black Sea to the west of Oczakoff.

Oczakoff, strongly fortified under the Sultan Achmet III by an Italian engineer during the reign of Peter the Great, commanded the mouths of the two great rivers of Southwest Russia, the Dnieper and the Bug, and virtually that of the Dniester. It was therefore a key position, and the Russians had determined to take it, cost what it might. The Russian army under General Suvaroff was to do the heavy work, while Jones was to prevent the Turks from reinforcing and supplying the garrison by sea. The operation as a whole was designed to clear the way for the long-dreamed-of Russian march to Constantinople and the Golden Horn — a march renewed at the beginning of the World War in 1914, but once more halted by the collapse of the Romanoff régime and the seizure of power by an entirely new force in human history — Soviet rule.

At Kherson, Jones got the first hint of what was in store for him. Admiral Mordvinoff received him with surly looks and gave him only the briefest instructions, without the least outline of the situation. An English aide, Lieutenant Edwards, had been assigned to Jones, and with him he now proceeded to the Liman and boarded his ship, the *Vladimir*, forty-eight guns, which Jones in his subsequent correspondence always persistently spelled " Wolodimer." Here he encountered further sulkiness. Alexiano, the Greek flag-captain, had assembled all the squadron commanders on deck; they confronted Jones in a pouting silence. Ignoring their failure to give him even the customary greetings, Jones procured a blackboard and proceeded to give them a lecture on operations and tactics, instructing them in the French system of signals invented by du Pavillon, which Jones had always maintained was superior to the

English. This lecture excited some discussion, during which Jones completely won over most of the assembled officers, including the Russian ones, and thereafter they gave him their loyal support. Others, however, remained furtively hostile. Among these were some of the English, of whom Jones says: " I own that their vexation, which I believe was generally known in and about St. Petersburg, gave me no pain."

It is doubtful as to how far Jones was justified in his tendency to see a conspiracy against him wherever he found a group of English officers. In London and other places after the war, his late enemies showed him marked courtesies and attentions. In Russia, however, some of them joined cabals against him, including Lieutenant Edwards, his own aide, whom at first he was disposed to praise. Admiral Greig, of the Russian Baltic squadron, alone was consistently friendly. Greig, however, was of Scotch birth, and his attitude may have been influenced by the tendency summed up in the saying: " Scotchmen of the world, unite! You have nothing to lose but the English."

VI

Jones made it his first task to inspect his squadron. He found it poor enough in men, guns, and equipment. It comprised seventeen vessels. There was a separate flotilla of about sixty light armed galleys commanded by the Prince of Nassau-Siegen. Jones at first supposed this satin sailor was to be subject to his orders. It was not till later that he learned the Prince had been directed to report only to Potemkin. But Jones, hamstrung by his worshipful attitude towards Catherine and Potemkin, made no further protest against this divided authority. For this he paid the penalty that never failed to follow his moments of weakness and fear of giving offense.

Jones next visited General Suvaroff to agree upon joint operations. South of Oczakoff was the Spit of Kinburn, a long sandbar on which rested the village of Kinburn, where Suvaroff had his headquarters. Jones pointed out the urgent necessity of fortifying the extreme end of the Spit. The old general agreed, but remarked " he had long ago learned to obey orders and say nothing." With a significant glance at Jones, he suggested the work could be done only if it were made to appear that the notion had come from Potemkin himself. Jones offered to take upon himself the responsibility of making the suggestion, if Suvaroff would start the fortification. Jones then wrote Potemkin congratulating him upon his genius and foresight; whereupon, sure enough, Cyclops replied with an order to begin building the fort, which by that time was almost completed.

" So far, so good," observed the world-worn Suvaroff. " But remember that wounds and death are not the only risks of war. Injustice is no less certain."

VII

On May 26, 1788, Jones hoisted his rear-admiral's flag. On June 5 the first attack was planned, and the Prince of Nassau-Siegen came around to say " if we gain any advantage, we must exaggerate it to the utmost." The Prince, whatever his defects, was a practical man, with both feet not only on the ground but not infrequently in the mud. In this, he was at the opposite pole from romantic, disdainful John Paul Jones, who tried to believe that, in courts and palaces at least, there was no such thing as mud.

At 2 o'clock on the morning of the 6th the Prince of Nassau advanced boldly on the Turkish vessels with his flotilla. The Turks at once came out bristling, whereupon the Prince recalled the definition of valor and retired with some celerity to the protection of Jones's guns. The Turks, much encouraged, counter-attacked the next day, and Jones formed his ships in an oblique line of battle, with the purpose of cutting off the enemy's advance guard. The Prince approved this and came on board Jones's ship to see it well done. To gain a better view, he placed himself within a few inches of Jones, where he firmly remained, praising the Admiral and begging him not to expose his precious life. Jones's manoeuvre succeeded. The Turks broke their line and fled, losing two of their flotilla.

Regarding this skirmish, Jones wrote to Potemkin, who was with his army on the River Bug: "The Prince showed great coolness and intelligence. I had the honour to act as his aide-de-camp, and he took all my suggestions in good part." He followed this with a report on June 8 saying: "Today we had the Te Deum sung in honour of the Prince of Nassau's victory over the flotilla of the Captain Pasha." And then he was astonished when Potemkin's letters of congratulation gave the greater praise to Nassau! Moreover, he was foolish enough to reply to Potemkin in these terms:

" I am greatly flattered by the letter which Your Highness did me the honour to write on the 8th of this month, to let me know you were satisfied by my conduct in the engagement of the 7th. It is a proof of your kind and generous spirit. I can assure you that I was not in the engagement for my personal advancement, but solely for the good of Russia, for I saw the first division of Her Majesty's flotilla in disorder and in a critical situation. M. Alexiano helped to establish order in the latter part of the engagement, and so if there are favours to bestow, I ask them for him; for myself I have not the least claim to them."

The result was what anyone more familiar with the Russian court might have expected. Potemkin showed by his subsequent attitude he considered Jones overrated, and believed Nassau and Alexiano his superiors. As for Nassau, he began to give himself the most pronounced airs. To Potemkin he described the skirmish as if he had been the sole person engaged in it.

"He has the air," complained Jones to the Chevalier Ribas, a Spanish officer and adventurer at Catherine's court, "of wishing to send me to the devil, for no other reason that I know, except that I loyally extricated him from his confusion and danger in the affair of the 7th for which he has got all the credit."

Thus did Jones at the very opening of his Russian career get off on the wrong foot, and in his over-eager desire to antagonize no one, seriously damage his own prestige. He began to feel an immediate change in the atmosphere, gave way to gloomy thoughts, and yielding to the reaction from his long journey south, took to his cabin bed. "I am unwell in my turn," he reported to Ribas on June 13. "Since I wrote you last I have been much indisposed." Half his unpleasant position was due to his ignorance of the mephitic influences around him; the other half was due to his own fault. In publicly giving undeserved praise to such varlets as Nassau, he had been guilty of Quixotic mendacity.

While he was still ill, word came from Suvaroff that Potemkin had reversed his order for the fortification of Kinburn Spit, and the Prince of Nassau notified Jones that in the future he would communicate with him only by letter. At the same time Nassau advised Potemkin that Jones seemed to be losing "that boldness which, it is said, he possessed."

The sarcasm contained in those weasel words, "it is said," could not have escaped Potemkin's single eye.

CHAPTER XXXI

Battles and Letters

I looked upon the rotting sea,
And drew my eyes away;
I looked upon the rotting deck,
And there the dead men lay.

I

ON June 16 the Turkish Pasha made another attempt to break through Jones's line and relieve the garrison of Oczakoff. He had loaded his numerous galleys with fire-balls and converted several vessels into fire-ships. With a fair wind at his back he himself led the grand attack into the Liman, his flagship steering straight for the *Vladimir*, which carried Jones. With the wind against them, the situation looked alarming for the Russians, but when about a mile and a half distant, the Pasha's flagship ran aground and the whole Turkish fleet halted uncertainly.

This mishap altered the whole situation, and Jones, recognizing his opportunity, called his captains around him and informed them it was now the time to win or die. They agreed enthusiastically, and Jones, masking the real weakness of his squadron, formed his ships into line of battle during the night, praying for a shift in the wind. At daybreak it came, and throwing his right wing forward, Jones, with an enveloping movement, swept down on the anchored enemy. The Pasha's ship had meantime been floated again.

The Turks were frightened by the formidable appearance of the Russian squadron, and in their hasty attempts to raise anchors and cut cables, got in each other's way and fell into confusion, their white sails eddying and drifting around like so many sheep. Jones, after vainly waiting for Nassau's lagging flotilla to come up, advanced with his squadron alone and opened fire on the huddled, churning enemy. The second largest Turkish ship ran aground, followed by the Pasha's. At the same time the Russian right wing advanced too far and ran into the Turkish flotilla, which hurled a bomb into the *Little Alexander* and sank her. Alexiano, in fright and without orders, then took it upon himself to drop the *Vladimir's* anchor. The Russian galleys at last came charging through the squadron, but instead of pursuing the Turks, swarmed around the two stranded ships and triumphantly retrieved the Pasha's flag which had fallen into the water. The Prince of Nassau seized it as his own trophy and Jones disdainfully let him have it. Jones had meantime begged Nassau to send over some galleys from his left wing to disperse the Turkish flotilla, but the Prince remained prudently in the rear, and it was Korsakoff who brought up the small boats.

The Russian failure to pursue enabled the Turkish ships to withdraw, with the exception of the two stranded vessels. These were now surrounded and set afire with *brandcougles,* a kind of combustible perforated bomb invented by the French. Jones at once condemned this as the useless destruction of two ships which could have been saved for the Russian navy; but it was too late. The Russian flotilla, under the separate command of the contemptuous Nassau, thought only of fire and massacre.

II

On the night of June 17 the defeated Turks tried to reassemble themselves and get out of the Liman. To do this, they had to sail by Kinburn Spit. The gunners in the fortification set up here through Jones's foresight and not yet dismantled, despite Potemkin's reversed order, now got an opportunity to prove the correctness of Jones's vision. As the Turks came up, they ran right into this unsuspected battery and in attempting to veer out of range, nine of their ships ran upon a sandbar. When daylight disclosed their plight, the galleys under Nassau attacked them with bloodthirsty fury. Jones could do nothing. The Prince of Nassau was responsible only to Potemkin and did as he pleased. Though the stranded ships were loaded with troops, the Prince did not trouble either to take them as prisoners or to save the vessels. The Turks fell on their knees, made the sign of the cross, and begged for mercy, but the Russians with savage exultation laughed at their cries and heaped the helpless ships with bombs, meantime firing not only upon the enemy but upon each other. More than three thousand Turks perished miserably, roasted alive in their burning ships.

To Jones, trained in a polite school of warfare and by nature entertaining almost exaggerated notions of chivalry, the spectacle was sickening. He realized that he had no place among such barbarians. He knew, furthermore, that Nassau and Alexiano would claim and receive the credit for a resounding victory.

He was right. Nassau made a glowing report to Potemkin, and the gratified Catherine at once bestowed on him a splendid estate in White Russia, making him lord over several thousand *moujiks,* and decorated him with the order of St. George. His officers received promotion and an extra year's pay. Alexiano was similarly rewarded, but death intervened to deprive the flexible Greek of those fruits of the earth and flesh to which successful Russian commanders had a right to look forward. He was stricken with a malignant faver and within a few days died on board the *Vladimir.* His companion in vainglory and invention, the Prince of Nassau, " neither visited him in his sickness nor assisted at his funeral." Jones merely received the Order of St. Anne, not truly a Russian but a Holstein decoration. However, he wrote he " could have been perfectlv satisfied, had others been recompensed only in the same proportion and according to the merit of their services. . . . The officers of the squadron under my command . . . obtained no promotion, no mark of distinction, no pecuniary reward."

III

Five days later Jones informed General Suvaroff that the way was now clear for the main army, of which the commander-in-chief was Potemkin, to cross the River Bug, and Suvaroff did so, investing Oczakoff from the north. He besieged the fortress and took it four months later, after enormous losses on both sides. Subsequently Suvaroff continued his successes, driving out the Turks from every stronghold north of the lower Danube, and two years later crowned his achievements with the historic victory of Ismail, where the defeated Turks, with their women and children, were butchered without mercy. These military and naval defeats were signals to Europe that the Holy Roman Empire was cracking and that a vast new power had lumbered out upon the field of Mars.

IV

Potemkin with his gorgeous suite now came down to visit the fleet, and dined with Jones in state on June 21. During the conviviality he requested the Prince de Ligne and the Chevalier Littlepage, a former Virginian who had become chamberlain at the Polish court, to make peace between Jones and the Prince of Nassau. They embraced before the whole company.

Jones had no doubt that henceforth he would receive the respect he regarded as his due; but as the campaign against the Turks developed, he found he was expected to act virtually as Nassau's aide, and later he learned that Potemkin had falsified his detailed report on the battle of the Liman to the Russian

Admiralty. To a man of Jones's pride, this was a galling position, and though he tried very hard to appear serene, his reports
to Potemkin became steadily shorter and blunter. Meantime
Nassau was writing to his wife: " I cannot keep telling you I am
pleased with myself."

Meantime from a certain lady in Paris, there came only a silence, and Jones finally appealed to Jefferson:

" I pray you to inform me if you possibly can, what has become of Mrs. T. I am astonished to have heard nothing from
her since I left Paris. I had written to her frequently before
I left Copenhagen. If you cannot hear of or see her, you will
oblige me by writing a note to M. Dubois, Commissaire du
Regiment des Guardes Français, vis-à-vis, la Rue du Vivienne,
Rue neuve des petits Champs, desiring to speak with him. He
will wait on you immediately. You must know that beside my
own purse, which was considerable, I was good natured or, if
you please, foolish enough to borrow for her four thousand
livres. Now M. Dubois knows that transaction and as she received the money entire from me for the reimbursement, I wish
to know if she has quitted the debt. When that fear is cleared
up, I shall be better able to judge of the rest."

v

More and more Jones was pushed into a subordinate position,
and then came a day when Admiral Mordvinoff came aboard
the *Vladimir* to hold a council of captains as to the best means
of linking up the Kherson and Sevastopol fleets. Jones was not
" apprised either by speech or writing." Moreover, Catherine
sent down twenty-four jeweled swords and a number of medals
to be distributed by Potemkin to deserving officers, but neither
Jones nor the men of his squadron received either. Potemkin
issued absurd and conflicting orders so fast that Jones found it
impossible to keep pace with them, whereupon Potemkin complained of his slowness. By October Jones was making reports

to Potemkin beginning with such melancholy words as " Our enterprise of last evening did not succeed," or " Luck was not with us last evening." When Potemkin peremptorily demanded a blockade of Oczakoff Bay to prevent the Turks from slipping supplies through to the garrison, Jones obeyed promptly, but protested when Potemkin ordered the small boats called in which Jones had ordered out as a screen. He addressed Potemkin in this fashion:

" Every thinking man is master of his own opinion. Mine is still that the return of these ships cannot produce other than an ill effect on the spirit of the enemy."

He was right. The Turks got several ships through the blockade.

Potemkin replied with a command which could not have been better designed to rub salt across the surface of Jones's smarting pride. In his answer Jones barely concealed his anger and alarm.

" Your Highness can yourself imagine how a military man, who fears nothing and has nothing with which to reproach himself, must have been affected by your order of the 13th. It told me to receive the enemy *courageously* and to do this without loss of time, for otherwise every ' *Negligence* ' would fail on my head! I was in despair! . . . Allow me, my Prince, to ask you how it happens that I have the misfortune to have lost your good graces? . . . Your Highness is so kind-hearted in every circumstance that you will pardon the vehemence which escaped me in my letter of the 11th. I am very anxious to continue my service. I do not need to recall either the promises or the offers which were made me. I am quite ready to do everything that can be asked of a man of honor in my position in the Imperial Navy, it lies only with you to keep me in Russia. But as I am not here in the least as an Adventurer, nor as a Mountebank, to repair a ruined fortune, I hope in the future to suffer no humiliation and soon to be in the position which was promised me when I was invited to enter Her Imperial Majesty's Navy. Perhaps I love honours too much; but as for fortune, although mine is not large, I have never bent the knee to that idol. I am well aware that riches do not secure happiness. I am certain of one thing, namely, that if I had once the good fortune to have your confidence that would suffice for my life; for I am not a fickle character."

John Paul Jones never wrote a weaker letter. By it he virtually threw himself on the mercy of Potemkin, who, often weak himself, despised weakness in others. Moreover, Jones's prayerful letter betrayed his fear that he was about to lose his job.

The appeal was the worst that Jones could have addressed to a man like Potemkin, who now definitely decided to get rid of him. On Oct. 18 Potemkin sent this message to Catherine:

" The sleepy Admiral Paul Jones has missed the transports to Otchakoff, and could not burn the ship which the Don Cossacks burnt. He was brave while he was a pirate, but he has never been at the head of many ships. No one consents to serve under him. Hence I have decided to send him to St. Petersburg under pretense of a special expedition to the North."

Mordvinoff was appointed to succeed Jones in command of the Black Sea fleet, and Catherine dispatched the following order to Kherson:

" According to our imperial desire, based upon necessity, the sphere of service for our Vice-Admiral, the Chevalier Paul Jones, is now fixed in the Northern seas. His Excellency the Vice Admiral will at once proceed on the journey to our capital. His Excellency the Vice Admiral will without ceremony present himself at our Palace of the Hermitage, where he will be made acquainted with our further wishes."

VI

Thus was Jones's service in the Black Sea brought to an abrupt end. But it is probable he learned of his recall to St. Petersburg with some relief. It meant his escape from a miserable position where he was bewildered, half-sick, and ineffective. The tenor of Catherine's order indicated that better things were in store for him, perhaps to succeed Admiral Greig, then dead, in the more respectable Baltic service; and it was with only a half-sigh that he hauled down his flag from the *Vladimir*.

Potemkin remained polite. He invited Jones to dinner, gave him a note to Catherine setting forth " the eagerness and zeal which the Rear Admiral Paul Jones has always shown in your majesty's service," and provided him with two of his favorite officers, Korsakoff and Edwards, to act as aides on his journey north. After dinner Jones relieved his feelings. He told Potemkin he had played an " unfair game " in compelling him to divide the command in the Liman, and that if promises had been kept, he (Jones) would have united the Kherson and Sevastopol squadrons and swept the Turks from the Black Sea. Potemkin remarked " it was too late now." Potemkin then broke into a violent denunciation of Nassau, whom he had " found out," he said, and told Jones if he had placated Mordvinoff at the outset, Nassau would never have found an opportunity for his intrigues. He then offered Jones sole command of a united fleet in the spring if Jones would consent to serve under Mordvinoff. Jones replied that one understanding had been broken, and he did not care to make another. He concluded by asking Potemkin to give the same rewards to Jones's officers that had been given to Nassau's. Potemkin promised, and Jones afterwards learned he had kept his word.

The recalled Admiral then started for Kherson, where after three days in an open galley, he again was taken ill, this time with bronchial pneumonia. After more than a fortnight in bed he resumed the journey to St. Petersburg about the time that Suvaroff made his bloody entry into Oczakoff. Passing through Minsk, Dvinsk, and Pskov, where he was entertained by army commanders, Jones reached the capital after eight months' absence, at the end of December, feeling very cheerful and expectant of greater things to come, for Catherine had not shown that she agreed with Potemkin's treatment of him.

to pursue my own Projects — Yet every one of these —
Armaments have fallen to nothing some of them even
the moment when I was taught to believe that the King's
Signature alone was wanting.

Thus have I been triffled with for near Five Months.
The best season of the Year, and such Opportunities of —
Serving my Country and acquiring Honor as I cannot again
expect in the Course of this War are lost. — I have written
to the Congress to reserve no Command for me in America
and to my inexpressible Mortification, having no Command
here, I am considered every where as an Officer in Disgrace.
Yet the Minister has made no Apology for all this either to
myself who did not seek after the connection, or to His Excellency
Doctor Franklin thro' whom it was accepted.

I am not an Adventurer in search of Fortune. On the
contrary I laid aside my Enjoyments in private Life, and Drew my
sword at the commencement of this War, only in support of
the Dignity and Violated rights of Human Nature. — Both my
Honor and my Duty prompt me steadfastly to persevere till
I see those Rights established — or loose my Life in the Righteous
pursuit.

But as I see no prospect of being soon relieved from this
Unworthy Situation; I have Written the within Letter to
His Majesty which I beseech your Royal Highness to —
Present. — You will thereby add a Singular Obligation to
what I already owe to your former condescending attention.

I should be supremely Happy to succeed thro' the influence
of so Amiable a Princess and so powerful an Advocate, whom
I perfectly Esteem & Respect; being truly and always in the
Utmost Sincerity of my Heart

Madam your Royal Highness' very Obliged

A son Altesse Royale   very humble servant
Madame La Duchysse De Chartres.   Wm Jones

CONCLUDING PAGE OF JOHN PAUL JONES'S LETTER TO
THE FAMOUS DUCHESS OF CHARTRES IN WHICH
HE BEGS HER TO CARRY HIS APPEAL FOR
SHIPS TO LOUIS XVI, KING OF FRANCE.

CHAPTER XXXII

Plots and Pleas

And I had done a hellish thing,
And it would work 'em woe:
For all averred, I had killed the bird
That made the breeze to blow.

I

ON the last day of the year Catherine affably received Jones in audience at the Hermitage. There was no hint that she considered him a disgraced commander, or even that she was displeased with him. On the contrary, he came away with the impression that he was to have an important command in the Baltic. As Russia was then at war with Sweden, this prospect appeared promising, and within a few days he sent word to the court that he was ready for action. Catherine replied that she must await the arrival of Potemkin before deciding what he should do. So Jones took lodgings in the capital, joined in social diversions, and employed his leisure in hatching dazzling plans and projects. One of them was for an alliance, political and commercial, between Russia and the United States which Jefferson had suggested. He laid this before the Vice Chancellor, who thought it important enough to refer it to Potemkin when that worthy returned about the middle of February. Potemkin sent for him, and once more the eager Scotch-American, who believed in everything, and the bored Russian, who believed in nothing, faced each other.

Potemkin glanced at Jones's outline and idly tossed it on a corner of his table. It contained some good ideas, he said, but the time was not ripe; it might arouse the suspicion of England,

and anyway, there was a peace to arrange with the Turks first. Thank you for bringing it to my attention. Good day.

II

When Jones came away, a man in inconspicuous clothing took up his trail and followed him to his door. Every movement of Jones since his arrival in the capital had been watched and reported. In fact, he had been under constant observation since Catherine had first thought of hiring him, all his friends and affairs having been recorded. In St. Petersburg he was watched by four sets of spies — Catherine's, Potemkin's, the British Ambassador's, and a fourth which had been freshly employed by as yet unknown persons.

In St. Petersburg at that day there were so many spies and counter-spies that they must have infringed upon each other's traffic rules. They were both home-made and imported. They founded a spy-tradition in Russia which was maintained through all reigns right up to that of Nicholas II, the last of all Russian Czars. His police employed the spy, Azeff, who, to strengthen his standing with the revolutionists, blew up the Czar's uncle and his favorite minister, but did not thereby injure his position on the imperial payroll!

III

Soon after returning to St. Petersburg, Jones had written to Jefferson in Paris proposing that Russia and the United States form a joint expedition to stamp out Algerine piracy in the Mediterranean. He now received a reply from Jefferson informing him that this had been the first letter received from Jones since he had left Copenhagen. Jones then realized, apparently for the first time, that all his mail, outward as well as inward, had been intercepted and sequestered, and that since arriving in Russia he had been virtually isolated from the world.

Had he been a little less naïve and trustful in courts, he might have discovered this for himself long before. Such practices were common not only in Russia but in other and presumably more civilized countries. As John Jay once wrote to Gouverneur Morris from Paris, " Seals are on this side of the water rather matters of decoration than of use." [1]

It would have been well for Jones if he had, at that fitting moment, resigned his position and left a country where he had received sufficient proof that he was surrounded by a network of enmity with which no blunt and unsubtle sailor could hope to cope. But still, led on by phosphorescent hopes, he hung on, pestering Count Besborodko and other ministers with importunate letters, until he had lowered his own prestige and paved the way for the culminating blow of his Russian career. We will accept his own account of the form it took.

About the middle of March a girl in her early teens came to his rooms and asked for garments to mend. When the porter had withdrawn, she " began some earnest and indecent allurements of person." Jones " advised her to beware of such a career, gave her a rouble in charity, and dismissed her." She refused to go, whereupon Jones " took her gently by the hand and led her to the door." There she raised an outcry, tore her clothing, and rushing out on the street to a woman she called her mother, screamed that Jones had assaulted her. The whole street — the Great Morskaya — gathered to hear the exciting details.

Jones at first failed to realize he had been victimized by a Russian variety of the historic " badger game," until the sympathizing porter told him the pair would be certain to " make trouble." Jones then summoned the only St. Petersburg law-

---

[1] That conditions in this respect have undergone little change is evidenced by the speech of Mr. A. Ponsonby in the English House of Commons, May 26, 1927: " We must really face the fact when getting on our high moral horse that forgery, theft, lying, bribery, and corruption exist in every Foreign Office and every chancellery throughout the world."

yer he knew — one Crimpion — who took down the facts and
departed. Two days later the lawyer sent word that " a high
authority " had forbidden him to act in the case. Recognizing
the gravity of his position, Jones tried to obtain other attorneys,
but they were all " busy." Then came a message from Catherine's deputy chamberlain forbidding him " to approach the
palace of Her Majesty, or to presume to send any communication to anyone in regard to the affair." Instantly he found himself immured in a great and silent wilderness. No one came to
see him, no communication arrived from any source. Even his
servants discovered promising positions elsewhere and left his
employ. In his despair he thought of suicide.

IV

After enduring this isolation for several days, his nerves became affected, and he sent a cry for help to the one man in the
capital to whom he now felt he might appeal, like himself a
friend of the amiable Duchess of Chartres. This was the
French Ambassador, the Count de Sègur. The Count came at
once and was shocked to find Jones looking grey and haggard,
with his pistols laid on the table before him. As the Count took
his hand, Jones broke down and sobbed. When he had listened
to his story, Sègur reassured him.

" Resume your composure," he said. " Give me the papers
in the case. You shall hear from me soon."

Among the numerous spies of the capital Sègur had no small
staff of his own. He at once put them to work on the case.
These agents reported that the girl who had accused Jones was
called Catherine Koltzwarthen, that her mother had left her
husband to become a procuress, and that this woman was in the
business of supplying young girls to hangers-on of the court.
Judging by the contents of a letter concerning the case which
Sègur sent Potemkin, he made more discoveries than he saw fit

to disclose to John Paul Jones, for he begged Potemkin to have the case hushed up and even offered to supply the money which he said Jones was willing to pay the woman to " assuage her greed."

It is probable that Sègur recognized the dangerous political broils that might ensue if the case attained the publicity consequent upon an open trial. He seems to have believed that Catherine's action in placing a ban upon Jones was not due so much to prudishness, of which she had odd attacks, as to her sudden suspicion that Jones had been entertaining offers from Sweden. She later wrote indignantly to Baron de Grimm: " During the war there was no need for him to become a Turco-Swede." The air was full of carefully manufactured rumors at the time, and one of them had it that Sweden, which was supposed to be receiving a Turkish subsidy, was negotiating for Jones's services. Sègur's survey seems to have convinced him that the disturbance made by the girl and her procuress-mother at Jones's home was not due merely to the attempt of unscrupulous women to obtain money, but it represented a plot by certain powerful but hidden influences to discredit Jones, to ruin his reputation in Europe, and finally to destroy his career. The European powers, then no less than previous to the World War of 1914–1918, were half demented with their jealousies of each other, and in their fear that one might obtain an advantage which would menace the security of the others, their diplomats resorted to the foulest measures. With a naval competition on, they regarded it as dangerous to have such an able commander as Jones, who had shown his capacities not only as a fighter but as a constructor of ships, at large and unemployed. They feared that as long as he was foot-loose, he might suddenly throw the weight of his experience on one side to the detriment of the other, and they therefore meant finally to dispose of him as a factor in the cannibalistic struggle which did not attain its climax until 1914.

V

The Koltzwarthen girl's charge was not the only one brought against Jones at this time. In his *Journal* of the Liman campaign written for Catherine II, Jones reminded her that " a Washington, a Franklin, a d'Estaing, a Lafayette, think the bust of Paul Jones worthy of being placed side by side with their own." He then remarked: " It is then certain that this is not the bust of one . . ." Here follows a passage which has been omitted from all printed editions of this *Journal*. Concerning this, the Hamilton biography of Jones says in a footnote:

" It appears . . . that accusations had been insinuated against him of a yet darker and more revolting character than the alleged murder of his nephew and the violation of a girl. Had not the latter calumny already been made public, as Paul Jones takes no notice of it in his Journal, we would scarce have polluted our pages by reference to it." [2]

At any rate, Sègur deemed it wise to address the following appeal to Potemkin:

" On Saturday, 25 April, 1789.

" My Prince,
" I have the honour to send you a letter which the Rear Admiral Paul Jones has begged me to bring before you. In the name of the friendship of which you have given me such frequent proofs, come to the aid of this brave officer and free him from a process whose publicity and continuance discredit a reputation won by the most brilliant valour. . . . He has enemies and powerful ones. In the last war I often heard them accuse him of actions the falsity of which I can, as minister, certify. . . . I pray you to obtain permission from Her Majesty to save Paul Jones, a famous man, from the shame of a trial, grievous when they make public the errors (*egarements*) of private life, always formidable when the accusers are advised

[2] *Life of Rear-Admiral John Paul Jones*, by James Hamilton.

by enemies. The war affords a thousand opportunities for sending Paul Jones honorably to Leghorn or elsewhere, while suspending the trial, and I answer for him that he will pay all the money that may assuage the greed of a woman whose charge has had no other object. If he needs money, mine will be at his service. As an American, a companion in arms, and a Chevalier of the King, I owe him this service."

Previously Jones had sent a long and excited letter to Potemkin to which no reply had been received. It declared:

" If this charge were true, I would not hesitate to confess my error to you frankly and to place my honor, which is a thousand times dearer to me than life, in the hands of the Empress. But that being far from the case, My Lord, I swear to you with the loyalty becoming a soldier that I am innocent."

He went on to relate that the girl in the case, after leaving his house, had gone to the home of a lady named Thevis where " she did not appear at all excited," and had actually returned to Jones's rooms for her gloves, " bowed to my secretary, and went out very quietly by the same rear door." Moreover, the girl had said to Mme. Thevis, " she would make no trouble about giving herself to a man." Finally he made this declaration:

" I love women, I avow, and the pleasures which one tastes only in the presence of (*aupres*) that sex, but enjoyments by force fill me with horror. I cannot even think how one can slake his passions at the expense of their freedom and their modesty; and I give you the word of a soldier and an honest man that if the girl in question had never passed through other hands than mine, she would still be a virgin."

VI

For one month Jones was permitted to exist in solitude; no reply came from anywhere; and then Sègur suggested that he write directly to Catherine. He did so in a long, too long, review of his case and his Russian career. In it he said: "Understanding neither the laws, the language nor the forms of justice of this country, I needed an advocate, and obtained one, but whether from terror or intimidation, he stopped short all at once and durst not undertake my defense." Sègur deemed this passage scarcely likely to help Jones's cause, since it intimated that justice was impossible under the conditions permitted by the Empress. Jones swore he would be " ever faithful to you as well as to the empire of which you form the happiness, the ornament and the glory," and concluded with this hint: " But if circumstances of which I am ignorant do not admit the possibility of my being employed during the campaign, I hope your Majesty will give me permission to return to France or America, granting, as the sole reward of the services I have had the happiness to render, the hope of renewing them at some future day."

There was another month of silence, and then Jones called on Count Besborodko to beg for news. A week later he wrote the Count, saying: " I ventured to promise myself that in two days I would be made acquainted with the ulterior intention of her Majesty, whether this was to give me a command, or a temporary leave of absence."

No reply came from Besborodko; instead, a curt message from Catherine's chamberlain informed the Admiral she had " granted " him leave of absence for two years, " with appointments belonging to his rank during his absence," at the rate of eighteen hundred roubles (about $1800, or £450) a year. He failed to obtain his pay in person, and was compelled to place his affairs in the hands of M. Genêt, son of " Citizen " Genêt, who had been his friend in France. He again called on Besborodko to ask for his passport, but that official evaded him by going out of a side door in sight of Jones, " without," Jones wrote, " a single expression of ordinary civility to console me for all the bitter mortifications I have endured in this empire."

VII

The Count de Sègur alone was loyal and sympathetic. He gave Jones numerous letters to the French ministers he might meet on his return to Western Europe, and prepared for insertion " in the Public Prints, and particularly in the *Gazette de France*," this item, which reveals how even at that date the technique of coloring the news and giving it a useful trend was well understood. The same dispatch was sent to General Arthur St. Clair at Philadelphia for publication in American newspapers:

" St. Petersburg, 21st July, 1789 — The Vice-Admiral Paul Jones being on the point of returning to France, where private affairs require his presence, had the honour to take leave of the Empress the 7th of this month, and to be admitted to kiss the hand of her Imperial Majesty, who confided to him the command of her vessels of war stationed on the Liman during the campaign of 1788. As a mark of favor for his conduct during this campaign the Empress has decorated him with the insignia of the order of St. Anne; and her Imperial Majesty, satisfied with his services, only grants him permission to absent himself for a limited time, and still preserves for him his emoluments and his rank."

Which proves that the Count was an ingenious journalist as well as able diplomat. Jones was permitted to take leave of Catherine at a public but not a private reception. She wished him a cool " bon voyage." She later wrote to Baron de Grimm:

" It seems to me I have nothing to say to Paul Jones: as I have emptied my bag and peace is almost concluded, he should be advised to go and attend his affairs in America."

VIII

On August 18, 1789, Jones completed the most wretched sixteen months of his life and left Russia. Catherine could easily have, on one pretext or another, dismissed him from her pay-roll; but she chose to keep him on a cord, obviously because, if dismissed, he might have, for aught she knew, taken service with Turkey, Sweden, or any one of the other countries with which her ambitions had thrown, or were about to throw, her cormorantic empire into war.

Jones had been run over and flattened by forces which he never understood, and which as a man of action and not of re-flection, he was incapable of understanding. He was a pebble caught between gigantic stones which in their revolutions ground him to powder. He was like an actor who, striding into the midst of a constructed set he thinks will afford him a mag-nificent background against which to perform, is astonished when it falls and buries him. What were virtues elsewhere became, in Russia, his defects. His self-confidence led him to oppose the Potemkin machine when a more flexible nature would have gone with it. His care in preparation for action was scorned by leaders who on slap-dash impulse loved to make impressionistic attacks. He was concerned to save lives and material when they cared for neither; while his numerous little punctilios they regarded as effeminate weaknesses. He was a man of the sea accustomed to working in great spaces, and he was assigned to the work of a lake-carrier in waters where his ships barely cleared the bottom. He was surrounded by men who did not wish him to succeed and they sabotaged his every attempt at unified action. It may have been true, as he egotistically contended in his *Journal*, that " *my operations* not only saved Kherson and the Crimea, but decided the fate of the war "; Oczakoff had to be taken, and it was Jones's strategy in blocking the Turks that enabled Suvaroff to take it and start his string of victories that culminated in the triumphant peace of Jassy; but it was not to Potemkin's interest to admit it.

IX

Jones's Russian *Journal*, which he sent to Catherine bound and sealed, could not, in any case, have helped his cause in her eyes. It was the work of a man badly shaken in nerves and health. It alternated between undignified boasting and the embittered criticizing of associates and subordinates. It was spotted with the rawest egotisms; for example:

" I have a soul too noble for that " (safeguarding his personal interests).

" I was known . . . to have given more alarm to their (English) three kingdoms during the war than any other individual had done."

" I am the only man in the world that possesses a sword given by the King of France."

" I am found too frank and too sincere to make my way at the Court of Russia without creating powerful enemies."

" Briefly, I am satisfied with myself."

The *Journal* rises to a climax in this extraordinary confession:

" If my heart has bled for the Americans . . . if I have exposed my health and my life to the greatest dangers, — if I have sacrificed my personal tranquillity and my domestic happiness, with a portion of my fortune and my blood, to set at liberty these virtuous and innocent men, — have I not given proofs sufficiently striking that I have a heart the most tender, the most elevated? — I have done more than all this. *So far from being harsh and cruel, nature has given me the mildest disposition. I was formed for love and friendship, and not to be a seaman and a soldier, to which I have sacrificed my natural inclination.*"

The italics are ours. This appeal, which produced not the slightest effect on Catherine's hard-boiled heart, would not have been written by John Paul Jones had it not ended upon a note containing more than a little self-complacency:

[261]

" I have the happiness to know that though my enemies
may not be converted into friends, my name will nevertheless
be always respected by worthy men who know me; and it is to
me a satisfaction and a signal triumph at the moment of my
leaving Russia that the public, and even the English in St.
Petersburgh, with whom I have no connexion, have now changed
their sentiments in regard to me, give me their esteem, and
regret my departure."

x

He left Russia as a man without a country. The United
States, in the midst of its struggles to establish a stable government after the inauguration of Washington as first President in
April of this same year, could give him no employment.
France was too absorbed in the labor-pains of her approaching
Revolution to pay attention to him. From the country of his
birth he had cut himself off with finality. As an admiral still
in the pay of Russia, he had been warned, for political reasons,
not to go to Denmark or Germany. He had no home, not even
a centre where among friends he could rest and recuperate.
His relations with Aimée de Tellison were such that he apparently felt no impulse to hurry back to Paris, where she was living in the little house bought by him with borrowed money.
And so, alone and introspective, he wandered back toward Western Europe, where in the atmosphere of courts, so congenial to
him, he was watched every step of the way lest he sell his services to this power or that, thus upsetting that hair-thin Balance
of Power assiduously nursed by England and her shifting
allies.

CHAPTER XXXIII

Back to Western Europe

How long in that same fit I lay,
I have not to declare;
But ere my life returned,
I heard, and in my soul discerned,
Two voices in the air.

I

IN his loneliness he was glad to accept the invitation of
Littlepage to come to Warsaw; and there the attentions of
the Polish court, which had no love for Russia, were so
soothing that he remained two months. Littlepage condoled
with him on his misfortunes at Catherine's court and informed
him it had been whispered to him that the plot against Jones
had been " conducted by a little great man behind the curtain."
Mrs. de Koven [1] identifies this "little great man" as the Austrian envoy to Russia, Count de Cobentzel, who, though representing a court allied with Catherine's, was himself an Anglophile who had been denounced by Count de Vergennes, the
French foreign minister, for his "indecent servility" to England. Cobentzel's appearance is described as "short, gross,
obese." He was an intimate and a flatterer of Potemkin during
Catherine's reign, and was later the Austrian envoy to France
under Napoleon's regime. His wife was a relative of the
Madame de Genlis, herself an Anglophile, who meantime had
come between the Duke and Duchess of Chartres.

At Warsaw he formed or renewed several friendships. One
of them was with the Countess de Valery de Tomatis, to whom

[1] *Life and Letters of John Paul Jones.*

[263]

he read the poetry of James Thomson and showed the manuscript of his Russian *Journal*, whose " faults and inaccuracies " he admitted, before he forwarded it to Catherine II. Another was with General Kosciusko, who, after returning from service in the United States, was fostering a movement to free his country from Russia.

What remains of the correspondence between these two late participants in the American war for independence leaves little doubt that Kosciusko laid before Jones certain proposals for joining the Swedish navy under Gustavus III, and that Jones, though cautious, did not repel them. The fact that Jones's late enemy, the Prince of Nassau-Siegen, had been appointed to lead the Russian northern fleet against the Swedes, may have tempted him just a little. Jones's parting letter to Kosciusko, November 2, 1789, gave his route to Holland in detail, also his permanent address in Amsterdam, and on February 15 following, Kosciusko addressed Jones in the following veiled terms, written in the General's unschooled English:

" I gave you the information to apply to the Minister of Svede at Hague or at Amsterdam for the propositions according to what M. D'Engestrom told me they both had order to communicate you. I wish with all my heart that it could answer your expectations. I am totally ignorant what they are; but I could see you to fight against the oppression and tyranny."

Jones replied " the delicacy of his situation " would not permit him to approach anyone, but that communications must come from the other side. However, rumors of these tentative negotiations got out, and Jones felt impelled to write to Catherine II, declaring he had no intention of entertaining any offer or commission from an enemy of Russia, but was preserving " the condition of an American citizen and officer."

" If I was ever tempted," wrote the Count de Sègur, commenting upon this letter, " to lose patience with him, it was in consequence of his inability of self-containment or to bide his time wherever he imagined his honor questioned or his fealty challenged."

II

From Warsaw he went to Strasburg, thence by Vienna where he met the Crown Prince who, as Leopold II, was soon to succeed the dying Joseph II. From there he sailed down the Rhine to Holland, arriving in Amsterdam December 18, 1789. Here he at once sought to re-establish his American contacts. He wrote to Washington, "Your name alone, Sir, has established in Europe a confidence that was for some time entirely wanting in American concerns"; and to Franklin he explained his "reasons for leaving Russia and the danger to which I was exposed by the dark intrigues and mean subterfuges of Asiatic jealousy and malice." He added a melancholy postscript: "It is this day ten years since I left the Texel in the *Alliance.*"

Franklin received this a few weeks before his death but was too weak to reply. The *Alliance* was then in the merchant service, but on reverting to the government, slowly rotted on the shore of Petty's Island, near Philadelphia, for lack of money to repair her.

Jones also wrote to Charles Thompson, secretary of Congress, asking about a small estate near Lancaster, and to John Ross at Philadelphia he mentioned his financial difficulties and his renewed wish for a "little farm" in America, where he might realize his old dream of "poetic ease." With a revival of spirits, he informed John Parish, in Hamburg, that he might be coming there soon to "pay court to some of your kind, rich old ladies." To Jefferson he wrote that, after consultation with William Short, then the American chargé at Paris, and Gouverneur Morris, he had decided to draw on Denmark for the small grant offered him there; but since he soon afterwards obtained a partial settlement from Bancroft's partner in the quercitron

[265]

bark importing business at London, Sir Robert Harries, there is no record that he actually did try to collect the Danish pension.

At London, to his surprise and obvious delight, he received hospitable attentions from the Earl of Wemyss, Lady Ossory, Horace Walpole, Charles James Fox and other notables, and at an entertainment there met his old supporter, the Duke of Chartres, who had meantime succeeded to the title of the Duke of Orleans. It is not likely, however, that the Duke told him exactly what he was doing in England.

At the end of May he was again in Paris, ill with a lung affection and a disturbing cough. His dark brown hair had begun to turn grey and his face to contract deep lines, though he was only forty-three years old. Gouverneur Morris made this note about him: " Paul Jones called on me this morning. He is much vexed at the democracy of this country."

* * * "It is by no means enough that an officer of the navy should be a capable mariner. He must be that, of course, but also a great deal more. He should be as well a gentleman of liberal education, refined manners, punctilious courtesy, and the nicest sense of personal honor.

"He should not only be able to express himself clearly and with force in his own language both with tongue and pen, but he should also be versed in French and Spanish * * *

"The naval officer should be familiar with the principles of international law, and the general practice of admiralty jurisprudence, because such knowledge may often, when cruising at a distance from home, be necessary to protect his flag from insult or his crew from imposition or injury in foreign ports.

"He should also be conversant with the usages of diplomacy and capable of maintaining, if called upon, a dignified and judicious diplomatic correspondence; because it often happens that sudden emergencies in foreign waters make him the diplomatic as well as military representative of his country, and in such cases he may have to act without opportunity of consulting his civic or ministerial superiors at home, and such action may easily involve the portentous issue of peace or war between great powers. These are general qualifications, and the nearer the officer approaches the full possession of them the more likely he will be to serve his country well and win fame and honors for himself.

"Coming now to view the naval officer aboard ship and in relation to those under his command, he should be the soul of tact, patience, justice, firmness and charity. No meritorious act of a subordinate should escape his attention or be left to pass without its reward, if even the reward be only one word of approval. Conversely, he should not be blind to a single fault in any subordinate though, at the same time he should be quick and unfailing to distinguish error from malice, thoughtlessness from

inconpetency, and well-meant shortcoming from heedless or stupid blunder. As he should be universal and impartial in his rewards and approval of merit, so should he be judicial and unbending in his punishment or reproof of misconduct.

"In his intercourse with subordinates he should ever maintain the attitude of the commander; but that need by no means prevent him from the amenities of cordiality or the cultivation of good cheer within proper limits. Every commanding officer should hold with his subordinates such relations as will make them constantly anxious to receive invitation to sit at his mess-table, and his bearing toward them should be such as to encourage them to express their opinions to him with freedom and to ask his views without reserve * * *

"A navy is essentially and necessarily aristocratic. True as may be the political principles for which we are now contending, they can never be practically applied or even admitted on board ship, out of port or off soundings. This may seem a hardship, but it is nevertheless the simplest of truths. Whilst the ships sent forth by the Congress may and must fight for the principles of human rights and republican freedom, the ships themselves must be ruled and commanded at sea under a system of absolute despotism.

"I trust that I have now made fairly clear to you the tremendous responsibilities that devolve upon the Honorable Committee of which you are a member. You are called upon to found a new navy; to lay the foundations of a new power afloat that must some time, in the course of human events, become formidable enough to dispute even with England the mastery of the ocean. Neither you nor I may live to see such growth. But we are here at the planting of the tree, and maybe some of us must, in the course of destiny, water its feeble and struggling roots with our blood. If so, let it be so! We cannot help it. We must do the best we can with what we have at hand!"

(U S.N.A.—1.12 26—200)

QUALIFICATIONS OF A NAVAL OFFICER AS OUTLINED BY JOHN PAUL JONES. THESE SENTIMENTS HAVE BEEN PRINTED IN LEAFLET FORM BY THE UNITED STATES NAVAL ACADEMY AT ANNAPOLIS AND ARE CALLED TO THE ATTENTION OF EVERY ENTERING MIDSHIPMAN.

CHAPTER XXXIV

A Changed Paris

And the bay was white with silent light
Till, rising from the same,
Full many shapes, that shadows were,
In crimson colors came.

I

THE inconsistencies found beneath the encircling epidermis of a man are, as has frequently been observed, endless and sometimes absurd. In America John Paul Jones took pride in assisting a rising, commercially-minded, middle class to free itself from a restrictive government. But in France he chose to remain an eighteenth century gentleman with the viewpoint of a retired member of the *ancien régime* and at first glance regarded the struggles of a similar class there with indignation.

On returning to his old Parisian haunts in 1790, he indeed found enough to disturb him. That lovely court at Versailles, where as a King's chevalier he had always been received with the pageantry delightful to the heart of an instinctive lover of the dramatic, had been ruthlessly broken up, and his benefactor Louis XVI and that "sweet girl," Marie Antoinette, had been brought to Paris under guard. His adored Lafayette was flirting with abhorrent, if moderate, ideas of a democracy. The Duchess of Chartres had been separated from the Duke and was living with her father, while her husband was following in the wake of Madame de Genlis in England. Such heroes of his own profession as d'Orvilliers, de Grasse, and la Motte Picquet were dead. Admirals Kersaint and d'Estaing were un-

[267]

easily facing a turbulent navy, but as yet not foreseeing the guillotine. To one coming from medieval Russia, France appeared to be a safe, serene and progressive land, and Jones could not understand why anyone should be dissatisfied with its government. He was all for shooting heads off. " I surely," he wrote, " would have made the thirty cannon of the courtyard teach to that mad rabble the lesson that grape-shot has its uses in struggles for the rights of man."

Later he abated these views considerably, but before giving attention to public affairs he was compelled to look after his health. His physical weakness continued until he was induced to consult physicians. They shook their heads over his cough, found he was suffering from a bronchial affection, and advised him against active service until he had had a long rest. A return to Russia, they advised, was out of the question.

Nevertheless he found it difficult to keep away from the anteroom of de Simolin, the Russian ambassador, and he was soon sending another long and imploring letter to Potemkin. In it he said: " I have been wrong and I avow it with a frankness which carries with it its own excuse. 1st, that I did not request of you a carte blanche and the absolute command of all the forces of the Liman. 2nd, to have written to Your Highness under feelings highly excited, on the 15th October, 1788. These are my faults. If my enemies have wished to impute others to me I swear before God they are a calumny." He hinted he was ready to answer a recall, suggested he would be pleased to receive the Russian order of St. George, and offered Potemkin a copy of the medal he had received from Congress. No answer ever came. A year later he had not yet rid his mind of the belief that Catherine might yet recall him, and he sent her a new appeal begging her " to withdraw me as soon as possible from the uncertainty in which I am placed."

He induced Grimm to forward to her a plan for a Russian *divertissement* affecting India, then governed by Lord Cornwallis, of Yorktown fame, in case England should take a hand in war on the empire. Catherine made no reply to him, but to Grimm she wrote at some length. Referring to a certain plan offered by " Sr. P. J." to Besborodko, she dropped into her native German capitalized: " GOTT WEISS WAS DAS IST! " (God knows what that is), and dismissed his other projects as impracticable. She remarked that if, as Jones contended, he alone had directed the operations in the Liman, " the commentator says that . . . it is certain he did not fight, because he was given order after order to advance and he never advanced, because of head winds, as he himself admits. He says the task given him was very difficult; that may be, but it was a question of attack, and in such a case it is wiser to give than to receive. . . . But this leave of two years was given Sr. P. J. so that he might leave here, it may be said between ourselves, without disgrace, for there was a suit against him for attempted violation which did no honor to his excellence or to his humanity, his justice, or his benevolence, and after this little affair, it would have been difficult to find anyone in the navy who cared to serve under the Rear Admiral. Aside from that, it was not very necessary that during the war, he should turn Turco-Swede. . . . In leaving he asked to kiss my hand, and never after the villainous affair described was he flattered by a private audience. . . . I hope that peace will soon be concluded, but if it is not, I will make my intentions known to M. Paul Jones. . . . He does not tell me of the audience which he asked for and obtained from the National Assembly, I do not know why."

Jones himself mentions in a letter to John Ross that, after observing the weakness of Louis XVI, he attended " some of the sessions " of the French National Assembly and compared it, to its disadvantage, " with the deliberations of our own Congress and the Constitutional Convention." Naturally, Catherine, as a despot, could not be pleased to hear, through her spies, of Jones's interest in the spreading revolution in France, even though he criticized the Assembly's proceedings as "theatrical" and the delegates as "a vast flock of sheep disguised as lions."

II

On July 9, 1791, he turned from his observations of the French struggle to forward to Catherine II a new plan for the Russian navy through Baron de Grimm, who had recently accepted a copy of Houdon's bust of Jones. The Admiral mentioned that he had met an old acquaintance who had invented a new type of ship which offered greater facility in navigation. Through this, he said, he had surmounted the obstacles which had prevented the completion of a ship devised by himself and Franklin. It " could be navigated without ballast, be ready for action at any time, draw less water and drive little or not at all to leeward." He offered to dedicate this invention to Catherine. Her reply to Grimm was short. She had " emptied her bag " of Jones, she said, adding: " Certainly I shall not be the first to apply the new construction of ships mentioned by him. Let him propose it to England."

By October of the same year, 1791, her Cyclops was dead. In his weakness, attributed to his foul diet and worse habits, Potemkin went to the south of Russia and thence to Jassy. Becoming restless there, he tried to reach Oczakoff, as if to find surcease at the scene of his greatest triumph, to which he could not admit that John Paul Jones had contributed. On the way he threw himself out of his carriage, stretched himself upon a rug beneath a tree, and there expired. To his memory Catherine II erected the Taurida Palace in St. Petersburg. In five years she was dead herself.

III

"Having too much time" on his hands, as he confessed, Jones wrote quantities of letters from his Paris apartment. He asked Short for his help in obtaining an American consul's post in Europe. He also urged upon Jefferson and Carmichael the necessity of doing something to redeem the American seamen captured and enslaved in Algiers.

And then he encountered a new interest. He met Bertrand Barère, afterwards known as "the Anacreon of the Revolution." Barère was a country-grown lawyer, a Gascon, and perhaps the first "publicist" of the modern type in French history. His hobbies were naval affairs and the "freedom of the seas." Barère saw the necessity of reorganizing the French navy and admitting to it aggressive young men of the middle class, if it was to hold its own against British naval domination in future. In communicating these ideas to Jones, he touched a vibrating chord in the Admiral, who had himself suffered from the fact that the French navy of the old régime had admitted as officers only men of aristocratic birth; and it was not long before Barère was introducing Jones to Frenchmen of those mercantile and professional classes which had determined to abolish the monarchy. Gradually Jones's hostility to the notion of a new and more democratic government in France abated measurably, and when Barère hinted to him the possibility that a new and better navy might find distinguished employment for a commander who had made his abilities everywhere known, Jones began to think better of the men who were threatening drastic things but had not yet done anything more violent than to destroy the Bastille, the key of which had been sent, both as a promise and a symbol, across the Atlantic to George Washington at Mount Vernon, where it is to be seen today. Before long Barère was also introducing Jones to members of the various Jacobin clubs, and to advocates of parliamentary government like Cambon, Carnot, and Lacoste. They sometimes argued affairs with Jones at the home of Madame Tellison in the rue Vivienne.

Some of these men were Freemasons, a fact which doubtless abated Jones's original prejudice against them. But the French Freemasonry of that day had but little in common with the club-like form developed in America or with the conservative type known to England and Scotland. It was socially radical, politically liberal, free-thinking, and permeated with the rationalism and skepticism preached in the prolific volumes of Voltaire, fellow member of Thomas Paine and Benjamin Franklin in the Lodge of the Nine Sisters. In consequence the tradition that Freemasonry is subversive of governments was set up on continental Europe, and this explains why to this day it is suspected and banned by certain rulers and dictators.

There is some evidence, found chiefly in the writings of Benoit André, his former secretary, that Jones promised French republicans, in case of attack by foreign powers, especially Great Britain, that he would join their navy as an admiral; but he was dead before the " sanitary cordon " of reactionary powers began to close in. There is a story that Napoleon, twelve years after Jones's death, realizing after Trafalgar and the Nile how British sea-power had nullified his plans for conquest in the East, asked: " How old was Paul Jones when he died? " About forty-five years old, he was told. " Then," said Napoleon, " he did not fulfil his destiny. Had he lived, France might have had an admiral."

IV

Meantime Jones's health continued to fail, and we find him writing to two women friends, Mmes. LaGrande, widow of his old banker, and Wolfe, who had invited him to their home in the south of France, that life had become a " nauseous draught."

" Love," he wrote, " frequently communicates divine quali-
ties, and in this light may be considered the cordial that Providence has bestowed on mortals to help them digest the nauseous
draught of life. Friendship, they say, has more solid quali-
ties than love. This is a question I shall not attempt to resolve
but sad experience generally shows that where we expect to find
a friend we have only been treacherously deluded by false appearances and that the goddess herself very seldom confers
her charms on any of the human race. I have had very bad
health almost ever since your departure. . . ."

He was then living at No. 42 (later No. 19) rue de Tournon,
Paris, a street which begins at the gate opening upon the building now occupied by the French Senate in the Gardens of the
Luxembourg. At the end of the year 1790 he wrote to his sister, Mrs. William Taylor, that he was unable to leave his rooms,
" having been for the most part obliged to keep my bed." He
urged Mrs. Taylor to end a family quarrel that had pained him,
by becoming reconciled to his other sister, Mrs. Lowden, which
name he spelled " Loudon." He cited a verse from Pope's
" Universal Prayer ":

> Teach me to feel another's woe,
> To hide the fault I see,
> That mercy I to others show,
> Such mercy show to me.

In another letter he mentioned his wish to be useful to his
nephews and nieces. " I wish I had a fortune to offer to each of
them," he said.

To Jefferson he wrote:

" I continued to be sensibly affected by the situation of our
poor countrymen at Algiers, the more so as I hear from the
pirate now here, who took the greatest part of them, that if
they are not soon redeemed they will be treated with no more
lenity than is shown to other slaves."

Jones often urged upon the American government the necessity of sending a relief expedition to the Barbary coast, but the country was too poor to raise the million dollars required to outfit it, and it was not until after his death that a commission arrived from the United States, authorizing him by act of Congress, May 8, 1792, to deal with the Dey of Algiers.

In another letter to Jefferson, Jones asked him to obtain for him the permission of Congress to wear the insignia of the Order of St. Anne, as he wished it to appear on a bust ordered for a North Carolina friend.[1] This seems to have been a second and less successful bust modelled by Houdon. On this Jones's formerly flattened hair appears rolled above his ears, and his features are thinner and more drawn than on the earlier bust. It also suggests the courtier rather than the sea captain.

v

By the beginning of the summer of 1792 he was much weaker, and was glad to spend much of his time lying in a sailor's hammock provided for him in the backyard of his rue de Tournon home by Madame Tellison. He began to exhibit symptoms of interstitial nephritis, known as Bright's disease, coughed fearfully, and suffered a severe attack of jaundice. At intervals he was cheerful and talked energetically with visitors, but his tendency to brood over his disappointments was not helped by his failure to collect from the French marine ministry arrears in pay due to the officers and men of the *Bon Homme Richard*. He addressed a letter on the subject to Bertrand de Moleville, the marine minister, but received in reply " a very

---

[1] The same difficulty arose when the French and other governments bestowed the various decorations on the American aviator, Charles A. Lindbergh, after his solitary flight from New York to Paris May 21, 1927. Lindbergh being a reserve officer in the United States service, it was, strictly speaking, illegal for him to wear a foreign decoration without the permission of Congress.

uncivil letter." To his successor, de la Coste, Jones sent a copy of this correspondence, saying:

" My losses and unavoidable expenses during my long connection with this nation amount to a large sum and have greatly lessened my fortune. I have given solemn proofs of my great attachment towards France, and that attachment still remains undiminished. I persuade myself that I may with full assurance repose my interests through your ministry on the national justice."

The reluctance of the three governments which Jones served, to settle his account is extraordinary. Knowing his love of glory, they seemed disposed to permit him to live on that exclusively. Of these not the least offender was the United States. It was not until 1848 that Congress settled his claims in full. It then paid to Francis E. Lowden, a descendant of Jones and administratrix *de bene esse*, $21,202.44 for Jones's share of prize money for the capture of the *Betsy, Union,* and *Charming Polly* by the squadron led by the *Bon Homme Richard;* also his pay from June 21, 1781, to May, 1788, $5,040, and $2,598.42 for moneys advanced by him to the government.

VI

On a Sunday in July 1792 Gouverneur Morris, the American minister to France and one of its chief social butterflies, visited Jones, finding him in his backyard hammock. " Mme. T. and two young ladies were with him," says Morris's diary. " He was extremely cheerful, and seemed better than for a long time previously. He did not cough much, and talked a good deal. Wonderfully interesting! "

But it was only at intervals that Jones roused himself. He sank slowly day by day, his face becoming yellow and emaciated. He lay for hours in his hammock, rocked gently by Aimée de Tellison.

[275]

" On thee, too, for country's sake, O Chevalier John Paul," wrote his fellow Scot, Thomas Carlyle, in his *French Revolution*, " be a word spent, or misspent. In faded naval uniform lingers Paul Jones visible here; like a wine-skin from which the wine is all drawn. Like the ghost of himself! Low is his once loud bruit; scarcely audible, save, with extreme tedium, in ministerial antechambers, in this or the other charitable dining room, mindful of the past. What changes, culminatings, and declinings! Not now, poor Paul, thou lookest wistful over the Solway brine, at the foot of native Criffel, into blue mountainous Cumberland, into blue Infinitude; environed with thrift, with humble friendliness; thyself, young fool, longing to be aloof from it, and even to be away from it. Yes, by that sapphire promontory, which men named St. Bees, which is not sapphire either, but dull sandstone. When one gets close to it, there is a world. Which world thou too shalt taste of! From yonder White Haven rise his smoke-clouds; ominous though ineffectual. Proud Forth quakes at his bellying sails; had not the wind suddenly shifted. Flamborough reapers, homegoing, pause on the hillside: for what sulphur-cloud is that defaces the sleek sea; sulphur-cloud spitting streaks of fire? A sea cockfight it is, and of the hottest, where British *Serapis* and French American *Bon Homme Richard* do lash and throttle each other, in their fashion; and the desperate valour has suffocated the deliberate, and Paul Jones is of the Kings of the Sea! The Euxine, the Meotian waters, felt thee next, and long-skirted Turks, O Paul; and thy fiery soul has wasted itself in thousand contradictions; — to no purpose. For, in far lands, with scarlet Nassau-Siegens, with sinful Catherines, is not the heart broken, even as at home with the mean? Poor Paul! Hunger and disappointment track thy sinking footsteps; once or at most twice, in this Revolution tumult, the figure of thee emerges; mute, ghostlike, as ' with stars dim-twinkling through.' And then, when the light is gone out, a National Legislature grants

' ceremonial funeral.' As good had been a natural Presbyterian kirk-bell and six feet of Scottish earth, among the dust of thy loved ones."

VII

On July 11, 1792, Jones raised himself with an effort, for his legs had begun to swell, and attended the session of the National Assembly where the threatening coalition or foreign powers was cited and France was declared to be in danger. Buell asserts it had been proposed that Jones should speak on the needs of the French navy, but he excused himself on the ground of his failing voice and weak legs. That night he attended a Jacobin dinner at the Café Timon, where he pledged himself to uphold French liberty and where he was toasted as " the coming Admiral of France."

On the 18th Col. Samuel Blackden, of North Carolina, and Major Beaupoil, of the French army, who had served at Yorktown, came to see him. His breath was short, and the swelling of his legs had crept up to his waistcoat. After one look at his shadowy eyes, they sent for Gouverneur Morris, in whose presence Jones, sitting in an armchair, dictated his will and made an inventory of his property. He named Robert Morris his sole executor, since Gouverneur Morris (the two Morrises were not related) made an excuse for not serving. He willed all his property as follows to his sisters, Mrs. Janette Taylor of Dumfries, Scotland, and Mrs. Mary Lowden of Charleston, S. C., later of Liverpool:

1. Bank stock in the Bank of North America, $6,000 with sundry dividends.
2. United States Loan Office certificate for $2,000, with long arrears of interest.
3. Balance in hands of John Ross of Philadelphia.
4. Lands in Vermont.
5. Shares in the Ohio Company (afterwards found to be five shares, covering 5,867 acres of cheap land).

[277]

6. Shares in the Indiana Company.
7. About £1800 due from Edward Bancroft.
8. Four years' unpaid Danish pension.
9. Arrears of pay and all prize money from Russia.
10. Balance due from the United States, and from unsettled European claims.

It is evident therefore that Jones did not die, as legend so long had it, in poverty.

His last request was that the sword given him by Louis XVI should be awarded to Richard Dale — "my good old Dick." It is now in the museum of the Pennsylvania Historical Society at Philadelphia.

Morris hurried away from the dying man's side to attend a dinner, and the visitors and the French notaries took their leave. John Paul Jones sat alone in his armchair.

Night fell, and still he sat.

The streets outside were quiet, but a keen ear listening at a microphone covering all Paris might have heard a hurried rustling, the sound of the French nobility deserting the sinking royal ship and stealthily fleeing to Coblentz.

Three weeks previous Louis XVI and Marie Antoinette had been brought back to Paris under arrest after the failure of their own flight.

The day before Lafayette had attacked with troops in the Champs de Mars the signatories of the manifesto declaring the King to be a perjurer, traitor, and fugitive.

Leopold II of Austria, whom Jones had met at Vienna, and Frederick William of Prussia were preparing to meet at Pillnitz to declare Louis's plight "a matter concerning all the sovereigns of Europe."

Jones's ears, if sufficiently attuned, might have heard the subdued murmurs, the growls, the screams, the protests, of the approaching Revolution running from Paris over all France, all Europe, on this soft July night.

Whatever were his thoughts, he refrained from putting them on paper. Perhaps, with his invincible expectation that tomorrow would bring him some new and glorious appointment, he persuaded himself that he would yet recover.

Tiring of his own musings, he picked up a book — said to have been one by Voltaire. But he could not anchor his mind upon it, and he suddenly arose and on his swollen legs, holding to the walls and furniture, made his way to the bedroom, threw himself face downward upon the bed with feet touching the floor, and there he died.

July 18, 1792. Aged 45 years.

VIII

It was deemed proper to notify the American minister, and Morris returned, accompanied by Madame Flahaut and Vicq d'Azyr, the Queen's physician. Jones's body was already cold.

" I must tell you," wrote Gouverneur Morris to Robert in May, 1793, " that some people here who like rare shows wished him to have a pompous funeral, and I was applied to on the subject; but as I had no right to spend on such follies either the money of his heirs or that of the United States, I desired that he might be buried in a private and economical manner."

It was in such a manner, indeed, that he was disposed of. Pierre François Simmoneau, commissary of the Paris section in which Jones died, paid with indignation the cost of his interment, the bill being 462 francs.

" I have since," continued Gouverneur Morris, " had reason to be glad that I did not agree to waste money of which he had no great abundance, and for which his relatives entertain a tender regard. I promised them to entreat your attention to their bequests, which will no doubt be somewhat troublesome, and consume the moments you can badly spare. . . . Thus, my dear friend, I have given you a history which ought to have

been communicated long ago. You will probably find it somewhat tedious now. . . . "

IX

On July 19 the National Assembly voted that le Brun, the
president, should appoint twelve members, including himself,
to " assist at the funeral of a man who has so well served the
cause of liberty." He named Citizens Cambon, Bouvet, Rou-
vier, Brival, Vernon, Chabot, Charlier, Dupetit, le Josnes, Rou-
baine and Deydier.

The body was placed in a lead coffin and taken to the St.
Louis Protestant cemetery, then in the suburbs, now near the
corner of the rue de la Grange aux Belles and rue des Ecluses
Saint Martin, in the quarter called, by a coincidence, " le Com-
bat." Henri Marron, a Swiss, former clergyman and member
of the Assembly, was selected to deliver the funeral oration.
The Americans present, so far as known, numbered three:
Thomas Waters Griffith Latimer, a tourist from Baltimore,
Md., who wrote " there was no priest, nor any funeral service,
but a few soldiers fired a volley of muskets in honor of the
naval hero over his grave " ; Colonel Blackden and Major J.
C. Mountflorence, former United States army officers.

Marron called Jones " one of the first champions of the liberty of America, of that liberty which so gloriously ushered
in our own. . . . Let his example teach posterity the efforts
which noble souls are capable of making when stimulated by
hatred to oppression."

In the following month Catherine wrote from Russia to de
Grimm:

" This Paul Jones was a very bad character (*une bien mau-
vaise tête*) and well worthy of being praised by a rabble of
detestable characters."

[280]

X

Time and its events flowed rapidly over the little foreign cemetery in which lay John Paul Jones. Napoleon arose, and the nineteenth century came hurriedly in, with its steam navigation and men who cut their hair short at the back; many of Jones's contemporaries lived to be very old men and no longer remembered with exactness the details of their association with the dead young Admiral; and soon Jones's grave was obliterated under several feet of earth on which grocers and tailors built their shops.

In 1831 Lieutenant A. B. Pinkham of the United States Navy found, when travelling in Scotland, the house where Jones was born and had it restored at his own expense.

In 1834 Congress authorized the naming of a ship after John Paul Jones, and twenty-eight years later this was done.

In 1845 George Bancroft, Secretary of the Navy and founder of the Naval Academy, was asked for permission to bring the body home, but legal complications interfered.

In 1861 the Secretary of the Treasury informed Congress that the prize money due to the officers and men of the *Bon Homme Richard* and *Alliance* then amounted to $91,024.34 for the former ship and $74,574.03 for the latter.

In 1899 General Horace Porter, United States Ambassador to France, resolved at his own expense to find the body of Jones. Much search located the forgotten cemetery at the end of a little street called by an odd coincidence, " Vicq d' Azyr," after the physician who had pronounced Jones dead. Excavation began in 1905. Three weeks of digging disclosed five lead coffins. Measurements and a process of elimination reduced the bodies examined to a nameless one about five feet seven inches in height, with brown hair and high cheek bones. It was preserved in alcohol. The studies of several distin-

[281]

guished French scientists convinced them it was John Paul Jones. The left lung indicated an attack of broncho-pneumonia. The kidneys had been affected by disease. Certificates were signed both by French and American officials that the identification had been satisfactory in every particular. The body was removed, the excavations subjecting General Porter to suits which lasted for years.

In 1905 President Theodore Roosevelt ordered Rear-Admiral Charles D. Sigsbee to proceed with a squadron to France and bring back the body. Escorted by French vessels, the American cruisers landed the casket and placed it in a brick vault on the Academy grounds at Annapolis in July.

Even in death John Paul Jones's name remained potent, for the guard posted at this vault was one night found to be missing. When traced, he explained that he had heard queer noises in the tombs — since supposed to have been made by squirrels — and he was sure that Paul Jones, impatient over his long wait, was coming out.

On April 24, 1906, commemorative exercises were held at Annapolis, with addresses by President Roosevelt, Secretary of the Navy Charles J. Bonaparte, the French Ambassador J. J. Jusserand, General Porter, and Governor Warfield of Maryland. After the naval and military exercises were over and all the attending officials had dispersed, the body was taken into Bancroft Hall, Annapolis, and placed behind a stairway. There, resting on two wooden sawhorses of the kind used by carpenters, it remained for seven years.

XI

It was as if destiny, which had in life inflicted upon John Paul Jones so many indignities, had returned, spectrally, to visit one more upon him in death. The thing became a scan-

[282]

dal, and a public outcry arose. In 1910 the press began to attack the Government for not making decent provision for the
housing of the hero's remains, and at last Congress, abashed,
appropriated $135,000 to complete the Naval Chapel, with a
crypt and mausoleum for Jones.

On January 26, 1913, 121 years after his death, Jones's
body, with due ceremonies, was placed in the crypt beneath
the domed chapel. It is truly a magnificent tomb, of marble
and porphyry, and is splendid enough to have pleased Jones,
who was at times so exacting and at others so self-denying.
Around the elevated casket runs a circle inscribed in shining
letters with the names of the ships he made famous: the *Ranger*,
the *Bon Homme Richard*, the *Alliance*, the *Ariel*.

No other United States naval commander has a tomb so
imposing, a shrine so lustrous. Had he been able with living
eyes to visualize it, John Paul Jones, even in his last solitary
hours, would have surrendered his life with alacrity, for above
all things he loved praise and human honors.

XII

Nothing he ever achieved in life, received unanimous praise;
hence it is not strange that voices should have arisen to dispute
the verdict that the body thus entombed was John Paul Jones's
own; and of course the proof, in the nature of things, could
not be absolute. It would indeed be in keeping with that ironi-
cal disappointment which so long pursued his unceasing efforts
and most effulgent dreams, if the body so majestically resting
in Annapolis belonged to a perfect stranger: some layman and
landsman who never smelled smoke or inhaled salt air; some
bourgeois who never did aught more exciting than to take a
Sunday walk; some sedentary clerk or professional who loved
his slippers better than any sword. But no expense, no pains,
were spared by General Porter's assistants and associates in ex-

amining, weighing and measuring every historical, medical and anthropological clue that would enable them to arrive at a decision regarding the authenticity of their discovery. Their findings were separately examined and compared. They were satisfied the body was Jones's and their verdict stands.

CHAPTER XXXV

The Man, the Victim, and the Knight

I

JUDGING by his achievements, his written projects, and the admiration of the accomplished men who knew him best, John Paul Jones was transcendently able as a sailor and man of action; yet frustration and disappointment waited at the end of almost every energetic movement, every daring plan. He never lost a battle, yielded in any naval contest, or failed in an errand; yet defeat, with light but repeated strokes, hacked his energy to pieces and eventually broke him down. He was like a prizefighter who, though unmarked and having wind and muscle unimpaired, suddenly falls heavily in his corner, his face clearly reflecting his astonishment and unbelief.

Like most men who have a touch of what is called genius, he was consumed by a desire for the unattainable. The walls of his imagination were painted with the artist's dream of perfection. He was haunted by the chimera of a Great Squadron which, sailing in perfect line, he was one day to lead across glittering seas into the harbor of the Minotaur and gloriously sink him and his combined fleet. He was a compound of Tom Sawyer, Don Quixote, Alexander the Great, and Sandy Mc-Phairson.

II

As human being he suffered from the common malady of a " split personality." He could not harmonize his own warring elements or coördinate his contending faculties. The hardy man of action was frequently halted by the intuitive artist. The sea captain was checked by the musing, undeveloped poet.

[285]

The man of resolution was in conflict with the sentimentalist. Only at moments of supreme excitement or crisis could his active talents function clearly; but even then the climb into the heights was often followed by exhaustion and desolating reaction. He was ridden by a *daimon* which would not permit either body or imagination to rest. His interest was too hot. He lacked an immovable something, a sense of mastering composure, an ability to withdraw himself and wait. He saw results, not as the logical outcome of a chain of processes, but as something to be immediately fought and struggled for. Without motion he fretted himself to ribbons. He bloodied his head against the wall of passing circumstance. His unchanneled restlessness made people uncomfortable. If they could not quiet him, they unconsciously sought to be rid of him. He had the genius to do, but lacked the genius not to do. He had the positive gift, but not enough of the negative. He could not gain the blessed relief of alternation from pole to pole, realizing that each phase — positive and negative — has its function and reason for being.

III

He was also seriously lacking in the virtue of coöperation. His was the genius of the lone hand. He could do the thing himself, but he could not successfully delegate. He visualized a perfect result so clearly that he could not understand why it did not occur. Not comprehending himself or human limitations, he often blamed subordinates or associates unduly. Primarily disposed to praise them, he often suffered a reaction and criticized them. He could communicate his arterial fire to the rank and file, but not always to his officers.

The hostilities, the prejudices, the treacheries, which were so often exhibited towards him by his fellow captains, were not due exclusively to their own defects. The innumerable quarrels into which Jones fell indicate a woeful shortcoming on his part. His associates were frequently incompetent, ill-trained, and weak men, but Jones, with head lifted aloft toward the perfect deed, did not sufficiently buttress himself against failings in the human factor; and when inevitably they occurred, his disdain took a form that permanently injured human feelings. He was deficient in tact, which may be defined as the ability to say nothing at the right time. He was needlessly hard to get along with. He was a little too aware of his own superiorities.

That John Paul Jones had genius there's no denying, but when that has been said about any man, we are no nearer to his core. Many definitions of genius have been written, but none are satisfying. Genius consists of certain attributes, between which exists something not to be separated or defined, a unifying and coördinating something which to a work imparts a final perfecting touch to the whole, a dazzling and electrifying lustre.

One mark of genius is the ability to accomplish great results with small means. The genius is careless about instruments: when the call comes, he seizes what is nearest to hand. John Paul Jones is remembered chiefly for two feats: the victories over the *Drake* and the *Serapis*. Yet both were relatively minor actions, and were fought upon vessels which today would scarcely be larger than tugboats. His genius lay not in the defeat of these stronger ships, but the use he made of ungifted men and sparse material. It is greatly to his credit that he lost no time complaining of the inferiority of the instruments assigned to him. He instantly set to work to make them better, and when he had improved them to the extent of his power, he wielded each as if it were Excalibur. Since the three men went to sea in a tub, never did ambitious warrior set foot upon a more inadequate vessel than that old barge, the *Bon Homme Richard*, yet with her Jones stamped his name high upon the list, as Carlyle has put it, of " the kings of the sea."

[287]

IV

Jones's *Journals* and numerous writings reveal his concentric limitations. Among his papers there is scarcely a line dealing with external events and objects, with observations of men, manners, and things. All are concerned exclusively with his own ambitions, thirsts, exploits, disappointments, and defeated plannings. He was a perfect example of the man to whom life is " the theatre for one's self." [1] Men and women belonged to a cast gathered " around " him. Events were subordinate parts of a drama designed to " feature " John Paul Jones. Things were outlines and colors of a setting especially painted for *him*. The naïveté of his beliefs in this respect palliates what in another kind of man might have been a disagreeable egocentrism.

It was his misfortune to be born a little too late. In another century, or even in the first half of the eighteenth, his romantic impulses, his knightly rôle, might have had fuller scope. But in the latter half of the eighteenth century, which saw him reach maturity, the world was hardening. With the birth of industrialism and the development of commerce, society was becoming " practical minded "; and so the Don Quixotry of a " Bayard of the ocean " appeared to some of his employers to be eccentric if not actually wild. The windmills, already feeling the colder currents of the approaching nineteenth century, broke his slender sword in pieces and tossed him to one side, unwanted.

It was also his misfortune to fall among men in America who understood him not. Even had they had a more ordered government, a richer treasury, it is doubtful if they could have used him better. Where he had romance, they had canny judgment. Their imaginations could not keep pace with his. Their slogans thrilled him, but their caution left him bewildered. In his frantic endeavors to make them see his own visions, he was

[1] See Nicholas Evreinoff's *The Theatre in Life*.

compelled to prod them incessantly, and these proddings sapped his energy. Their delays aged him before his time. A dim realization that Jones received ill at the hands of the young country which he so ardently adopted, is perhaps the reason for the almost superfluously splendid mausoleum which houses his worn body at Annapolis.

v

Certain comparisons between Jones's temperament and Napoleon's suggest themselves. Both were small men, somewhat dainty in build, and it was perhaps to compensate themselves for their small stature that among their fellows they were wont to affect a bold and hardy demeanor. Both were soft in the hands of women. Both were born obscurely and rose rapidly in a difficult and alien atmosphere. Both had object-grasping minds, could foresee a concrete situation readily, and act upon it swiftly. Both loved danger while dealing with it circumspectly. Both had a demoniac energy, were indifferent to petty hardships, and when greatly spurred, could exhibit a dazzling personal courage. Both were egotists. But Jones was no careerist like Napoleon, and altogether lacked the Corsican's single-minded ruthlessness and ability to bend his fellows to his own purposes. Early in life Napoleon knit together the two halves of his own warring nature, and so completely realized himself as an instrument for France, for Europe and for himself. Beside this exploiter of men and material, Jones appears as an almost foolishly romantic and unselfish figure — generous, warm, devoted, incapable of petty meanness, and happy in the thought that he was helping Washington, Franklin, Jefferson, Thomas Paine and Lafayette to cleanse oppression from what was bound to be a new and shining world.

"Napoleon," said Emerson, "was an agent of the middle class of society." And Jones was another. "Men's actions," said Emerson again, "are too strong for them." True, as regards both Napoleon and Jones. "The measure of action," said the Concordian a third time, " is the sentiment from which it proceeds."

That criterion gives John Paul Jones's bust the right to hold its head very high, for the sentiment upon which he acted ran, throughout his service to the United States, clear, ardent and strong. It was not his fault that he was not an even greater contributor to history.

Afterword

HISTORY is outwardly the most respectable of dames. Her prestige is still enormous. But those who have visited her dwelling place and rummaged through her *escritoire* have experienced the impulse to denounce her claims as frequently suspect if not fraudulent. Her closets are filled with strangled, stunted or mutilated facts; her shelves are lined with suppressed or unopened documents; while the lady herself, in unguarded, or perhaps merely naïve, moments, has manifested bias, prejudice, furtiveness, and even spleen, occasionally breaking out into barely concealed objurgation and invective, in accordance with her epoch, her race, her religion, her nationality, her social class, and sometimes even in accordance with the opinions of her native village. It is when she declares she is wholly objective that she is so subjective as to deserve the attentions of psychanalysts. Pretending to be a detached observer, she is frequently the advocate, propagandist, and even *agent provocateur*. Assenting her lofty, if not divine, origin, she reveals herself as all too human.

History has many times dealt with John Paul Jones and his period. She has occasionally permitted herself to be dazzled by his boldness and gallantry; at other moments she has donned the garments of a prosecutor, or Mrs. Grundy, and belabored him. Rarely has she tried to disentangle the inner from the outer man, or separate the essence from 'the froth. As with her other subjects, she has too often been content with the mere chronicle of triumphs and defeats, never asking: What were his motives, what his purposes, and did he greatly 'try?

The statements made concerning John Paul Jones, particularly his early life, often conflict. From this welter we have endeavored to select that which appeared to be correct or convincing; but much is still lacking regarding Jones's obscure life in Virginia, particularly his property and affiliations there. According to the Honorable W. R. Jones, of the Arkansas House of Representatives, who calculates that he is the seventh cousin of the Admiral, John Paul Jones was descended from Cadwallader Jones (of the Welsh line of Rodri the Great) who came to Virginia from Wales in 1623, but who went to Scotland in 1699. He left an estate on the Rappahannock to which William Jones, John Paul Jones's uncle, succeeded. William Jones's heir was William Paul, of Fredericksburg, who changed his name to Jones on taking charge of the estate. It was this inheritance to which his brother, John Paul, it is asserted, succeeded, and he then likewise changed his name to Jones. According to Buell's biography, this estate was ravaged by Lord Dunmore, the Tory governor of Virginia, and Jones lost everything. Mr. W. R. Jones's forthcoming brochure on *The Lands of John Paul Jones* may clear up these disputed points, just as Dr. F. A. Golder's recently published work on *John Paul Jones in Russia* has illuminated phases of his career under Catherine the Great.

The bibliography concerning Jones is copious. He has several times been the hero or conspicuous figure of romances, notably those of Alexandre Dumas (*Le Capitaine Paul*), J. Fenimore Cooper (*The Pilot*), Allen Cunningham (*Paul Jones: A Romance*), Herman Melville (*Israel Potter, His Fifty Years of Exile*), Winston Churchill (*Richard Carvel*), and most recently James Boyd (*Drums*). Lives and studies which, besides those mentioned, we have found useful are as follows:

The Life and Letters of John Paul Jones, by Mrs. Reginald de Koven.

Paul Jones, Founder of the American Navy; a History, by Augustus C. Buell, who has been assailed by Mrs. de Koven for alleged inventions.

Life of Paul Jones, by Alexander Slidell McKenzie.

Life of Paul Jones, by Edward Hamilton.

Commodore Paul Jones, by the Rev. Cyrus Townsend Brady.

Life of Paul Jones, by James Otis.

Life and Character of John Paul Jones, by John Henry Sherburne.

Paul Jones, by Hutchins Hapgood.

Paul Jones, His Exploits in English Seas, with a complete Bibliography, by Don C. Seitz.

John Paul Jones Commemoration at Annapolis. Government Printing Office.

We have also consulted numerous books on naval affairs, on America, French and Russian history, and on Freemasonry. Every effort has been made to obtain accuracy; but correctness is not the synonym of truth; it is only a minister of it. A fact, object, or event is the observed plus the observer.

Special thanks are due for assistance, or for permission to examine documents, to the United States Naval Academy authorities, the Congressional Library, the American Philosophical Society, the Pennsylvania Historical Society, the J. P. Morgan Library, the New York Public Library, Dr. A. S. W. Rosenbach, Mr. W. R. Benjamin, Mrs. V. M. Fleming of Virginia, and Mr. J. LeGrand Everett, Masonic Past Grand Master of North Carolina.

PHILLIPS RUSSELL

APPENDIX

[ROSTER OF OFFICERS, MARINES, AND CREW OF THE *BON HOMME RICHARD* IN FIGHT WITH THE *SERAPIS* (COMPILED BY BUELL)]

COMMISSIONED OFFICERS

Paul Jones, Commandant of the Squadron. Captain of the *Bon Homme Richard*.

Richard Dale, First Lieutenant, wounded.
Samuel Stacey, Acting Master.
Laurens Brooke, Surgeon.
Matthew Mease, Purser, wounded.

Edward Stack, Lieutenant.
Eugene Macarty, do., wounded.
John Mayrant, Acting Lieutenant, wounded.

WARRANT OFFICERS

John C. Robinson, boatswain.
Nathaniel Fanning, midshipman.
Thomas Potter, midshipman, wounded.
Benjamin Stubbs, midshipman, wounded.
Reuben Chase, midshipman.
Robert Coram, do
John West Linthwaite, midshipman.

Jonas Caswell, master's mate, killed.
John Gunnison, carpenter, wounded.
William Clarke, sailmaker, wounded.
Arthur Randall, gunner, wounded.
Henry Gardner, acting gunner, wounded.

(Stephen Lee, Jr., Captain's clerk.)

PETTY OFFICERS AND ABLE SEAMEN

Jacob True.
Thomas Turner, killed.
Ichabud Lord.
Daniel Russell.
Edward Garrett, wounded.

Jonathan Wells, wounded.
John Murphy, killed.
Francis Campbell.
Michael Langstaff, killed.
Elijah Perkins.

Thomas Miller.
William Phisic, killed.
James Connor.
Robert Steel, killed.
Robert Towers, wounded.
William Thomson.
John Woolton, wounded.
Robert Stevens.
Thomas Macarthy, killed.
Thomas Davis, killed.
Thomas Knight, wounded.
Pierre Gerard (Fr.).

———

Peter Nolte.
Gilbert Crumb.
Thomas Wythe, wounded.
Henry Martin, killed.
John Brown, wounded.
William Fox.
Duncan Taylor.
John McKinley.
Robert Hill, killed.
Lewis Brown.
James Evans, wounded.
John Earl.
Robert Doherty, killed.
John Brown, wounded.
William Clisdell.
James Nicholson, killed.
John Connor, wounded.
John Walker.
George Johnston, wounded.

Hugh Wouton, killed.
John Williams, killed.
William Sturgess.
John Thomas, wounded.
John Madden.
John Hughes, wounded.
John Peacock.
John Burbank, wounded.
Josiah Brewster, killed.
James Quinn.
John Weaver, wounded.
David Cross.
John Turpin.
John Carrico, killed.
John Burnet, wounded.
John Thompson.
John Frankford, wounded.
Charles Peterson, wounded.
Daniel Emblen.
Peter Biorkman.
Benjamin Gartineau.
Peter Molin, wounded.
Oliver Gustav.
Elijah Johnstone.
Pierre Carreau (Fr.), killed.
Jacques Lorziere (Fr.).
Jacques Maziani (Fr.).
Jacques Carrons (Fr.), wounded.
Nicolas Muhé (Fr.).
François Etienne Maré (Fr.).
Alexandre Antoine (Fr.), killed.
Jean Baptiste Ferry (Fr.), killed.
Jacques Loria (P.*), killed.

* " (P) " means Portuguese and (Fr.) means Frenchman, when placed after a name in this roster. The Irish, Scotch, and Scandinavians in the crew are not specially indicated, because they either then were or afterward became American citizens — such as survived the battle.

[296]

Andrew Ryan.
Samuel Matthews.
Lawrence Furlong, wounded.
James McKinley, wounded.
John McCaffery.
Thomas Mehanney.
James Riley.
James Lenn, wounded.
Joseph Collinson, wounded.
Joseph Weira (P.*), wounded.
Antoine Alcantara (P.).
Joseph Mare (P.), killed.
Joachim Joseph (P.), killed.
Vincent Ignace (P.), killed.
Leonard la Roche (Fr.).
Pierre Fanchot (Fr.).
Jean Moulin (Fr.), wounded.
Jean Fanchot (Fr.).

Louis Rolé Tomise (P.), killed.
Jacques Baterga (P.), killed.
Thomas Watt, wounded.
John Lyons, wounded.
George Trefathen, wounded.
Richard Williams, wounded.
John McIntyre, wounded.
Hugh Euroney, wounded.
Aaron Smith, wounded.
Richard Hughes, wounded.
William Hamilton, wounded.
Nicolas Borela (Fr.).
Louis Joly (Fr.), wounded.
Pierre l'Eveque (Fr.), wounded.
Modiste Tardif (Fr.).
Jean Constant (Fr.).
Jean Tardif (Fr.), wounded.
Jean Paul (Fr.), wounded.

ORDINARY SEAMEN, LANDSMEN, AND BOYS

John Downes, wounded.
Anthony Jeremiah (Narragansett
   Indian).
John Redway, killed.
John Jordan, wounded.
Francis Perkins, killed.
Joseph Crooks, killed.
James Parry.
William Lister, wounded.
Isaac Hobshaw.
Thomas Hammett, wounded.
Stephen Soley, killed.
Nicholas Rodgers.
Andrew Mason, killed.
Nathaniel Kennard.

Robert Lyons, wounded.
Laurent Verness.
Daniel Swain, wounded.
John Duffy.
William Knox.
Abram Martell.
Nathaniel Bailey, killed.
James Mehanney.
William Wilkinson.
George Harroway, killed.
Thomas Clarke, killed.
Antoine Francisque (P.),
   wounded.
François Darros (P.).
Ignace Silveira (P.).

William Collingwood, wounded.
Benjamin Bickert.
James Cunningham.
James Halliday, wounded.
Robert Upham, wounded.
Joseph Bartlett.
William McCullough, wounded.
Samuel Fletcher.
James MacMichan, wounded.
John Kilby.
William Simpson, wounded.
Nicholas Caldwell.
Jerry Evans.
Patrick Quinn.
William Garth, wounded.
Daniel Pryor.
Joseph Cooper.
William Murphy, killed.
Mark Paul.
Antoine Cazziero (P.), killed.

Mathieu Antone (P.).
Josef Rodrique (P.), killed.
Mathieu Josef (P.).
Joan Ignacio (P.).
Joan Praçia (P.).
Josef Maçeda (P.), killed.
Manuel Viera (P.).
Joan Silveira (P.).
Manuel Priezra (P.).
Joan Josef (P.), killed.
Antoine Foustade (P.).
Manuel Antone (P.), killed.
Mathieu Francisque (P.).
Josef Ignacio (P.), killed.
Antonio Silvestre (P.), killed.
Joachim Joseffa (P.).
Manuel Castaino (P.).
Luis Antonio (P.), killed.
Robert Bruman (Fr.).

COOK AND COOK'S MATES

George Campbell.
Charles Priestly.
Joseph Holland.

Louis Ferrine.
Augustin Garat.
Olivier Relaut.

FRENCH MARINES (VOLUNTEERS)

Commissioned Officers.

Paul de Chamillard, Captain wounded.
Wibert de Mezieres, Lieutenant.

François de la Bernerie, Lieutenant, killed.
François Kuelain, Ensign, killed.

Non-Commissioned Officers.

Pierre Mongue, sergeant-major, killed.

Denis Bouchinet, sergeant.

François La Frayé, sergeant, wounded.

Barthelemy Pellé, sergeant.

Charles Conconnier, corporal, wounded.

Antoine Longpré, corporal, wounded.

Jean Brousseau, corporal.

Pierre Lusson, corporal, wounded.

Charles Quentin, corporal, killed.

Nicolas Forêt, corporal, killed.

The foregoing were all regular marines, loaned for the cruise from the Royal Dockyard of l'Orient.

Private Marines.

Jean Margue.

Georges Wiebert.

Pierre Daniel, killed.

Balthazar Audibert, wounded.

Jean B. Flandrin.

Louis Macé.

Joseph Revellant.

Charles Quédon, killed.

Michel Langlois.

Jacques Langlois, wounded.

Joseph Olivard, wounded.

Joseph Beillé.

Jacques Pegorier, wounded.

Jean B. La Porte.

Louis Gandalin.

Gabriel Oillie, wounded.

Joseph Gourgeon, wounded.

Ambroise Launay.

Guillaume Le Brun.

René Murat, wounded.

Julien Ligonne, killed.

André Bronége.

René Brousseau.

Jean Guerrier, killed.

Jean Peroussel, wounded.

Louis de la Maré.

Renaud Cavelet, killed.

Jacques Core.

Pierre de la Haye, wounded.

Jean Fillier, killed.

Jean B. Deschamps.

Jean B. Lubin, killed.

René Rousselain.

Pierre Georgelin, wounded.

André Duvinique.

Jean B. Janique.

Louis Néant, wounded.

Claude Rousseau.

François Salerné.

Pierre Guillard, wounded.

Ambroise Daniaud.

Mathurin Ledée.

Yves Geoffrin.

Joseph Deliarme, wounded.

Mathurin Leger.
Jean Ferront, killed.
Jean Gaspardin.
Guy Brissard, wounded.
Baptiste Quentin, wounded.
Jean Denée.
Manuel Chaussepied, wounded.
Denis Bernard.
Louis Jacquenot.
Pierre Menard, wounded.
René Joué.
François Chapon, killed.
François Vallée, wounded.
Vincente Roland.
Manuel Le Deirne, wounded.
François le Roté, wounded.
Pierre Bouillait.
François Aline, killed.
Jacques Ribout, killed.
Pierre Ollivier.
Laurent Clérge, wounded.
Pierre d'Amour.
Mathurin Chevrance.
Jean Macé.
Jacques Chaouest, killed.
François Lesconnée, wounded.
Pierre Viaud, wounded.
Louis Latiner, wounded.
Louis Jeannot.
Jean Saligan, killed.
Joseph Paule.
Mathurin Lepeine.
Jean Orgérot, killed.

Claude La Maitre.
Jean Routier, killed.
Pierre Louis Lemoine.
Jean Denis Jaquet, wounded.
Henri Ystreau, killed.
Joseph Bosquet.
Jean Frené, wounded.
Pierre Maudin, wounded.
François Chaillon.
Christophe Billiere, killed.
Jacques Datté, wounded.
Antoine La Bastier, wounded.
François Duclos.
Jean Antoine Auger, killed.
François Victor Noël, wounded.
Antoine Perrigat, wounded.
François Legué.
Toussaint Gautier, wounded.
Pierre Antoine Vouän, killed.
Antoine Villéger, wounded.
Bernard Tabournier, wounded.
François Maçeré.
Pierre Fr's Languille, killed.
Baptiste Macheret, wounded.
Gérome Doux-Ami.
François Ambellon, killed.
Pierre Pillon.
Juline Laurent, wounded.
Jean Paterne.
Louis Roule Johonnot, wounded.
Jacques Laziere, killed.
Jean Baptiste Travaillé.

(The private marines were mostly infantry soldiers who volunteered from the garrison of l'Orient for the cruise. A few of them were civilian volunteers, who had never seen service of any kind before.)

[300]

ABSENT AND NOT IN ACTION

Cutting Lunt, Master.

Henry Lunt, Second Lieutenant.

James Gerald O'Kelley, master's mate. (Sent to France in command of a prize.)

John White, master's mate. (Sent to France in command of a prize.)

Beaumont Grubb, midshipman.

William Danill,   do

Louis White,   do

Richard Watt,   do

Gilbert Watt,   do

William Lee, petty officer.

John Pearce,   do

Thomas Jones,   do

William Roberts, do

John Brussen, ordinary seaman.

John Jones,   do

Joseph Burns,   do

John Pinkham,   do

Henry Humphreys,   do

Elijah Middleton,   do

John Hackett,   do

James Fogg,   do

Adolphe la Berniere, surgeon's mate.

James Smith,   seaman.

Edward Lewis,   do

George Walker,   do

Alexander Cooper, do

Richard Taylor,   do

David Pritchard,   do

Thomas Forrest,   do

John Colbraith,   do

James Hareham,   do

Jacob Henzies,   do

James Powers, ordinary seaman.

Peter Richardson,   do

Joseph Stewart,   do

Aaron Goodwin,   do

Richard Lawson,   do

Manuel Quito (P.), do

Joseph Galois, corporal of marines.

Felix Marrel, marine.

Louis Guinot,   do

Jean Rousseau,   do

Yvon Hierry,   do

Nicolas Abelard, do

Joseph Pennetier, do

Guillaume Valmont, marine.

Bernard Noguez,   do

Index

[303]

INDEX

INDEX

North Carolina, 35–36, 43, 54, 104, 277

Northwest Territory, 214

" North Carolina Captain," the (Hewes), 56

O'Kelly, Irish Lieutenant, 141

Old St. Patrick's Churchyard, 188

Olney, Joseph, 55

" Order of the Cincinnati," 218

" Order of St. Anne," 244, 259, 274

" Order of St. George," 244, 268

Ormoy, Mde. la Presidente d', 175, 194–195, 196

Orvilliers, Comte d', 92, 116, 267

Osgood, Samuel, 217

Ossory, Lady, 266

Paine, Thomas, 118, 272, 289

Pallas, 136–137, 142, 158, 159

Paris, 8–9, 38, 84, 86, 92, 101, 103, 105, 116, 117, 127, 160, 162, 163, 165, 171, 172, 185, 190, 193, 199, 211, 215, 217, 218, 223, 224, 225, 246, 252, 253, 262, 265, 266, 267, 271, 278

Parish, John, 265

Pasha, Capt., 235, 237, 240, 242, 243

Paul, George, 16

Paul, John (J. P. J. referred to as), 7, 10–12, 14, 16–20, 22–25, 27–31, 33–36, 40, 46, 57, 88, 94, 95, 97, 99, 142

Paul, John (J. P. J.'s father), 16, 29, 292

Paul Jones, Founder of the American Navy, 34–35

Paul, William, 17, 19, 35, 40

Pavillon, M. de, 237

Payne, Frances, 41, 43

Peace of Jassy, 260

Pearson, Capt., 149–159, 161, 164, 173, 176

Pennsylvania, 11, 198

Pennsylvania Academy of Fine Arts, 175

Pennsylvania Historical Society, 278

Pensacola, Florida, 79

Pezakoff, 237, 238, 242, 245, 247, 250, 260, 270

Philadelphia, 41–42, 48, 49, 50, 51, 58, 64, 68, 78, 79, 80, 83, 86, 108, 128, 143, 180, 192, 198, 203, 208, 209, 211, 259, 265, 277

Picquet, la Motte, 267

Pillnitz, 278

Pindar, John, 198

Pinkham, Lieutenant A. B., 281

" Pirate," John Paul Jones, 94, 161, 166, 213

Pitcher, Jonathan, 55

Plaince, Capt., 129

Plymouth, England, 33, 134

Polignac, Countess, 119

Poor Richard's Almanac, 124

Pope, Alexander, 37, 129, 273

Porter, General Horace, 281, 282, 283

Porter, Thomas, 64

Porto Cabello, 210

Porto Rico, 107

Portsmouth, England, 5

Portsmouth, N. H., 8, 82, 83, 180, 205, 206

Potato, Irish, 20

Potemkin, 176, 226, 227, 232–233, 234–236, 238, 239, 240, 241, 243, 244, 245, 246, 247, 248, 249, 250, 251, 252, 254, 255, 260, 263, 268, 269

Potter, Thomas, 140, 169–170, 222

Profiteering (privateering), 69–72, 121, 197

Providence, 8, 61, 63, 64, 65, 66, 72, 75, 77

Pulaski, Count, 118

Putnam, 118

INDEX

LEON UNDERWOOD
27.